The Ritual of Rights in Japan demonstrates that rights-based conflict is central to Japanese legal, political, and social practice. Challenging cultural stereotypes about harmony and consensus, the author spent three years in Japan analyzing groundbreaking battles over AIDS policy and the definition of death. His vivid descriptions of these struggles supports an innovative conclusion – that Japan is a nation where rights are potent weapons in battles over politics and policy, asserted by those seeking both individual remedies and social change.

Eric A. Feldman is Associate Director at the Institute for Law and Society, New York University. He has been a Fulbright Fellow at the University of Tokyo, a Robert Wood Johnson Health Policy Research Scholar at Yale University, and an Abe Fellow at the Institut d'Etudes Politiques in Paris. He is co-editor of *Blood Feuds: AIDS, Blood, and the Politics of Medical Disaster* (Oxford, 1999), and has written for publications including the *Journal of Asian Studies*, the *Los Angeles Times*, the *Hastings Center Report*, and *Social and Legal Studies*.

CAMBRIDGE STUDIES IN LAW AND SOCIETY

Series editors

Chris Arup, Martin Chanock, Pat O'Malley
School of Law and Legal Studies, La Trobe University
Sally Engle Merry, Susan Silbey
Departments of Anthropology and Sociology, Wellesley College

Editorial board

Richard Abel, Harry Arthurs, Sandra Burman, Peter Fitzpatrick, Marc Galanter, Yash Ghai, Nicola Lacey, Boaventura da Sousa Santos, Sol Picciotto, Jonathan Simon, Frank Snyder

The broad area of law and society has become a remarkably rich and dynamic field of study. At the same time, the social sciences have increasingly engaged with questions of law. In this process, the borders between legal scholarship and the social, political and cultural sciences have been transcended, and the result is a time of fundamental re-thinking both within and about law. In this vital period, Cambridge Studies in Law and Society provides a significant new book series with an international focus and a concern with the global transformation of the legal arena. The series aims to publish the best scholarly work on legal discourse and practice in social context combining theoretical insights and empirical research.

THE RITUAL OF RIGHTS IN JAPAN

Law, Society, and Health Policy

Eric A. Feldman

Institute for Law and Society
New York University

CAMBRIDGE
UNIVERSITY PRESS

PUBLISHED BY THE PRESS SYNDICATE OF THE UNIVERSITY OF CAMBRIDGE
The Pitt Building, Trumpington Street, Cambridge CB2 1RP, United Kingdom

CAMBRIDGE UNIVERSITY PRESS
The Edinburgh Building, Cambridge CB2 2RU, UK   http://www.cup.cam.ac.uk
40 West 20th Street, New York, NY 10011-4211, USA   http://www.cup.org
10 Stamford Road, Oakleigh, Melbourne 3166, Australia

First published 2000

Printed in the United Kingdom at the University Press, Cambridge

Typeset in Goudy 11/13 pt. [WV]

A catalogue record for this book is available from the British Library

Library of Congress Cataloguing in Publication data

Feldman, Eric A.
The ritual of rights in Japan: law, society, and health policy/Eric A. Feldman
    p.   cm.
ISBN 0 521 77040 8 (hb.). – 0 521 77964 2 (pbk.)
1. AIDS (Disease) – Patients – Legal status, laws, etc. – Japan.
2. Dead bodies (Law) – Japan. 3. Transplantation of organs, tissues, etc. – Law and legislation – Japan. 4. Actions and defenses – Japan. 5. Law – Social aspects – Japan. I. Title
KNX3098.F45 2000
340'.115'0952 – dc21   99–23257   CIP

ISBN 0 521 77040 8 hardback
ISBN 0 521 77964 2 paperback

CONTENTS

PREFACE

This book began as a study of Japanese public policy, more specifically the legal, ethical, and political dimensions of health policy debates in Japan. Having studied medico-legal conflicts in the United States, and the tensions they generated between public health and individual rights, state power and personal privacy, medical paternalism and patients' rights, I decided to examine how such concerns were addressed in Japan with regard to AIDS policy and the definition of death. Would HIV lead to policies of isolation? How would the Ministry of Health and Welfare handle reporting requirements, access to treatment, and anonymous testing? Would hemophiliacs infected with HIV through the blood supply demand compensation? If so, from whom, and in what venue? How would the impact of traditional views of life and death affect the determination and definition of brain death? What position would the Japan Medical Association take with regard to organ transplantation, and how would it influence the process of legalizing a definition of death and implementing an organ transplant program? Who would have the power to make decisions about extracting and implanting organs – doctors, patients, their families, or some combination of these parties?

AIDS and the definition of death were interesting for a variety of other, more general reasons. First, both issues in Japan had experienced quite different life cycles than they had in the United States. Whereas the definition of death as brain death in the United States happened quickly and with minimum controversy, AIDS policy was a vocal and visceral battle. Quite the opposite appeared to be the case in Japan; there, it was the definition of death, not AIDS, that was a major controversy. I was interested in learning why.

Second, both AIDS and death invade personal, private realms of social life, such as the family, sexuality, and health. Examining how legal and policy conflicts arose and were resolved with regard to these issues promised to be revealing of how conflict in less intimate areas would progress. Third, both AIDS and the definition of death afforded the opportunity to study Japanese law and legal institutions in a variety of contexts. These were not cases that played out in isolated courtrooms. Instead, they both were infused with law on a variety of levels – courts, legislatures, executive committees, professional codes, and more general social norms and practices – and thus provided a rich assortment of approaches to Japanese law well beyond the realm of litigation.

As I accumulated literature and interviewed participants in the controversies, I discovered that the Japanese word for "rights," *kenri*, was frequently and widely invoked. Perhaps this should not have been a surprise; discussion of both AIDS and the definition of death in the United States had long been framed in the language of rights. But the literature on Japanese law and policy strongly suggested that rights in Japan were peripheral, a non-issue in the study of disputes, not even worth an index entry in a work titled *Conflict in Japan* (Krauss et al. 1984).

This disjuncture between empirical, case-based observation and received wisdom piqued my curiosity; I decided to take a long look at rights in Japan. Doing so led me to review the writings of Japanese and Anglo-American historians, and carefully examine their findings to determine whether the assertion of rights in contemporary health policy conflicts was a postwar phenomenon or had deeper roots. It caused me to study the etymology of *kenri*, a word that was created by Meiji reformers to translate European codes. It required that I examine Japanese and Western scholarship on Japan's legal culture that has strongly influenced the conventional view of rights in Japan. And it persuaded me to undertake two analyses of contemporary policy conflicts, one over the definition of death, the other over AIDS. The details of the policy conflicts are presented in Chapters 4, 5, and 6, once the necessary historical and legal background is provided in Chapters 2 and 3. Readers who desire a fuller discussion of rights in Japan may want to first read Chapter 7, where I focus on their sociolegal dimensions.

Induction, rather than deduction, is the method I used to study rights in Japan, but in fact they are closely related. The idea that research consists of formulating hypotheses on the basis of theoretical ideas, gathering data, and testing hypotheses has been called "the folklore of mainstream social science" (Ragin, *The Comparative Method*, 1984). In practice, there is an interplay between concepts and facts, and both develop and confound as a project progresses.

Robert Ellickson, in *Order Without Law* (1991), describes how he abandoned "library-based legal scholarship" in favor of fieldwork. Ellickson sought to explore the Coase Theorem by studying cattle trespass disputes in rural California. "Although vaguely confident from the outset that fieldwork in Shasta County would turn out to be enlightening in one way or another," Ellickson writes, "I began with no particular hypotheses in mind." Ellickson concludes that "[i]n many contexts, law is not central to the maintenance of social order," despite the assumptions of law and economics, and the perception that Americans are attuned to formal legal rules. My method is similar, but my conclusions are the inverse – that in contrast to the vision of Japan as having a premodern legal system and no tradition of rights assertion, many conflicts are pervaded by rights talk and brought to the courts. In short, this book presents and analyzes a series of observations and conclusions that contradict the conventional view of Japanese law and dispute resolution.

ACKNOWLEDGMENTS

When I started to read Japanese texts in preparation for writing this book, I discovered that I was spending large blocks of time struggling through difficult academic writings and coming up empty handed. Why is it, I wondered, that I seem to be reading so much, and learning so little? I had honed my critical reading skills as a graduate and law student at the University of California at Berkeley, but suddenly I was experiencing the frustrations of a first time reader of some types of philosophy – the kind that make you realize that the deeper meaning of the words is eluding your grasp.

So I sought the counsel of a friend who had spent many years in Japan, and asked if he had some suggestions as to how I could be a better consumer of Japanese scholarship. As he listened to my travails, he smiled knowingly. Don't expect the original insights of the author to be placed prominently on the first page, he told me. Don't even look to the conclusion for a summary of the author's contribution. Instead, look for the unexpected. A jarring transition, a naked *non sequitur*, a confusing connection – those are the signs that an interesting and original thought is on the way.

What he told me has paid dividends, I hope, not only in how I have approached the written word in Japan, but also how I have observed social, legal, and political interactions. Meaning resides no further below the surface in Japan than in any other place I have spent time; the Japanese "mask" offers no greater disguise than do those in other cultures. But one must remain attentive to a new range of sounds and smells, voices and vices, if the goal is to be a sensitive observer of Japanese life.

I was reminded recently of the importance of a broad scholarly gaze when I sat in on an undergraduate architecture class at Yale University. In the concluding lecture of the semester, the professor was summing up the message of his course, and presented two contrasting images: the pyramids of Egypt and Ise Shrine in Japan. Both were built for a combination of religious and secular purposes; both represent the height of creative and aesthetic grace from cultures at a certain point of maturity. Yet in glorious contrast to the stoney permanence of the pyramids, the aerial view of Ise Shrine shows two adjacent, mirror-image sites. From ground level, visitors might feel as if they are within an enduring, holy monument from Japan's past. Yet every twenty years the structures on one site are ripped down, and activity shifts to the newly built version of this ancient place of worship. It was a stunning visual demonstration of the deep connection between cultures and their structures, between the rituals of social and political action and the institutions through which they are manifested. If my discussion of the ritual of rights in Japan moves some readers to think about those connections, the aim of this book will be met.

The debts that I owe – intellectually and more literally – to those who have contributed to my work on this book feel more like the enduring pyramids of Egypt than the grassy shrines of Ise. My intellectual debts began with the first audience for this work, the three people who were on my dissertation committee; Malcolm Feeley, Martin Shapiro, and Chalmers Johnson. Each of them was generous with both criticism and praise. Without them, I would not have mustered the sustained energy needed to finish this project.

At the University of Tokyo, I was hosted by Shibagaki Kazuo at the Institute of Social Science, and Fujikura Kōichiro and Watanabe Hiroshi at the Faculty of Law. Their kind and gracious welcome made my stay in Japan a pleasure in every way. A number of friends and colleagues have read and/or talked with me about earlier versions of this book, in whole or part. They are Ronald Bayer, Robert Bullock, John Campbell, Ikegami Naoki, David Johnson, David Kirp, Kitamura Yoshinobu, Robert Leflar, Margaret Lock, Theodore Marmor, Ugo Mattei, Miyazawa Setsuo, David Nelken, Dorothy Nelkin, Nudeshima Jiro, Mark Ramseyer, Donald Richie, Frank Upham, Wada Mikihiko, Charles Weathers, David Wolff, Yonemoto Shohei, and two anonymous reviewers at Cambridge University Press. I am grateful to them all. At New York University's Institute for Law and Society, I am fortunate to work with Christine Harrington. She has provided me with a wonderfully collegial institutional home, and has been unsparing in her willingness to discuss my work and offer her always thoughtful views. Alexandra Kowalski-Hodges and Tsutsui Yuko have taken time from their own work and provided me with invaluable research assistance. At Cambridge University Press, Finola O'Sullivan has shepherded this book through the publication process with intelligence, precision, and grace.

It was my good fortune to have been well cared for during the research and writing of this book. I thank the Japan–US Educational Commission (Fulbright), the Social Science Research Council/American Council of Learned Societies, the US Department of Education (Foreign Language and Area Studies Fellowship), the Japan Society for the Promotion of Science, the Toyota Foundation, the Center for Interdisciplinary Research on AIDS (Yale University, NIMH and NIDA Grant No. P01 MH/DA 56826-01A1), the National Science Foundation, the Robert Wood Johnson Foundation's Scholars in Health Policy Research Program, and the Japan Foundation Center for Global Partnership for their generous support.

Lastly, three special bows of gratitude. First, I will always be thankful for the friendship and guidance of the late Gregory Vlastos. He has described how he "toiled and moiled" over his first book manuscript in 1953, only to "junk it" because he decided that it was "a lemon." I too have toiled and moiled; were I to have fully incorporated the wise Professor Vlastos' advice, I too might have "junked it." Though still a long way from internalizing the exacting standards that he set for himself, his capacity for honesty and self-criticism remain my template. Second, I am grateful for the extraordinary support and encouragement of my parents Gloria and Saul Feldman, and for all they have taught me about rights and rituals. With Stephanie, who came into my life in Tokyo with the permanence of an Egyptian pyramid and the grace of a Shinto shrine, I have found happiness and harmony in abundance. To all of them, I dedicate this book.

Note: As custom dictates, all Japanese names in this book are written last name first.

CHAPTER ONE

RECONSIDERING RIGHTS IN JAPANESE LAW AND SOCIETY

This book challenges the belief that the assertion of rights is fundamentally incompatible with Japanese legal, political, and social norms. In doing so, it explores evidence in a variety of sociolegal arenas: in linguistic and conceptual predecessors to the Japanese word for "rights," *kenri*; in Japan's tradition of protest; in the growth during the late nineteenth century of the Movement for Freedom and Popular Rights; in the "new rights" movements of the 1960s and 1970s; and in contemporary policy disputes over AIDS and the definition of death. Analysis of each of these domains points to the same conclusion; rights in Japan have been, and continue to be, asserted and fought over, if not always secured.

Many of the most erudite and influential commentators on Japan have reached very different conclusions. They argue that the persistence of premodern legal and political values in Japanese society has inhibited the articulation and emergence of rights.[1] Political analyst Karel van Wolferen writes that "[t]raditional attitudes, reinforced by contemporary practice, obstruct the establishment of an unambiguous concept of 'rights,'" and he dismisses the seriousness of groups that frame their arguments in the language of rights.[2] Susan Pharr, Harvard's Reischauer Professor of Japanese Studies, claims that "most Japanese continue to view the official ideology [postwar democracy and egalitarianism], with its linkage to a notion of individual rights, as basically 'Western,'" and goes on to argue that Japanese political culture is antithetical to an idea of rights.[3] Traditional Japanese scholarship has supported these views, emphasizing the disjuncture between

Japanese culture and rights,[4] sometimes dwelling on Marxist theories about the state control of rights.[5] Abe Haruo says that in the postwar era rights were "suddenly handed down from above," indicating that Japan was rights-less for most of its 2,000 year history.[6] Takayanagi Kenzō identifies a Japanese preference for mediation, and argues that it is in part the result of "the Japanese national character, that the Japanese people are less assertive of their rights than Anglo-Saxons or Germans . . ."[7]

Hyperbolic descriptions of a rights-laden United States have influenced scholars of Japanese law to describe a radical disjuncture between rights assertion in the United States and Japan. The University of Chicago's Leon Kass, for example, opines:

> It has been fashionable for some time now and in many aspects of American public life for people to demand what they want or need as a matter of rights. During the past few decades we have heard claims of a right to health or health care, a right to education or employment, a right to privacy (embracing also a right to abort or to enjoy pornography, or to commit suicide or sodomy), a right to clean air, a right to dance naked, a right to be born, and a right not to have been born. Most recently we have been presented with the ultimate new rights claim, a "right to die."[8]

Kass's critique of what he perceives of as an overindulgence in "the liberal – that is, rights-based – political philosophy and jurisprudence to which we Americans are wedded" coincides with the theme of Harvard Law School Professor Mary Ann Glendon's *Rights Talk: The Impoverishment of Political Discourse*. Glendon describes an America gorged on rights, with individuals unable or unwilling to control their rights assertions, and who are unburdened by a conception of a common good. Even worse, the people who inhabit Glendon's America have the most limited and crass understanding of rights:

> American rights talk is set apart by the way that rights, in our standard formulations, tend to be presented as absolute, individual, and independent of any necessary relation to responsibilities . . . we have observed a tendency to formulate important issues in terms of rights; a bent for stating rights claims in a stark, simple, and absolute fashion; an image of the rights-bearer as radically free, self-determining, and self-sufficient; and the absence of well-developed responsibility talk . . . and a consequent carelessness regarding the environments that human beings and societies require in order to flourish.[9]

While Kass and Glendon are harsh in their condemnation of American rights talk, they are not alone in considering the United States unique with regard to the frequency and vigor of rights assertion. Political scientists Stewart Scheingold and Michael McCann, for example, in their separate studies of rights, mobilization, and social change in the United States, both remark on the exceptional way in which rights function in American society.[10] R. Shep Melnick, discussing special education policy, cites a "peculiarly American" reliance on the orientation to and language of rights.[11] Starting with de Tocqueville, who observed that in America most public men were lawyers and legal discourse pervaded the culture, the so-called American obsession with law and rights has become an almost conventional wisdom.

Japanese scholars like University of Tokyo legal philosopher Inoue Tatsuo, and other prominent Japanese intellectuals, can hardly be faulted for accepting the views of their American colleagues and using them to construct a similarly unidimensional analysis of rights in Japan. Inoue, summing up the work of Glendon and others, bluntly states that "[T]he American people are well known for stressing the role of individual rights within society."[12] He offers a critique of Japan that explicitly builds on Glendon's view of the United States. In contrast to America's rights saturation, he sees Japan as barren:

> individual rights are an endangered moral species in our Land of Community. They are chronically endangered . . . We have an urgent need to save them because our human lives are now impoverished, devastated and even destroyed by the same moral environment that has been causing, and is caused by, their atrophy and suffocation.[13]

Glendon pleads for a greater sense of community in America; Inoue cautions about the tyranny of community. Inoue implores Japan to strengthen its commitment to individual rights; Glendon condemns the American infatuation with rights as a "caricature of our culture."

Conventional accounts of rights in the United States and Japan are similarly flawed. Recent sociolegal scholarship in the United States points to both qualitative and quantitative data indicating that the American obsession with litigation and rights has been vastly overstated.[14] In the United States, it turns out, there are surely people who are vigorous rights asserters, but so too many conflicts are settled without resort to rights. There has been little comparable rethinking of rights in Japan. Instead, without looking to countries in Europe or

Asia, where the frequency and tenor of rights assertion may be much like Japan, analysts of Japan have fixed on the perceived clamor of rights assertion in the United States. Against the artificially constructed landscape of a rights-obsessed America, they have constructed a myth that there is no rights assertion in Japan.

To better understand the contours of the alleged contrast between the United States and Japan, it is critical to distinguish between jurisprudential rights, cultural myths about rights,[15] and the strategic assertion of rights. Jurisprudentially, for something to be a right in the most fundamental legal meaning of the term, it must be guaranteed by a code or constitution and/or protected by a court – that is, it must be legally enforceable. In both the United States and Japan, there is much jurisprudential literature on precisely what claims should be treated as "rights," and how rights should be distinguished from a range of other legally protected interests. In neither country is there widespread agreement on the precise meaning of rights, nor on which rights should be protected.

Cultural myths about rights concern the relative importance attributed to rights in a particular society by popular and academic writers, as well as by laypersons. The power rights are imagined to possess, the frequency with which they are supposedly invoked, and how they are thought to define the identity of a people are the key components that fuel the creation of a myth about rights. In examining litigiousness in the United States, for example, an issue closely related to rights, Carol Greenhouse writes not about litigation itself, but about the interest Americans have in it. What animates her work is "the observation that many Americans are ready to believe in, almost to the point of insistence, their own allegedly litigious national character, even when evidence for this characterization is absent, ambiguous, or contradictory."[16] Just as Greenhouse notices a gap between Americans' perceptions of litigiousness and the actual amount of litigation in the United States, there is also a gap between the perception and reality of rights assertion in the United States, Japan, and elsewhere.

The strategic assertion of rights refers to what Stewart Scheingold calls "the politics of rights." It requires an analysis of how social actors use rights to frame, discuss, and debate issues relevant to social policy; paying attention to the language of such actors engaged in social movements, particularly the context and timing of rights assertion; determining the efficacy of invoking rights for mobilizing like-minded individuals; and evaluating the success of those who use rights in pursuit of particular social ends. Concern with the strategic assertion of rights often supersedes questions about the jurisprudential nature of rights; even if an asserted "right" is not (yet) protected by courts or constitution, it may generate a fierce political struggle. The right to die, for example, was widely discussed and contested in the United States well before it was recognized, in part, by the courts.

In emphasizing sociolegal rather than jurisprudential aspects of rights in contemporary Japan, this book focuses on the interplay between cultural myths about rights and the strategic assertion of rights. Like the gap identified by Greenhouse between unspectacular litigation rates in the United States and beliefs among Americans that they are inherently litigious, the gap in Japan with regard to rights separates the cultural myths about rights – that rights are incompatible with Japanese culture, so that Japanese people will go to great lengths to avoid asserting a right to anything – from a more empirical or case approach that examines who asserts rights, why, and with what effect. Because the interplay between the myths about rights, the strategic use of rights assertion, and the legal and political outcomes of rights-related conflict varies over time and place, I refer to it as a ritual. It is the ritual of rights in Japan, illustrated in the battles over AIDS and the definition of death, that this book seeks to illuminate.

Rights in Japan do matter, but they exhibit differences from, and matter in different ways than, rights in the United States. Living in Japan and in daily contact with Japanese, one is aware of how rarely the word *kenri* (right) is used in daily conversation, even when there is an overt dispute that from an American perspective seems to involve rights. When individuals are angry, or feel cheated, or abused, they are likely to walk away, or to change the subject, or to act extraordinarily polite, rather than to claim that their rights have been aggrieved. Such behavior is not an indication that the parties fail to understand rights, but that rights are not an acceptable tool of one-on-one argument. It is a bad strategy to start talking about rights, because the other party will recoil, the relationship will be severely damaged, and the possibility of a fast or advantageous solution will vanish. Thus, the public, aggressive assertion of rights is reserved for particular types of conflicts, generally those in which the hope of continuing a superficially harmonious relationship between the parties has been abandoned, and the possibility for informal agreement is stalled.

I can support this observation with an array of anecdotal material, some from my own experience. Several weeks after I had (at the lessor's insistence) read every clause of an apartment rental contract, signed it, paid a deposit, and received the key, and only five days before moving in, the landlord appeared at my apartment with a large box of cookies and a formal apology because her cousin wanted to live in the space I had rented. Neither of us referred to the contract, nor the laws governing landlord–tenant relationships and rights. Both of us appealed for sympathy and understanding. We knew that the worst course of action would be to assert our rights and go to court. She offered me a different, less expensive apartment; I saved a substantial amount of rent.

On another occasion, I had an accident in a rental van. Unfortunately, the car that I hit was waiting at a red light, immobile. The other driver worked at an auto body repair shop, which explained his ability to immediately estimate the cost of repairing his company car at $700. Cash on the spot, he demanded, or we would have to call the police. If the police came, it would mean three or four hours making chalk marks on the street to determine the exact angle of my turn and estimate speed. There would be endless paperwork. In the end all would conclude that I had hit a stationary vehicle and had to pay. But the other driver also had better things to do. So we went to his shop, I apologized to his boss and gave him a ceremonial basket of fruit, and we settled on $200.

Neither of these incidents, had they occurred in the United States, would have led to court. Nor would the outcomes have been significantly different. But the choice of a strategy for engaging in the interaction – the repertoire of rituals and rhetoric – would have been distinctive. In the United States, I would have asserted my rights as a tenant, the landlord would have countered with the rights of property owners, and in the end we would have settled. Similarly, after hearing the sound of metal on metal, I would have gotten out of the car, but may not have apologized. He would have acted enraged and demanded my insurance information. I would have offered him $200. One important difference between rights assertion in Japan and the United States, therefore, is the selection of occasions to, or not to, assert them. There are many more occasions in Japan when it is better to be silent, or polite, or apologize, not because one is unaware of the legal rules, though in some cases that too is true, but because one is more likely to reach a satisfactory solution.

How can one sensibly approach the study of rights in Japan when the definition of "rights" and the occasions for rights assertion in the United States and Japan may be so different? Take an example from an entirely different area. The meaning of dance to Webster and others is "to move with rhythmical steps or movement, usually to music." There is a good fit between that definition and the waltz, the polka, and even the monkey. It can reasonably be applied to jazz and modern dance, though experts may insist that the definition needs some fine-tuning. But what of Japanese *butoh*? There is often no music, movement is rarely rhythmical, and artists sometimes remain with their feet planted for long periods of time. Look in a Japanese dictionary, however, and the word "*butoh*" is translated as dance. Ask a Japanese performing artist, and they will tell you that *butoh* is dance. Go to a performance, and you will see an art form that looks like dance. It is neither sensible nor interesting to conclude that since *butoh* does not conform to Mr. Webster's definition of dance, there is no dance in Japan. For those who are interested in the art form called "dance," it would be much more illuminating to observe Japanese *butoh* and think about how it challenges and complexifies their idea of dance.

Like *butoh*, examining rights in Japan provides an opportunity to look beyond the familiar (though contested) Western terrain of jurisprudential approaches to rights, cultural myths about rights, and the strategic assertion of rights. By setting one's gaze upon Japan, one discovers that far from a nation barren in rights and rights assertion, both have a long history and a rich present. The sensible question about rights in Japan is not whether or not there are any. Rather, as with dance, the challenge is to critically examine the historical background of rights, and to look at contemporary instances of rights assertion to learn by whom rights are asserted, when, and with what impact.

Kawashima Takeyoshi, the godfather of the view that contemporary Japanese are unusually reticent about asserting their rights, discussed the values animating legal behavior in Japan and the West as part of a theory of Japanese modernization. In contrast to rights-based Western legal systems, where individuals assert rights without fear of social condemnation, Kawashima claimed that the Japanese legal system was based on duties and lacked a concept of rights. Although in postwar Japan people continued to avoid courts and rights assertion, in Kawashima's view the gap between rights assertion and litigation in Japan and the West would narrow as the Japanese legal system became more modern. Kawashima presented his theory about Japanese law and legal behavior in *Nihonjin no Hō Ishiki* [The Legal Consciousness of the Japanese], widely acknowledged to be a masterpiece of postwar sociolegal scholarship.

Kawashima identified cultural factors as the most important cause of Japanese legal behavior. An orientation toward groups rather than individuals, a preference for consensus over conflict, and a propensity to feelings of shame and indirect communication in situations of tension were among his explanations for why rights assertion and legal conflict were limited. In short, according to Kawashima, Japanese culture, more specifically legal culture, accounts for the infrequency of rights assertion.

John Haley, a University of Washington law professor and Japanese legal expert, offered a powerful critique of Kawashima's ideas.[17] Haley presented a contrasting position that emphasized the power of structural factors in containing legal struggles. Strict controls on the number of people permitted to pass the bar examination, high filing fees when going to court, and a long, cumbersome legal process are just a few of the many structural features of the Japanese legal system that he said discouraged the use of the courts.

Despite their disagreement about the relative importance of culture and structure, however, Kawashima and Haley share a common framework; both accept that there is a fundamental difference between rights assertion in Japan and the West, and seek to explain *why*. Attempts to answer that question have consumed more energy and resulted in a greater range of publications than any other single issue on the agenda of sociolegal scholarship about Japan. With few exceptions, observers and laypersons interested in contemporary Japan have accepted the view that Japanese rarely assert rights, use courts, or engage in other law-related behavior.[18]

In fact, Japan already exhibits certain characteristics of rights talk that would agitate critics of rights in the United States. An article on subway renovations in Tokyo, for example, reported claims that "not providing bathrooms or making males and females share the same lavatories at public lavatories are violations of human rights."[19] A Korean resident of Japan, engaged in a long-standing battle regarding the family registration system, contended that "a person's name is an important matter involving human rights, so it should be registered correctly . . . not to be correctly called by one's name is a violation of those rights."[20] A dispute over the decibel level of public address systems is portrayed as "the rights to free speech pitched against appeals to the right to peace and quiet."[21] Measured by a jurisprudential yardstick, the interests being asserted would probably not be considered legal "rights" by Japanese courts. Viewed as examples of how people in Japan articulate their grievances, however, they defy the conventional wisdom by illustrating an unexpectedly broad use of rights rhetoric in Japan.

This book rejects the sharp contrast between rights assertion in Japan and the United States. The contrast is revealing for what it suggests about the creation and reproduction of cultural norms and beliefs, but it fails to provide an accurate picture of the role of rights in either society. Borrowing insights from writing on the legal, historical, sociological, and political dimensions of rights, this analysis examines the function and power of rights in Japan, treating the invocation of rights as one important strategy that groups use to publicize their concerns, to mobilize supporters, and to seek policy change. Although the book is primarily concerned with an analysis of rights in Japan, it also contains an implicit critique of the tendency of scholars in the United States to treat American rights talk as singular. Without diminishing the importance of differences between rights talk in the United States and Japan, I suggest that there are intriguing similarities that have been consistently overlooked by observers in both nations.

Stuart Scheingold, with reference to civil rights struggles and other social movements in the United States, describes how rights are used to galvanize support by those seeking political change, and of the role played by courts in affirming the symbolic power of rights.[22] In Scheingold's account, it is a "myth" to treat rights as entitlements that are secured by litigation. Instead, in his view, rights are better suited to manipulation than realization – asserting rights is a way to influence the balance of political forces, which in turn may affect public policy.

Writing about the history of bioethics in the United States, for example, David Rothman describes a clash between the authority of the medical profession and the demands of patients.[23] In the climate of the 1960s and early 1970s, with the civil rights movement in full bloom, patients were the oppressed. Rothman likens them to tenants in a housing project, to women, to the poor on welfare, powerless in the shadow of physician power. The movement toward patient empowerment, accompanied by great distrust and hostility, expressed itself through rights assertion and litigation. Indeed, it was sometimes criticized for overly exalting individual rights and infringing on the proper domain of medicine. Rothman understands the power of the rights-based approach, remarking on "the extraordinary power that the movement drew from the fact that it was building on this sense of patient as minority and then scaffolding onto it autonomy and all the ancillary issues of consent that go with it."[24]

In his study of the pay equity movement in the United States, Michael McCann elaborates Scheingold's approach to the politics of rights.[25] McCann argues that litigation and its attendant rights discourse may not lead directly to the implementation of new policies that recognize and protect rights, and he alludes to the ways in which rights may inhibit or constrain political action. But he does underscore their symbolic power in providing pay equity activists with a vocabulary and strategy around which to organize their movement, advertise their goals, and broadcast their victories. My study of Japan adopts a similar perspective; it is the use of rights as symbols and resources, in both litigation and in debates over public policy, that makes them an important element of change in Japanese law and society. The move from the jurisprudential to the socio-political context of rights, highlighting the myriad ways that rights are interwoven with the cultural and institutional characteristics of conflict, is the defining characteristic of the ritual of rights in Japan.

In exploring law and rights in Japan, it would be unwise to ignore the view that there is something inherent in Japanese culture that minimizes the importance of rights and the resonance of rights assertion. That claim, similar to but significantly more overstated than assertions about the American propensity for rights assertion, is part of a general tendency to think of the Japanese nation and people as singularly unique. Such beliefs fail, Miyoshi Masao writes, because "exclusivism and essentialism are ethnocentric and fantastic, and as such both dangerous and groundless."[26] Yet there is a persistence to the claim that Japan is "uniquely" unique, a circular argument that Japan is unique because Japanese culture is unique, and Japanese culture is unique because Japan is unique, a corollary of which is that law, legal institutions, and legal behavior in Japan are also unique.

In an attempt to slay the "myth" of Japanese uniqueness, Stephen Reed writes that "[O]ver the years, most scholars, both Japanese and Western, have argued that Japan is a unique country, sui generis, a country unlike any other." He concludes that "[T]here is no need to create a special category for Japan. It is a normal country."[27] This conclusion is unfortunate. Just because Japan is not unique, it does not follow that Japan is like every other place, "normal," conforming to some sort of universal standard. Political economists studying Japan have made exactly that point.[28] They have argued, for example, that Japanese capitalism is not the same as capitalism in the United States, and does not conform to all of the assumptions made by neoclassical economists. While unsympathetic to the idea that Japanese culture is unique, these political economists demonstrate that Japan is different, particularly with respect to institutional arrangements. A central intellectual challenge in studying Japan is thus to identify the ways in which it is similar to and different from other places, rather than assuming exogenous difference that cannot be explained. Such an approach accepts that Japan is not so different that it is singularly "unique," nor so "normal" that it lacks differentiation. It is one on a spectrum of nations, all different in profound respects, and similar in others.

To consider Japan as singularly unique (that is, more different from all other nations than is any other nation) is to accept that it is virtually impossible for non-Japanese to make valid observations about Japanese legal, social, or political practices. Some have made such claims, and they are taken to task by Reed, Peter Dale, and others who make the case for a "normal" Japan and expose the ideological underpinnings of the "uniquely unique" perspectives.[29] But there are various aspects of Japan that are interestingly different from the United States and other nations, and it is necessary to find a way to talk and write about them without lapsing into language or conceptualization, that imply either uniqueness or sameness. The task of studying rights assertion in Japan partly depends upon an approach that recognizes relevant differences while identifying similarities.[30]

Although this study of rights is not an ethnography, it confronts a challenge analogous to that faced by anthropologists interested in describing and analyzing non-Western law. With roots in

THE RITUAL OF RIGHTS IN JAPAN

Wittgenstein's arguments about the influence of Indo-European languages on conceptions of reality, anthropologists have debated the validity of using Western legal concepts to analyze non-Western systems. In *Justice and Judgment Among the Tiv*, for example, Paul Bohannan argues that it is a cardinal error to classify the practices of another system into categories derived from one's own society.[31] He writes: "It would be possible to consider *jir* which concerns 'releasing livestock' as cases of breach of contract. Little purpose would be served by so doing, for Tiv do not have a concept 'contract', and if we do so classify them, there is very grave danger of forgetting that we have applied the notion 'contract' from our own culture."[32] Bohannan's apprehensions are minimized by Max Gluckman, who is confident that Western legal language is adequate for analyzing non-Western systems. Gluckman comments: "Clearly we must not force tribal law into a Procrustean bed of Western jurisprudential concepts, but we may with care use those refined concepts for comparison and analysis."[33]

Those who reject the applicability of Western terms to non-Western systems stress the differences between legal systems, whereas those who stress their applicability emphasize similarities. Gluckman, for example, attacks Bohannan's rejection of the concept of "truth" in relation to Tiv legal proceedings, claiming:

> I would suggest that Bohannan has been misled in his comparison . . . other concepts in English deal with the same phenomena as he finds in Tivland: the white lie, tact, and discretion are but three. I wish to insist on this equivalence as against Bohannan, because he represents a school which stresses mainly the differences between African law and European law, and overlooks similarities. I think that on this point he has gone astray.[34]

Emphasizing the connection between reliance on Western terminology and an emphasis on similarities, Gluckman approvingly cites E. E. Evans-Pritchard's study of the Nuer: "The Nuer has a keen sense of personal dignity and rights. The notion of right, *cuong*, is strong. It is recognized that a man ought to obtain redress of certain wrongs."[35] Gluckman emphasizes similarities between systems, and uses Western terms to do so; Bohannan concentrates on differences, and is uncomfortable with using Western legal language.

Aside from vocabulary, there are other factors in the choice of whether to stress similarity or difference when analyzing legal systems different from one's "native" system. Legal comparativists in the late nineteenth century, for example, emphasized the differences between legal systems and the loss of a common legal culture, a consequence of the codification of Continental law and the emphasis it placed on the distinctiveness of each nation's system.[36] As interest in formal legal rules and institutions gave way to a concern with their actual functioning, comparativists began to stress similarities between jurisdictions. More recent trends in comparative legal scholarship, according to Mary Ann Glendon, include a concern with the underlying principles of the law, as well as with the interaction between law and social change.[37] Both of these issues make room for the identification of similarities and differences.

This study is attentive to both the similarities and differences in rights assertion in Japan and the United States. Western terminology is used throughout the volume, but that should not obscure the fact that "rights" in Japan does not have the same meaning as "rights" in the United States, just as "rights" in the United States does not have the same meaning as "rights" in Germany. Thus, despite the presence of rights talk in many areas of Japanese social relations, rights talk in Japan can be distinguished from that in the United States. Countervailing forces like a strong state bureaucracy willing to intimidate or suppress rights assertion, institutional barriers that make using the courts difficult, conservative judges and a hierarchical court structure that moderates judicial innovation, statutes or administrative guidance that require conciliation, and a 2,000 year history, all shape the assertion and recognition of rights in Japan. These differences are real; but they do not justify the all too common claims about the insignificance of rights in Japan.

Reinhard Bendix was confronted with a related dilemma when studying economic development in Western and non-Western settings. Bendix connects the use of Western terms to the conclusion that societies do not progress or evolve in a universal pattern. He writes:

> As we turn today to problems of development in the non-Western world, we employ concepts that have a Western derivation. In so doing, we can proceed in one of two ways: by formulating a new set of categories applying to all societies, or by rethinking the categories familiar to us in view of the transformation and diversity of the Western experience itself. These studies adopt the second alternative in the

belief that the insights gained in the past should not be discarded lightly.[38]

Once Bendix accepts that processes or results of development differ between nations, the use of Western terms and conceptual categories becomes problematic. Rather than jettison the categories and language that make up the Western analysis of modernization, he seeks to expand and improve upon them.

By applying this approach to Japan, it is possible to preserve the vocabulary developed to discuss political and legal practices in the West, and at the same time refine and revise the original concepts. Much of Chalmers Johnson's analysis of Japanese capitalism has followed such a course. In discussing the idea of ownership in Japan, for example, he refers to ownership and control as they developed in capitalist economies. Johnson claims that in Japan, the distinction between ownership, which depends upon the number of shares possessed by individuals or organizations, and control, vested in professional managers who run the business in the interests of owners, has become blurred. In Japan, he writes, "the managers are ascendant and the owners have become invisible to the point that the concept of ownership no longer means much of anything."[39] By using the term "ownership" to analyze Japanese corporations, Johnson uncovers a critical aspect of Japanese corporate governance, and increases our understanding of the limitations of neoclassical economic theory for explaining Japan. Johnson believes that capitalism in Japan can be understood, but only through detailed research on the history and development of Japanese institutions and organizations, not through the language and theories of Western economics or political science.

It would have been difficult for Johnson to describe the relationship between financial and managerial roles in Japan without using the Western vocabulary of ownership. Like ownership, the Western term "rights" has analytic power when applied to Japanese rights assertion; given the lack of alternatives, it is the best available conceptual tool for understanding the Japanese experience. Just as answering the question "are there political parties in Sierra Leone," for example, with a "yes" or "no" does little to increase understanding of social and political organization there, a simple answer to "are rights asserted in Japan" is not terribly informative. In both cases, there is a need to go beyond terminological argument, the "yes there is, no there isn't" variety of scholarship. What is needed is a description of different attributes and experiences that are linked by a common quality, and a reasoned argument that the naming of that quality fits the data. I call the thread that connects the historical and contemporary Japanese material discussed herein "rights"; an examination of some of the attributes and experiences that it connects forms the body of this book.

CHAPTER TWO

RIGHTS IN JAPANESE HISTORY

THE ROOTS OF "RIGHTS"

Concepts functionally similar to rights can be found early in Japanese history.[1] Until Japanese legal experts began translating European law during the Meiji Restoration (late nineteenth century), however, there was no word that directly translated as "rights" in Japanese.[2] The translation of the word "rights" is therefore important in framing the discussion of rights in contemporary Japan. In itself an interesting piece of intellectual history, the translation more importantly indicates that the social and political significance of rights was understood in Japan by government officials, intellectuals, and social reformers. Were rights merely a foreign import lacking resonance in Japan, it is unlikely that the translation would have been so hotly contested.

Meiji reformers set off in the 1870s to study European legal systems and codes. Some went to Holland, others to Germany, still others to France and England. Their objective was to create a new legal system for Japan, in large part to avoid the humiliation of foreign extraterritoriality laws. Much of their work entailed gaining proficiency in foreign legal languages so that they could translate codes and other legal documents into Japanese. In doing so, they transformed virtually the entire range of legal language, from narrow technical terms to words describing entire categories and concepts.[3] Most new words, created through a process in which Chinese characters were combined into new blends of sound and meaning, generated little controversy. But "rights," central to the law of each European jurisdiction studied by the Japanese reformers, became the focus of a prolonged debate between proponents of different translations.

Those impressed by the absence of rights in traditional Japan viewed the translation of "rights" as particularly problematic. Carmine Blacker, for example, writes:

> At the beginning of the Meiji period the enormous majority of Japanese were entirely ignorant of its [rights] meaning, for the reason that there had been no idea even remotely equivalent to it in the old Confucian philosophy . . . Having no idea of rights, the Japanese naturally had no word to express the idea – and their difficulty in grasping its meaning is well illustrated by their difficulty in choosing a suitable word.[4]

Even those who saw a connection between certain Japanese concepts and "rights" found the translation of "rights" difficult, particularly because they were starting with a variety of European words for "rights" that had similar, but not identical, meanings. To Blacker and others, the difficulty of selecting an appropriate combination of Chinese characters to capture the meaning of "rights" exemplified the difficulties of recreating Japanese law, the foreignness of Western legal thought, and the alleged limitation of the Japanese language in capturing the precise definitions of foreign legal concepts.

Most accounts of the translation of Western legal texts begin with Mitsukuri Rinshō. But it was his grandfather, Mitsukuri Genpō, who was the pioneer in translating European legal codes into Japanese. A resident of Okayama prefecture, where there was a tradition of Western studies, Mitsukuri Genpō was trained as a doctor and went on to become an official translator of the Bakufu. He helped to translate books about geography, military affairs, mining, geology, and foreign affairs, and served as a translator during Matthew Perry's 1853 visit.[5] In 1839, he was asked by the Japanese government to translate the Dutch legal codes. His primary focus was the Code of Civil Procedure, which he completed in 1855.[6]

One of the first challenges facing Mitsukuri Genpō was the lack of an appropriate Japanese vocabulary with which to express European legal concepts. The difficulty this presented was encapsulated by the translation of the Dutch word *regt*. Like the German *recht*, French *droit*, and Latin *ius*, *regt* combined the meaning of the English terms "law" and "right." Mitsukuri had to create a word from Chinese characters that captured the breadth of these concepts while selecting characters with meaning to literate Japanese.

He settled upon *seiritsu*, combining the word for correctness and justice (*tadashii*) with that for law or regulation (*ritsu*). As possibly the first translation into Japanese of the European words for "right," this was not a bad choice, retaining the character of both "law" and "rights" found in the originals. Based upon Mitsukuri's translation of *regt* as *seiritsu*, Dutch legal historian Frans Verwayen concludes that for Mitsukuri *regt* was "something legal, that could belong to a person, and could be damaged, both elements which are more consistent with the meaning 'right' than the meaning 'law' of the word *regt*."[7] While Mitsukuri's translation does not encompass the entire range of meanings of "right," it is a considerable achievement, and suggests that at least some Japanese scholars did not find the translation of "right" so daunting. In fact, from almost the same period, class notes of Nishi Amane and Tsuda Masamichi, two Japanese intellectuals studying law in Leiden with Simon Vissering, include a discussion of law, rights, and natural rights indicating that Nishi and Tsuda were able to follow the lectures and describe them in Japanese with a high degree of accuracy.[8]

Still, none of the above scholars created the word for "rights" that has been in use for more than a century. That word, *kenri*, first appeared in William Martin's Chinese translation of Weaton's *Elements of International Law*, published in Beijing in 1864 and introduced in Japan by Mitsukuri Rinshō in 1865. Like his grandfather, Mitsukuri Rinshō excelled at languages and legal study; like most translators he was considered an expert on law, not simply a linguist. He spoke fluent Dutch at the age of twelve, and on his way to becoming an important figure in the Ministry of Justice became proficient in French to facilitate his translation of the French codes.[9]

Soon after the introduction of the word *kenri*, a debate began among Japanese scholars about which Chinese characters most appropriately captured the meaning of rights as used in European law. The word *kenri*, as used by Martin, consisted of two ideograms. *Ken*, written 権, originally meant quantity, amount, or volume, and was used when discussing the measure of quantity.[10] It later came to mean measure in general, and was sometimes used to describe spiritual measure. As is often the case with Chinese characters, it was combined with other characters to create new meanings. *Ken* became part of the character *kenni*, meaning authority, power, dignity, and prestige, and *kensei*, meaning power or influence. The association of *ken* with authority and power continues in the present.

While there was little disagreement about the use of *ken* as part of the character compound representing rights, two different characters were proposed for *ri*. One, written 利, carried an original meaning of something that went smoothly, good circumstances, and good situations. Later, it took on the meaning of profit, gain, benefit, and advantage. The other character for *ri*, 理, means reason, justice, truth, and principle. From the late 1860s, and continuing for several decades, two different translations of rights, 権利 (K1) and 権理 (K2), both pronounced *kenri*, were being used in Japan.

Martin's version of rights, K1, was used in legal codes, court papers, regulations, and other official documents. K2 was used by many prominent intellectuals, such as Fukuzawa Yūkichi, Nishi Amane, Ono Azusa, and Katō Hiroyuki. Some writers used both versions of *kenri* in their work.[11] Fukuzawa, for example, used K2 to mean the general concept of rights in modern law, and K1 to indicate the consciousness of legal rights by people since feudal times. Others had ideological reasons for favoring one or the other of the words. K2 was favored by members of the Movement for Freedom and Popular Rights, particularly those former samurai influenced by feudal law who liked the association of rights with reason and disdained the connection between rights and secular profits.

Eventually, K1 came to be used not only in official government and legal documents, but also in the writings of intellectuals, journalists, and others wishing to discuss rights in Japanese. It is not clear why K1 prevailed over K2, but many considered it unfortunate. Had K2 become common usage, the Japanese word for right, *kenri*, would have combined power or authority with reason or principle. Instead, it combines power or authority with profit or interest.[12] This version of the word lacks any ideographic connection to morality, justice or correctness, and lends support to the scholarly and popular view that to assert a right in Japan is to be self-centered, profit-seeking, and self-righteous.

With the derivation of *kenri* from the combination of Chinese characters for power and interest has grown the view that there can be no understanding in Japan of rights.[13] Devoid of any moral sense of rights, the word *kenri* itself is seen as the ultimate example of a Japanese inability or unwillingness to grasp complex Western legal concepts. The choice of *kenri* proves, according to this view, that in Japan rights have been misunderstood as related exclusively to the exercise of power and narrow self-interest.

This interpretation ignores two important points. First, K2 was a powerful contender for the official character for rights. Had it been accepted, its rise to prominence would probably have been more the result of political maneuvering than moral philosophy. Would scholars then have had a basis for claiming a particular Japanese appreciation for the subtleties of rights in Japan? The choice of a character is interesting, but it can be overemphasized. Second, while rights in the West are related to morality and justice, they are not exclusively so; there is also a strong association with power and interest. Asserting rights, seeking legal sanctions, and disputing are all closely connected to the exercise of power. An even closer link between rights and power is demonstrated by the association of rights assertion with state regulation and suppression in Japan. Rights are not only about power, but in the realm of law and politics the Japanese linguistic connection is not entirely misleading.

RIGHTS BEFORE *KENRI*: EARLY ANTECEDENTS

The translation into Japanese of the Western words for "rights" could not and did not create rights in Japan. In fact, the impossibility of a nation successfully importing wholesale another nation's concept of rights has been derided by Mary Ann Glendon: "We cannot, nor would most of us wish to, import some other country's language of rights. Nor can we invent a new rhetoric of rights out of whole cloth. A political Esperanto without roots in a living cultural tradition would die on the vine."[14] That does not mean, however, that the idea of rights was alien. One must be careful to distinguish between the absence of a *concept* of rights and the lack of a *word* for "rights." Despite the absence of a vocabulary for "rights" and the influence of the Chinese legal tradition in Japan, my interpretation of the work of historians of Japan is that there were certain legal relationships that were based on concepts similar to Western rights. Indeed, some commentators now argue that Japanese legal history cannot be understood without a focus on rights. Mark Ramseyer, for example, concludes his recent study *Odd Markets in Japanese History* by writing: "In significant part, the history of law in imperial Japan is a history of the way courts enforced claims to scarce resources. More simply, it is a history of property rights."[15]

In the eleventh and twelfth centuries, there emerged in Japan an estate (*shōen*) system that constituted the core of medieval economic organization. As the system developed, relationships between peasants (*hyakushō*) and proprietors evolved and were redefined, particularly with regard to land use, occupancy, and profit. Rules were intricate, with the proprietor both conferring and guaranteeing the peasant's status, as well as serving as the court of redress, and the peasant sharing in the exercise of authority in a system of "mutual dependence and empowerment."[16]

Within such a system, conflicts were bound to arise. As they did, a procedure of peasant petitions (*hyakushō mōshijō*) appeared, in which peasants wrote their grievances about problems like excessive rent and greedy managers and submitted them to the proprietors.[17] Historians are divided on how to understand this process of conflict resolution; some view it as based in contractual rights and others as merely peasants pleading and proprietors exercising power by fiat.[18] But all agree that peasant petitions were to some extent dependent upon the fact that both peasants and proprietors accepted the idea that the powerless had at least a general, abstract expectation of assistance from the powerful, and that the powerful were obligated to help. There were certain intolerable conditions, therefore, that could spawn justified claims by peasants against proprietors, and which the proprietors had an obligation to grant. These claims may not have entailed all the elements of a modern claim of rights; but they contained some of their core features, as described by Gregory Vlastos in his seminal essay "Justice and Equality."[19] According to Vlastos, rights are "justified claims," which means that rights are "something which could be claimed with justification, i.e. a claim which others have the obligation to grant if (but not, only if) it is asserted." Under this definition, there were rights-like relationships in the *shōen* system.

During the same period, an aspect of the estate system known as *shiki* was refined. Already in existence for several centuries, during the medieval period *shiki* came to describe the entitlements to income from estates. All administrative and economic interests in estates took the form of *shiki*; proprietors, local administrators, and high-ranking peasants all had some type of *shiki*.[20]

In effect, *shiki* were a complex network of rights that gave one benefits flowing from cultivated land.[21] They were negotiated, disputed, litigated, and delineated through the highly developed legal systems of the Kamakura and Muromachi Bakufu, complex systems that were the origin of the rule of law in Japan.[22] John Haley describes "the development of rights of proprietorship beginning with the enforcement of offices [*shiki*] entitling their holders to income from particular parcels"[23] as an early example of a legal rule that developed through adjudication. Legal historian John Carey Hall supports this claim, describing the shift from centralized rule during the Kamakura period to the ensuing feudal system: "[T]he distinction between boundaries of legal jurisdiction and outright control had been largely obliterated. Within this area, the complex division of rights which characterized the *shōen* system had given way to the holding of land in fief."[24] Not all commentators are comfortable equating *shiki* with rights. Japan's most influential postwar legal sociologist, Kawashima Takeyoshi, for example, describes interests in land, forests, personal effects, and other things in traditional Japan as "entitledness." He insists "that there has been no clear and definite notion of 'right' to the effect that the person who has the right is entitled to demand other persons to act in conformity with his interest invested in the 'right'."[25] Kawashima's idea of rights – that rights mean having the ability to make demands and have them satisfied – suggests that in the absence of a clear enumeration of rights that can be asserted and enforced there is no concept of rights. Because he recognizes the significance of *shiki*, however, Kawashima makes the unusual argument that in traditional Japan there were "rights that are not rights." Stated differently, it appears that Kawashima is saying that there were rights in Japan, but they were not the same as rights in the West. Rights (Japanese) that are not rights (Western).

Shiki has a strong resemblance to what are now called "rights." That does not mean that the word *shiki* should be translated as "rights," nor that the concepts underlying *shiki* and "rights" are identical. Instead, as Japanese legal scholar Carl Steenstrup puts it, Kamakura "was a rights-conscious society, or, rather, the central power was weak enough to permit competing groups to speak up and call their claims for more of the cake 'rights.'"[26]

RIGHTS, PROTEST, AND REBELLION IN TOKUGAWA JAPAN

Analyses of social upheaval during the Tokugawa (1603–1868) period provide evidence that both prior to the minting of the word *kenri* and immediately after it entered the Japanese vocabulary, rights-like entitlements were vigorously asserted and violently defended (until *kenri* was created, the Bakufu used the Dutch *regt* to mean rights[27]). There was much continuity between Tokugawa and Meiji rebellions; despite formal changes in the law, the Meiji Restoration did not cause a "radical fissure" in how Japanese claimed their rights.

Tokugawa Japan was a rigidly feudalistic society, in which peasants were denied education, freedom of movement, and freedom to choose an occupation. They were treated contemptuously by the elite, perhaps more so than peasants in European feudalistic societies. One early nineteenth-century description reads:

> Those people whom we call peasants are no better than cattle or horses. The authorities pitilessly compel them to pay heavy taxes ... The arrogant behavior of these officials is like that of a heartless driver of some horses or ox; after loading it down with a great weight he proceeds to rain blows upon it; then when it stumbles he becomes more and more angry, cursing it loudly and striking it even with greater force – such is the fate of the peasant.[28]

Still, peasants were not completely intimidated by the authority of Tokugawa lords and rulers. Historians estimate that during the Tokugawa period, there were between 3,000[29] and 7,000[30] peasant rebellions. Protest ranged from the filing of legal appeals to violent confrontation.[31] It took place throughout the nation, and included riots (*bōdō) and house smashings (uchikowashi)* involving the destruction of property. The aims were sometimes specific – a protest against a single administrative act – but many were also quite general. Rather than targeting a single grievance, they sought to transform the economic and political conditions under which peasants lived. Peasants called such protests *yonaoshi,* meaning "world renewal" or "world rectification," and a variety of such incidents have been carefully documented.[32]

Tokugawa rule was cloaked in the mantle of benevolence, consistent with Confucian thought, which posited a natural social hierarchy of higher and lower beings and linked the legitimacy of rulers to the goodness of their acts. Peasant protest is thus frequently understood as a demand for the benevolence that the elite had a *duty* to display, as opposed to a justified claim of rights. Hashimoto Mitsuru, in his discussion of peasant uprisings seeking *yonaoshi,* describes the desire to return to the "good old days" of peasant life: "Restoration of morality in the fallen world thus took the form of rebellion against whoever exploited "good" peasants. In uprisings and in the new religious movements, peasants rejected what had been authoritative and sought a more benevolent and merciful rule."[33] The objects of protest were usually village officials or higher-status peasants. Peasants continued to accept the legitimacy of Meiji state officials, despite the anger and violence displayed at the local level.[34] The fact that they protested is squarely within the Chinese tradition of disposing of evil rulers and bad government.[35]

The question, then, is not when or whether there were peasant protests, but how to interpret such protests. Were they clearly distinguishable from rights-based claims as conceived of in the West, and as claimed by those who find no tradition of rights assertion in Japan? Do they signal a tradition in Japan that can legitimately be evaluated as rights assertion?

One approach to this issue is suggested by the work of historian Irwin Scheiner, who describes the consciousness of Tokugawa peasants:

> While peasants accepted their obligations, they did so conditionally, however, and with an "if" clause . . . They "respectfully" bound themselves to pay taxes, but they did so with the provision that the lord would realize his bounded duty to oblige them when they demanded it. Notably, they also had a sense of what was a proper tax, and they believed that past law limited present actions and that traditional practices set precedent for future policy . . . This sense that they lived in a world of conditional loyalties, established duties, and mutual obligation may be seen most clearly when the peasant asserted his belief that he might remove himself from service to the *han* [area] if justice was not given or aid refused . . .[36]

Scheiner describes a web of loyalties, duties, and obligations between peasants and lords. Although he does not invoke legal language, the relationships Scheiner discusses indicate that peasants and lords had reciprocal rights and duties. A similar point of view is expressed by Japanese legal scholar Takayanagi Kenzō. Takayanagi acknowledges that theoretically Tokugawa civil justice was administered as a matter of grace, not right. However, because certain types of interests were protected by law, he thinks it reasonable that jurists could have "worked out a scheme of rights based on the categories of remedies which had regularly been recognized."[37] Unfortunately for the peasants, they had little power to enforce their rights when they sensed that "justice was not given," even when they were correct in understanding past practice. Their only recourse was protest, and as they felt themselves increasingly abused, the tenor of protest increased.

In *The Agrarian Origins of Modern Japan*, Thomas Smith describes the importance of water in the Tokugawa period as one concrete example of private rights-based peasant conflict. Water, always essential to farmers, was often scarce, and required some means of rationing. As a resource frequently held in common by the community, it was distributed in accordance with rules established by the village administration. Beyond the small circle of privileged families, which always took part in community management, those wishing to be involved had to win office. Consequently, there was constant conflict over who had the right to determine water allocation, which became increasingly tense as the Tokugawa era progressed: "Wherever conflicts did break out the issues were similar: either a disenfranchised party demanded equal political rights in the village, including the right to hold office, or they demanded the dismissal of incumbent village officeholders, which was in effect an attempt to exercise the right of selecting officials."[38] Whereas Smith emphasizes the administrative function of village leaders in water distribution, Japanese legal specialist Mark Ramseyer highlights individual claims in his discussion of the development of Japanese water law. In both accounts rights play a critical role, with the allocation of water hinging on the successful assertion of rights by those who needed to irrigate and those who desired to expand their fields.[39]

Political scientist Roger Bowen, who identifies a series of rights and obligations that bound Tokugawa rulers and the ruled,[40] recognized the limits Confucian traditions placed on protesters. He distinguishes between rebellions that *appeal* through violence and those that *demand* as a result of official recognition of rights.[41] Bowen argues that during the Tokugawa period neither rulers nor ruled were concerned with political rights – by which he means rights that could be asserted by peasants against the authorities. He locates the genesis of such rights in the "quasi-political right of subsistence," the economic "right" to have enough to eat. From that "right," he argues, sprung a "right" to appeal to "benevolent government ameliorative action in times of severe dearth, [and] when flood or famine or a dishonest tax collector infringed on [the] 'right to subsist.'"[42]

Bowen in this way distinguishes full-fledged political rights, that would allow peasants to make demands on authorities through established, official channels, and the quasi-political "right" of subsistence, that led to entreaties: "While feudal in *form*, like the European version, having certain established relationships involving rights and obligations between rulers and ruled, it was nonetheless Confucian in *substance* and therefore highly restrictive of the manner by which the ruled could press the rulers to honor traditional feudal obligations."[43] By distinguishing between the form and substance of peasants' claims, Bowen's argument goes to the essence of the debate over whether there is a tradition of rights assertion in Japan. There is not, his writing suggests, if one seeks as evidence substantive political rights recognized by Tokugawa rulers and peasants, backed up by legal means of appeal and enforcement. But if one takes a broader view, and characterizes peasant revolts as seeking action from authorities in recognition of economic interests that would now be called "rights," then Bowen's work describes a tradition that strongly resembles what is now considered rights assertion.

What emerges from viewing Tokugawa peasant uprisings as a consistent and concerted assertion of rights is an understanding of how and why peasants united, protested, and sought to have their interests recognized and satisfied.[44] Tokugawa peasants were engaged in a process of *yonaoshi*, embedded in an ethos of benevolence and honor, and victims of a brutal feudalism. They were unable to resort to independent and just legal or judicial mechanisms, because none existed. They were unable to demand "rights" *per se*, because there was not a word for "rights" that would serve as an appropriate slogan. Still, they utilized a variety of means, both peaceful and violent, to voice their grievances. While not explicitly demanding or asserting something called "rights," they were engaged in protests that attest to the existence of a general sense of rights. As Herbert Bix writes:

> The right to resist unjust exactions, the right to land, and the right to fair treatment by privileged power holders were three such general rights repeatedly expressed in rebellions. But there were other rights, of a more specific nature, which became manifest as the Tokugawa political economy and its culture developed through specific historical stages.[45]

The translation of "rights" as *kenri* did not lead immediately to the diffusion of a new vocabulary in which to express one's demands. There remained a process of public explanation and popularization, as legal theorists, scholars, and officials discussed and debated the substance of this new word.

THE MOVEMENT FOR FREEDOM AND POPULAR RIGHTS

As Tokugawa isolation ended late in the nineteenth century, the frequency of peasant uprisings declined. Peasant dissatisfaction with living conditions was expressed through new channels, as violent revolts were translated into battles for political control. Higher offices in the new government came to be occupied primarily by members of two previously powerful domains, Satsuma and Choshu. Most officials were ex-samurai, who with the collapse of feudalism were discarded by their lords. Known as *rōnin*, or masterless samurai, they had social standing and prestige, and were eventually absorbed by the rapidly growing government bureaucracy.

Itagaki Taisuke, one such official, soon entered a struggle for power connected to his interest in political reform. Itagaki led a group of politicians in demanding a Japanese military expedition to Korea. When the demand was dismissed, they resigned from the government in protest and helped found one of the most prominent movements of the Meiji era, the Movement for Freedom and Popular Rights (*Jiyū Minken Undō*, hereinafter PRM). One manifesto of the movement states:

> We, the thirty millions of [sic] people in Japan, are all equally endowed with certain definite rights, among which are those of enjoying and defending life and liberty, acquiring and possessing property, and obtaining a livelihood and pursuing happiness. These rights are by Nature bestowed upon all men, and therefore, cannot be taken away by the power of any man.[46]

While the exact size of the movement is difficult to calculate, there were hundreds of affiliated local organizations with membership in the hundreds of thousands.

A direct causal link between Tokugawa peasant uprisings and the PRM is difficult to demonstrate, but both demonstrate a similar style of social conflict. W. G. Beasley, for example, points out the similarities in character and social composition between violent uprisings by supporters of the PRM and those of peasants. Such links, he suggests, "signaled the danger, which was not overlooked by those who made Meiji policy, that traditional forms of protest, not yet removed, could be given political direction by modern ideologies."[47] Historian Peter Duus also affirms the links between these different periods of protest, while crediting the PRM with initiating "a new tradition of legitimate political dissent" and instigating a broadening of political consciousness.[48]

Founders of the PRM were the first in Japan to make political use of the newly created language of rights. Embedded in the very name of the *Jiyū Minken Undō* was the contentious character for rights, the *ken* of *kenri*. It arrived there via the Ministry of Justice, run by the ambitious Etō Shimpei. Etō recruited Mitsukuri Rinshō to translate European legal codes. In the process of doing so Mitsukuri encountered the term *"droit civil."* He translated it as *jinmin kenri*, soon shortened to *jinken* (human rights) or *minken* (civil rights).[49]

It is instructive that the PRM chose to use this new word as part of its name, rather than use a more traditional and perhaps more easily recognizable name. Combined with *jiyū* (freedom, also a word that was recently coined to translate a Western term), the use of *jiyū minken* to name the movement indicates that the leaders were bent on identifying themselves with new, "Western-style" concepts. Leaders of the PRM were politically sophisticated, and understood that a movement championing rights would attract attention and support. While neither leaders nor followers of the PRM may have been concerned with the epistemological subtleties of *minken*, they did know how to invoke the new language of rights in their quest for political and social change.

The use of the word *"minken"* also served to highlight its linguistic and conceptual relationship to *kokken*. Linguistically, both words share the Chinese character *ken*, used in *kenri*, meaning power or authority. Changing the first character, however, replaces a character meaning person or people with one meaning state or nation. The civil, individualistic meaning of *minken* thus contrasts with the communal, nationalistic sentiment pervading *kokken*.

Those opposed to the development of discrete civil rights in Japan, or to the PRM more generally, promoted the idea that *minken* and *kokken* were mutually exclusive, similar to the split between selfishness and patriotism.[50] Others viewed *minken* and *kokken* as natural complements. Fukuzawa Yūkichi, for example, wrote:

> Recently we Japanese have undergone a great transformation. The theory of human rights has flooded the land and has been universally accepted. However, equal rights does not merely mean that all men within a single country are equal. It means equality between a man from one nation and a man from another nation, as well as between one nation and another nation; it means that, regardless of power or wealth, everyone's rights are exactly equal.[51]

Ueki Emori, a writer, intellectual, and leading figure in the PRM, disagreed. While Ueki believed that the rights of individuals and states were closely correlated, he worried about the rise of nationalism and strategically decided to advocate for individual rather than state interests.[52]

Tension between the promotion of individual rights, and the relationship between those rights and the interests of the state, also arose in the debate over whether the creation of a popular assembly or the promotion of private rights should take precedence. Donald Calman quotes one critic who claimed that PRM leaders could not appreciate the relationship between citizens and the state. "They still appeared to think that the government was in some way of a higher status than the people, and could not convince themselves that the tasks entrusted to the government were in no way superior to those performed by the people."[53] By promoting a system in which individuals could participate in government but could not assert their rights against it, PRM leaders were accused of perpetuating a strong state structure unresponsive to citizens. In addition, influential thinkers like Etō Shimpei believed that without public appreciation of rights, and the legal institutions to support them, a popular assembly had little value. He championed the view that people had a right to go to court against government officials. Such appeals to a rule of law and the creation of civil rights were firmly rejected by government authorities. Etō's reward for attempting to spearhead legal reform and the rule of law was prosecution, forced confession, and the public display of his disembodied head.[54]

Evaluations by historians and others of the PRM's impact are divided.[55] Some denigrate its importance by seeing it as a vehicle for leaders who were primarily interested in personal gain, and used their positions in the movement to secure comfortable government jobs. Fukuzawa Yūkichi, for example, complained about the elitism of the PRM leaders: "So whenever [leaders of the PRM] start talking about equal rights it is hard to listen to them without some impatience. If one does not eat of a certain dish, he cannot appreciate its true taste. If one has never been a prisoner himself, he cannot speak of the real sufferings of imprisonment."[56] Hane Mikiso agrees, arguing that the attainment of liberty and rights was essentially a foil for the ambitions of the leaders, who desired to wrestle some power from the rulers and find jobs for unemployed ex-samurai.[57] PRM leaders, critics claim, were socially and economically elite, and their movement was neither democratic nor popular. It was not democratic because it used violence to achieve its goals; it was not popular because it considered "people" only those of above-average socioeconomic standing.[58] The implication is that PRM advocates had little interest in broadening political consciousness or rights assertion.

Most experts of the PRM, however, see it as continuing a tradition of protest and contributing to the legal, social, and/or political development of rights. Irokawa Daikichi writes that "the spirit [behind the fight for freedom] was definitely not an import. Those grass roots [of democracy] were nurtured within feudal society, stemming from primitive forms of democratic practices."[59] Beasley contends that farmers who supported the PRM "showed a remarkable degree of political awareness and understanding."[60] According to Bowen, "Meiji commoners gave demonstrable proof of possessing a political consciousness of their rights . . ."[61] Duus wrote that "the long-run significance of the popular rights movement was . . . [that] it established a new tradition of legitimate political dissent."[62] Koga, citing an increase of civil suits at the time of the PRM, argues that it was the last time rights were truly understood and asserted in Japan.[63] Indeed, the public began, literally, to hum the tune of popular rights. The lyrics from the "Country Song of Popular Rights," by Ueki Emori, the equivalent of a nineteenth-century top forty hit among the peasants, went in part:

> Man is free; The head thinks and the heart feels; The body moves and runs; Man surpasses all other wonderful creatures; The heart and body are comparable to the universe; Man's freedom does not allow a dearth of liberty; We are free; we have rights; The people of Japan must claim their rights; If we do not, then our companion is shame.[64]

Clearly, a political and legal sensibility called "rights" was not a stranger to nineteenth-century Japan. The power associated with invoking rights was understood by the PRM leaders and others both within and outside the movement, who regularly engaged in the ritual of rights. Some evidence points to the use of litigation as a way to publicize a rights consciousness and attack government policy. As a tactic to stop the building of a new road, for example, protestors turned to the courts, justifying their litigiousness by claiming that legal action was one way to "guarantee happiness and to regain rights for our members."[65] Such an understanding of rights challenges claims about the lack of a tradition of rights assertion in Japan, and the inability of the Japanese to comprehend "Western" legal concepts.

After all, only ten years before the beginning of the PRM, in 1864, did Mitsukuri Rinshō introduce the word *kenri* (rights) to Japan. If it were indeed a radical legal transplant, the Japanese body politic was extraordinarily fertile.

STATE POWER AND THE CONTROL OF RIGHTS

In *Gakumon no Susume* (An Encouragement of Learning), Fukuzawa Yūkichi, perhaps the most influential interpreter and popularizer of rights in Meiji Japan, explained the idea of rights to his nineteenth-century countrymen. Fukuzawa drew a distinction between social status, which varies between individuals, and rights, which everyone has in so far as they concern the preservation of life, property, and honor.

> For a samurai to strike down a merchant, or for a *daimyō* to tax a peasant unjustly was a violation of the rights of the merchant and peasant. A coolie had a right, just as much as a *daimyō* had, to protect his life. A poor pedlar of sweetmeats had as much right to preserve his four farthings as a wealthy merchant his million gold pieces.[66]

In a similar vein, he tried to explain rights by using the idea of *bun*, which concerns one's allotted station in life. A samurai would say his *bun* was infringed if he was insulted, and employers would be infringing on the *bun* of their workers if they did not adhere to the terms of their contract.[67] Fukuzawa used these examples to suggest that a concept functionally similar to rights was present far before the actual translation of the European term.

This type of analogic reasoning is reminiscent of the *Laches*, where Socrates discusses the qualities embodied by courage. The word "courage" already existed in Greek, but its meaning was limited to describing the bravery of soldiers in battle. Socrates identified a number of other situations where the quality of courage could be found, thereby imbuing the concept of courage with the broad meaning it has today. He argued:

> For I meant to ask you not only about the courage of heavily armed soldiers, but about the courage of cavalry and every other style of soldier; and not only who are courageous in war, but who are courageous in perils by sea, and who in disease, or in poverty, or again in politics, are courageous; and not only who are courageous against pain or fear, but mighty to contend against desires and pleasures, either fixed in

their rank or turning upon their enemy. There is this sort of courage –
is there not, Laches?[68]

Socrates did not invent courageous behavior, and unlike the Japanese
reformers he did not have to create a word. But he did provide a
conceptual framework for categorizing and analyzing behavior that
existed but had not previously been thought of as connected.[69]

Like Socratic courage, the translation of "rights" into Japanese provided a new way of understanding, linking and describing certain
behaviors and relationships that were previously separate. Fukuzawa,
through his examples and analogies, attempted to explicate the new
links. Whether labeled "rights" or given another name, there was a
concept similar enough to rights in Japan that people could cultivate
their fields, rent their land, and engage in a broad range of social
interactions with reasonable assurance that if conflict arose they could
make claims and adequately protect their interests.

Perhaps the most vivid indication of the extent to which rights
demands were frequent, widespread, and threatening in pre-World
War II Japan is the number and variety of techniques the state used
to control them.[70] The most subtle was the promotion of particular
perspectives and beliefs that can be classified under the rubric of ideology. Gluck, for example, describes the effectiveness of *tennōsei* ideology: "many Japanese accepted the emperor and the nation 'without
question,' just as they knew that it was 'not done' to mention social
protest in the presence of an official."[71] Myriad other beliefs and practices were similarly internalized. The emphasis on moral (*giri*) over
legal obligations (*gimu*) and humaneness (*ninjyō*) over rights (*kenri*),
for example, appealed to national values and traditions at the expense
of individualism and justice.[72]

Political theorist Maruyama Masao, in his influential postwar essay
"Theory and Psychology of Ultra-Nationalism," compares the relationship between individuals and the state in Japan and in the West.
He contends that in Japan, there was (and is) no split between the
formal institutions of state control and the internal values of citizens,
a split that he believes is vital for modernization. As a result, he
argues that Meiji reformers failed to appreciate the need to change
traditional morality as an essential step to securing individual freedom
and political change.[73] Instead, they concentrated on securing formal
political rights, such as a popular assembly, rather than on transforming fundamental social or political relations.

The strong link Maruyama cites in Japan between the internal sphere of the individual and the external sphere of the state is connected to the reliance on natural rights theory by nineteenth-century reformers. They advocated natural rights as a way of justifying opposition to the state, and identifying particular rights they thought deserving of explicit legal protection. Few of the natural rights that were advocated, however, required internal and external spheres to be demarcated in a way inconsistent with prior social arrangements. The state could legally recognize natural rights, and still be identified as a moral entity superior to individuals and determinative of values. When the rights advocated by the reformers eventually were seen as a threat to the state's monopoly on determining civil relations and practices, the state responded with power and repression.

Linked to Maruyama's insight about the relationship between individuals and the state in Japan is the different way in which public and private are distinguished in English and Japanese. Public in English is defined as "of, relating to, or affecting the people as an organized community"; its meaning can be synonymous with civic, national, common, and government, depending upon the context. In Japan, the meaning of public (*kōteki*, *ōyake*) has less to do with any sense of the common good, or the collection of individuals that make up civil society, though exactly what it does mean is elusive. Barshay argues that the public sphere was born during the creation of the modern state in Imperial Japan (1868–1945), and that public came to be identified as identical to the state.[74] More specifically, public was connected to the emperor and to imperial government, as well as to the interests of private corporations.

Private (*shiteki*, *watakushi*), as in English, can refer to individual persons. But in Japan, its content and nuance are not always so clear. Chalmers Johnson criticizes what he considers the myopia of Western economists, for example, who talk about the Japanese private sector as if it were not amply populated by former bureaucrats and financed by large amounts of government capital.[75] From a different perspective, private is more generally associated with the sense of a disconnected, selfish, unrepresentative person, rather than a citizen who takes a public stand in the common interest. The consequence is one of social control – the common interest comes to be identified with the interests of the state, not the people, and private interests are considered narrow and self-serving.[76] The implications for contemporary Japan are well stated by Patricia Boling in her analysis of the public/private distinction:

> Even when rights exist on paper, individuals are reluctant to assert them, afraid of being perceived as troublemakers or whiners. They cannot overcome the feeling that what pertains only to them (as they see it) is selfish and illegitimate, and so they do not feel they are in the right to argue that others respect their privacy or beliefs.[77]

In other words, private is pejorative, public is positive, and conflict between them is to be avoided.

Assertion of rights was not only regulated through such ideological means. A more concrete method of regulating rights was to require that disputes be conciliated rather than litigated. Conciliation was aimed both at disputes between private parties and those that involved the state, since each represented a threat to maintaining an image of Japanese culture as valuing harmony over conflict and group solidarity over individualism.[78] In cases where conciliation rather than litigation was used to resolve disputes, precedent was not established, legal rights were not enforced, and the growth of law was limited.

As early as the Kamakura period, with its newly simplified and elegant *Bukeihō* legal code, a system of conciliation, or *wayō*, was in place. According to Ōki, because of a high degree of legal awareness (more accurately, perceived injustice), there were a great number of claims, and handling them outside the court system led to similar results at lower cost.[79] Dan Henderson's 1965 work remains the best and most comprehensive English-language treatment of conciliation (*chōtei*) in Tokugawa Japan.[80] Examining conciliation from a variety of perspectives, he concludes that "by resolving the vast majority of civil disputes before they reached the stage of formal trial, the Shogunate conciliation process had the effect of stunting the rate of growth of Shogunate legal precedents throughout the Tokugawa period . . ."[81] While ultimately attributing the prevalence of conciliation to the early stage of development of Tokugawa law, he demonstrates the extent to which it was involuntary, "always on the side of authority," and functioned to "circumvent the enforcement of the rights underwritten by the codified law."[82] The eminent legal historian Ishii Ryōsuke, in discussing Henderson's book, sums up by stating that "the policy of encouraging and even coercing didactic conciliation meant that those who had just legal claims but were weak in a de facto situation had no legal rights."[83] Or, stated differently, the assertion of rights was limited not by a cultural aversion to rights or an inability to understand them, but because the state did not want people to assert them. The Meiji government copied European law by decreasing the sovereignty of the family and making disputes within families actionable as conflicts over rights. But it used the school system to inculcate values to ensure that courts would not be used in such cases, and then instituted a system of required conciliation. A similar pattern of formal law, limited by required conciliation, was followed with regard to labor, unions, home rentals, business, loans, and other areas, evidence that "the mediation system was created through the use of national power to systematically 'avoid law' and to promote informality and the traditional morality of Japan."[84] When conciliation was not mandated, the power of the government was emphasized by cases holding that no compensation was required when a government warehouse exploded, or firefighters caused damage, or a doctor at a state hospital injured a patient, because all existed for public benefit.[85]

More recent examples of conciliation are discussed by Frank Upham. He details the dispute resolution procedures that resulted from conflict over environmental pollution and employment discrimination.[86] Upham persuasively argues that litigation, while not often successful in attaining its narrow objectives, is an important element in forcing bureaucratic action. By reasserting power over a particular issue or area, the bureaucracy often creates a conciliation scenario. This does not necessarily mean that disputes are then settled through extra-legal means. As Martin Shapiro argues, litigation and mediation (here, conciliation) both occupy a place on the continuum of dispute resolution processes.[87] Either one may provide insight on the degree of law and conflict in a society. But the high degree of forced conciliation in Japan enabled the state to reinforce the ideology and the image of a harmonious, consensual society, to repress the assertion and exercise of rights, and to control the process and outcome of disputes in a more subtle and effective way than would direct manipulation of the courts. Even in situations where conciliation was possible but not required, the conciliation option was often made so much more attractive than litigation that parties may well have experienced a coercive pressure to avoid the courts.

Enacting repressive legislation was another way to limit both substantive rights and rights assertion. It was facilitated by linking political dissent with lack of patriotism. No concept of loyal opposition existed in Japan; rights-asserters therefore opposed the state, or at least failed to obey it and could be labeled as disloyal.[88] Laws like the *Kenka Ryō Seibai Hō* of 1831, for example, made disputing itself punishable.[89] Other well-known Meiji laws limiting the growth and assertion of rights were enacted to control farmers' protests against land tax reforms and other state measures that affected their incomes.[90] The Press Law (1875) and Law Prohibiting Libel and Slander (1877), originally envisioned by Ono Azuza, a Meiji reformer and vice-chief of the Civil Law Section of the Ministry of Justice, as a way of protecting individuals from libel and slander came to be used as a way of suppressing political opponents of the government by jailing newspaper editors who expressed seditious views;[91] the Public Meeting Law imposed restrictions on meetings in order to control political associations. Slightly later was the Peace Preservation Law (1925), enacted to control mass organization and political dissenters, particularly socialists and communists.[92]

Laws like these sought to ensure that rights demands would cease or become tempered, as the price for making such demands became increasingly severe. "Don't tell people the rules," went one Edo period saying, "and make them obey."[93] But despite the apparent triumph of power over substantive individual rights, the ritual of rights was tenacious. Kawashima, for example, describes the suppression of the PRM, the rebirth of rights after World War I because of unions, tenant farmer associations, lessee associations, and various rights claims, and their subsequent suppression through indoctrination and forced conciliation. Nonetheless, he believed that rights would eventually flourish:

> the desire for democracy and civil rights has existed ever since the Meiji Reform on a national scale, though we might get an opposite impression when we look at the official ideology disseminated and imposed upon the nation, which was nothing but a means of the government to overcome the democratic ideas persisting within the nation, which constituted the evidence of the existence of democratic ideas. Democracy in Japan is now firmly grounded in the minds of the people, and any political attempt to infringe upon democracy and civil rights will encounter the strong opposition and the resistance of the people in the future.[94]

This chapter suggests that the social and political salience of rights has a long history in Japan. While the instances of contemporary rights assertion recounted in the following chapters have met with mixed success, the prevalence of rights talk in today's Japan would not come as a surprise to Kawashima. In chapter 3, I describe the profusion of social movements built around rights assertion in the 1960s and 1970s, and closely examine one of them – the movement for the rights of medical patients.

CHAPTER THREE

PATIENTS, RIGHTS, AND PROTEST IN CONTEMPORARY JAPAN

"NEW RIGHTS" MOVEMENTS AND TRADITIONAL SOCIAL PROTEST

Student activism in the 1960s, and citizens' movements organized around controversial social issues in the 1970s, presented a challenge to the paradigmatic view of Japanese legal behavior that emerged in the postwar period. That paradigm portrayed Japan as a unique, tradition-bound nation where the power of culture overwhelmed the importance of law or rights. Far from confirming Japan as a nation devoid of rights assertion, events of the 1960s and 1970s provided a patina of possibility to the image of Japan as a litigious, rights-oriented society. The transformation from an absence to an abundance of rights assertion, while more sudden than predicted, accorded with the expectations of legal scholar Kawashima Takeyoshi and others who had claimed that the forces of modernization would cause a shift in various aspects of Japanese legal behavior. As industrialization and urbanization proceeded, according to Kawashima, Japan increasingly would come to resemble a Western nation, and the assertion of rights (as well as their enforcement) would occupy an ever more prominent place in its social interactions.

The emergence of citizens' movements in pursuit of rights temporarily focused the attention of Japanese legal sociologists on the possible transformation of traditional Japanese legal culture. By the late 1970s, however, the social movements that appeared to signal a profound shift in Japanese legal behavior had largely disappeared, and the transformation from a rights-denying to a rights-affirming society had seemingly stalled. The evolutionary view of rights assertion in Japan, which had appeared on the verge of being validated, was instead rebuked. If scholars had taken a longer look at the historical record, they may have recognized that the "new rights" (*atarashii kenri*) movements of the 1960s and 1970s were not so new at all. The movements were squarely within a tradition of Japanese social protest that stretched back many centuries. Japanese citizens had regularly and aggressively asserted their interests when they believed that they had been aggrieved. What made the movements and the rights they invoked new was the availability of a vocabulary that enabled them to encapsulate in a single word or phrase the legal, political, and moral components of their demands. Rights-like concepts had long been present in Japan, and social protest has an extensive pedigree, but in the 1960s and 1970s "rights" came to be used as the vocabulary of social protest. The novelty was the fusion of rights talk and protest, and the scholarly interest in the movements that emerged. By the early 1980s, much of that interest had dissipated. The issues raised by the new rights movements were addressed, for better or worse; the expectation that Japan was on the verge of creating a new civil society dwindled; and legal scholars returned to the task of explaining the tenacity of traditional legal consciousness.

STUDYING THE "NEW RIGHTS"

Social movements that emerged in Japan from the late 1960s through the 1970s shared a number of characteristics. Perhaps most significantly, they were directed at achieving the recognition and protection of what were called "new rights" (*atarashii kenri*). The rights the movements sought – environment (*kankyō ken*), sunlight (*nisshō ken*), taxpayers' (*nōzeisha ken*), personal integrity (*jinkaku ken*), and others – were "new" in the sense that they were not enumerated in the Constitution and were not attached to a particular jurisprudence. But the designation "new" referred only in part to the recent emergence of those rights. More importantly, "new" described the way in which the rights were pursued. All were advanced by citizens' movements rather than isolated individuals, organized around a shared interest, and framed in the language of rights.

While the movements have pursued rights through various strategies, litigation has been at their core. In contrast to the "reluctant litigants" who are said to have once peopled Japan,[1] individuals joined social movements in order to pursue rights in court, and filed lawsuits meant to bring attention to those rights, despite potential economic hardship, political criticism, legal obstacles, and moral and social opposition.[2] Many movements were drawn to the courts for reasons other than winning positive judgments. Though a clear win is always desirable, winning was not considered to be the only objective. Other goals included the desire to attract publicity, to garner new supporters, to increase public awareness of alleged injustice, and to pressure defendants to reach a more acceptable informal solution than would otherwise be possible. Criticism of the new rights, frequently aimed at those who asserted the rights, censured the trend toward "rights inflation" (*kenri infure*), insinuating that the value of such assertions was becoming increasingly diluted. Still, the movements persisted; despite the ample survey data indicating that people have a negative view of others who litigate or assert their interests, those same people express a willingness to assert their own rights.[3] In the "new rights" movements, they asserted vigorously.

Some scholarship aimed at understanding and mapping the "new rights" is taxonomic. Yamada Takao classifies the type of rights being asserted by the subject of the right (human, animal, ecosystem, etc.), people with rights (criminals, consumers, patients, etc.), the "merit" of the right (a right to do something, a right to access to some service), and the authority supporting the right (constitutional, legal, extra-legal).[4] Inamoto Yonosuke categorizes new rights as those established by agreement (*shōhinteki kenri*), fundamental rights that are asserted by social movements and accepted by a majority of citizens (*kihonteki kenri*), and rights that are privileged by law (*tokkenteki kenri*).[5] Konishi Minoru distinguishes between rights that are not yet recognized by established law, already recognized rights, expansions of previously recognized rights, and rights that are based on new grounds, like sunlight and the environment.[6] Awaji Takehisa groups new rights movements as non-legal, legal, and super-legal, and Kobayashi Naoki also offers a model for understanding and distinguishing the various new rights.[7]

All of these models are aimed at grouping the new rights into categories depending upon their basis in established law. Other approaches to new rights have been more philosophical. Tanaka Shigeaki, for example, a scholar of jurisprudence and the sociology of law, has written on citizens' movements and dispute resolution.[8] He discusses rights and rights consciousness in Japan, and criticizes other legal sociologists for not being analytically or definitionally precise.[9] Although Tanaka argues that Japanese law cannot be understood from the perspective of what he labels American "universalistic" law,[10] his theoretical focus is on the development and meaning of "rights" in the Western legal tradition.[11]

Rather than taxonomy or philosophical aspects of the meaning of "new rights," most scholarship directed at new rights has focused on their institutional and sociological significance. It has taken the form primarily of mobilization studies, examining particular rights and the movements they generated, or similarities between different rights-related movements and corresponding litigation. Some such studies conclude that the new rights movements indicate that Japan is on its way to becoming a pluralist society, at last unleashing the democratic forces, indigenous or imported, that will make it more like its Western democratic counterparts. Citizens' movements and the rights they advocated, it is said, were evidence of "a change in, or a transformation of, our rights consciousness, or way of thinking about rights."[12]

The "big four" environmental cases, for example, prompted tremendous attention. One expert writes:

> These four pathbreaking cases ... demonstrated that the judicial system could be used to protect ordinary citizens against abuses by powerful institutions, and thus to break down the well-known reluctance among Japanese to use the courts ... Thus these cases have greatly affected Japanese legal culture in addition to legitimizing litigation as a tool of citizen participation.[13]

The same author, using the environmental arena to indicate the significance of citizens' movement in general, states:

> Their [citizens' movements] message is home-grown, not imported, indicating that Japanese political culture had an indigenous potential for democratic "evolution." To the Japanese who have become active in citizens' movements, the idea they have something called "rights" which have been "unjustly" trampled upon, that the system itself owes them some recourse, that democratic procedures are actually devices that exist precisely for the situation in which they find themselves, is attractive and satisfying.[14]

This assessment shares much with the evolutionary view of Japanese law and society propounded by Kawashima. It accepts the description of traditional Japanese legal behavior as averse to courts and assertions of interest. It posits that Japanese society, and its political and legal systems, are changing. And it treats rights assertion as a newly discovered domestic activity. In short, the emphasis is on sharp change rather than on historical continuity.

Hasegawa Kōichi's excellent discussion of new rights and social movements identifies shared characteristics of a variety of new rights lawsuits. According to Hasegawa, the lawsuits over new rights are: (1) group based, relying on the joining of many separate suits since class action is not available; (2) seek a variety of compensatory damages, which are allocated individually, since the difficulty of obtaining an injunction denies the group the possibility of a shared victory; (3) utilize both administrative appeal procedures and courts, since they are separate; (4) use the media, public hearings, and other means of publicizing their complaints.[15] These four features capture important aspects of the new rights movements. Unlike reformers in the US, whose belief in the power of courts frequently leads them to place undue emphasis on legal decisions,[16] those involved in new rights movements in Japan sought their goals through multiple channels. They understood the political and social power of rights rhetoric and rights assertion, and they used litigation as one way to publicize and accelerate their grievances.

Observers who believed that an increase in citizen participation, pluralism, and rights assertion in Japan were positive developments came to realize that bureaucratic control and authority were not easily weakened. As social transformation was stymied by political reality, studies of social and legal conflict such as those by Frank Upham[17] and Susan Pharr[18] cast doubt on the power and effectiveness of citizens' movements. They emphasized instead the way in which the state marginalizes protesters and contains conflict by manipulating legal rules, avoiding generalizable decisions, and retaining power and control over the pace of social change. Other analysts began to explore the characteristics of both the Japanese state and the dynamics of citizens' movements to explain the apparent failure of new rights-related movements to usher in profound or lasting change.[19] One explanation echoes arguments that use institutional factors to explain Japanese legal behavior. Even though there are rights in Japan that are explicitly guaranteed by law, courts are reluctant to enforce, expand or interpret them, judges are hierarchically organized and conservatively inclined, and the number of attorneys is insufficient.[20] While courts may satisfy certain needs of movements, like being good vehicles for publicity, they are inadequate if expected to articulate innovative legal doctrine.[21]

Another explanation of the failure of the "new rights" movements concerns the relatively recent vintage of many aspects of law in Japan. Most important, the postwar constitution is less than fifty years old, and it may be that its values and declarations have not yet had a determinative impact on legal institutions or the legal culture of the population they serve. Since the constitution is the ultimate foundation of rights, both those that it explicitly includes and others that are asserted and defended as having a legal basis, the failure of courts to consistently recognize and support the assertion of new rights is a co-factor in perpetuating a gap between constitutional guarantees of rights and the real possibilities of exercising and expanding the new rights promoted by citizens' movements.[22] Yet another explanation for the difficulties encountered by new rights movements suggests that bringing about change is no less difficult using channels outside the courts. Using the power of a movement to influence politicians in order to achieve legislative reform, or pressuring the bureaucracy to bring about change through administrative action, are both fraught with complications.[23]

Advocates of the expansion of new rights have criticized the tendency of social movements to be insulated from each other. Instead, they argue that the rights are all related with regard to their emphasis on social justice, equality, and freedom, and that the rights movements of citizens, workers, and others should be unified.[24] Some also believe that despite the problems with using the political process for achieving new rights, it offers the greatest possibility of success, leading them to suggest that disparate movements should unify in order to increase the amount of political pressure they can exert. Finally, in response to criticism about "rights inflation," the perceived tendency to add *ken* (right) to every claim, some argue that the proliferation of rights talk is an improvement over the traditional view of rights assertion as shameful, greedy, and egoistic, and over the suppression that was experienced during the Meiji era.[25]

PATIENTS' RIGHTS AS "NEW RIGHTS": CONCEPTUALIZATION, LITIGATION, LEGISLATION

In retrospect, it is clear that the interpretation of citizens' new rights movements as the dawning of a new era was vastly overstated. Some did achieve limited success, in the form of bureaucratic largesse, mediated solutions, and even legal judgments. But for the most part, the grand claims of imminent change in the Japanese social, political, and legal systems did not come to pass. "Rights inflation" in the sense of a widespread acceptance that *all* claims would soon be framed as legal rights turned out to be bankrupt; the transformation of legal consciousness reflected little more than wishful thinking; litigation as a vehicle to social evolution was stymied by a powerful and entrenched bureaucracy.

Still, the forces that pressed for the institutionalization of "new rights" have had a certain long-term impact. At the very least, they laid bare the reality of rights in Japan – that rights are not remote, alien, misunderstood entities of a foreign legal system; that "the Japanese" are not unable to articulate rights claims; that the culture of Japan is not so harmonious, consensual, or hierarchical that conflicts are solved through informal channels to the satisfaction of all parties. "New rights" also provided a model for groups that had grievances and needed both a process and framework for pursuing them. While organizing a movement, seeking publicity, going to court, and applying pressure on politicians and the bureaucracy were no guarantee of success, they were the best, and perhaps the only feasible strategies. And so the procedures followed by many of the 1970s movements have been emulated by subsequent groups.

One of these has clustered around the theme of patients' rights, a contentious subject in every industrialized democracy with a well-developed health care system.[26] Patients' rights describes a variety of prerogatives and liberties that can be exercised by individuals in their interactions with physicians or the medical system generally. Access to care, the intensity and longevity of treatment, choice of physician and facility, and many other things may be included as patients' rights, depending upon the organization of a nation's medical system. Japanese patients are spared a battle over some of these issues, since Japan has a relatively equitable health care system with regard to access and availability of care.[27] What is lacking in Japan is a legal guarantee that patients can exercise some control over treatment decisions. Foremost among the rights demanded by Japanese patients, therefore, are those that relate to diagnosis and treatment information and decision making, often grouped under the term "informed consent" (*setsumei to dōi*, or *infōmudo konsento*).

The doctrine of informed consent, first enunciated at the Nuremberg trials, was affirmed in the 1970s by patients' rights declarations in the U.S. and Europe, and received support from the World Health Organization in the Lisbon Declaration of 1981. It has been extensively litigated in the US.[28] Some of its requirements include: that consent be voluntary; that the patient be competent; that physicians describe treatment risks, probabilities of success and failure, potential problems with recovery, the chance of death, and other factors; and that a patient understand the physician's explanation and sign a prescribed form. Weak versions of informed consent may simply order doctors to verbalize warnings and get on with their work. But taken seriously, the doctrine of informed consent requires a reallocation of information and authority in the medical setting. In Japan, where physicians traditionally have operated with almost unbridled discretion, affirming the doctrine of informed consent means changing the medical power structure. Given the strength and prestige of the Japan Medical Association and other professional organizations, the history of medical paternalism, and expectations that patients be deferential to medical authority, those desiring to institute the doctrine of informed consent clearly face substantial resistance.[29]

Moreover, there are numerous institutional barriers obstructing the implementation and practice of informed consent. Unrelated to its legal or moral aspects, for example, is the current reimbursement practice that leads physicians to treat up to one hundred patients per day, each for only several minutes. On the occasions when obtaining informed consent may be necessary, appointments are simply too short for any meaningful discussion between doctor and patient.

Another barrier affecting the creation of a doctrine of informed consent in Japan is most easily illustrated with reference to the US. American law on informed consent owes its development to medical malpractice litigation brought under tort law (as well as contract and criminal law), refined through a series of cases, and ultimately codified by state legislatures and in the professional conduct rules of medical organizations. Without contingency fees, a sufficient number of attorneys, easy access to courts, class action, and useful legal doctrine, informed consent (and patients' rights more broadly) would not have developed. The legal system in Japan, however, contains multiple roadblocks to successful litigation, such as protracted court proceedings, a small number of attorneys, and hierarchically organized, conservative courts. Consequently, courts hear a relatively limited number of cases related to patients' rights, and their decisions have not encouraged others to litigate.

Patients in Japan thus lack a variety of the rights held by their American counterparts. They have no right to examine their medical records. Their right to information about diagnosis and treatment is contingent on physician discretion, which in practice means that many patients are not given an accurate diagnosis. Patients do not have a right to decide which course of treatment to pursue. And in what may be the nation with world's highest rate of prescribed and ingested medication, patients lack the right to know about the intended and unintended effects of what they are consuming.

Echoing the literature on rights in other contexts, some claim that even now, the idea of patients' rights is unsettling in Japan. A Japanese medical ethicist has written:

> [Right] is originally an alien notion for the Japanese, and hence not only the notion of "patients' rights," but also the notion of "sharing information" and "shared decision-making" between patients and physicians is still quite radical for many Japanese patients and particularly for many paternalistic Japanese physicians.[30]

Likewise, a radical physician who runs an advice center for patients in the Tokyo area thinks about patients' rights in the context of a transplant metaphor: "Japanese society is still not based on contracts but rather on human emotions. So we have to discuss what kind of informed consent system can fit Japanese society because imported concepts from overseas don't work here."[31] Others like Bai Kōichi, however, founder of the Japanese Association of Law and Medicine, have spent decades writing about the relationship between rights and health care, and advocating fundamental changes in the provision of medicine.[32] And there are many individuals committed to bringing about legal change at both the adjudicative and legislative levels.

The movement for patients' rights began in earnest in the early 1970s, although academic discussion of informed consent had begun some years earlier.[33] Hirasawa Masao describes the formation of several of the first patients' rights citizens' groups.[34] One, the Saitō Hospital Victims' Group, was made up of patients living in proximity to the hospital where they each claimed to have been a victim of medical malpractice. Because they lived in the same area, and had suffered from similar mistreatment, their interests and actions were congruent.

That was not the case with other groups, which consisted primarily of individuals who had not been affected by poor medical treatment. The Kitakyūshū Citizens Medical Conference, for example, was brought together for the more generic mission of fighting for citizens' rights. It consists of members with a variety of professional and personal commitments who share an interest in progressive politics. Labeling patients involved in disputes over treatment "victims" (*higaisha*), they identified with the plight of weak individuals whom they believed were unfairly treated by the powerful. These associations were derided by the medical establishment; the president of the Japan Medical Association, Takemi Tarō, called them "truly despicable" (*iyashimu beki shūdan*).[35] Yet they persisted, organizing plaintiffs who claimed to be victims of malpractice and taking physicians and hospitals to court.

One of the most litigated issues related to patients' rights in Japan concerns the treatment of cancer patients. For many years, Japanese physicians have withheld information about cancer diagnoses, sometimes telling families but claiming that the loss of hope experienced by patients upon hearing that they have cancer would expedite death. Patients at the National Cancer Center, and even the Emperor Shōwa, whose cancer was reported in media throughout the world, remain uninformed. A recent judgment by the Nagoya District Court, upheld by the Nagoya High Court, held that "how much information should be given is in the discretion of the doctor to the extent that the patient's right to self-determination is not infringed."[36] The fact that the court explicitly recognized a right to self-determination may appear encouraging to patients' rights advocates. But, in practice, the court affirmed the wide degree of discretion allocated to physicians.[37] As interpreted by one expert on law and medicine in Japan, "Japanese courts are willing to recognize the inviolability of the patient's body but this willingness does not extend to the patient's right to self-determination or autonomy with respect to the selection of treatment courses."[38]

The lack of overt success at securing patients' rights through the courts has surprised no one, but litigation is only one part of a strategy that also includes political pressure. It is not clear to what extent litigation alone has been a factor in attracting attention and members to patients' rights groups, influencing professional associations to formally recognize patients' rights, or persuading the Ministry of Health and Welfare and the Diet that patients' rights are good polit-ics. But it is apparent that litigation is one part of a strategy to attain more patients' rights through all available channels. This is made explicit by an activist attorney in the prologue to a book on patients' rights legislation:

> In the West, medical malpractice litigation was an important element in the unfolding of the patients' rights movement. In Japan, however, patients' rights and informed consent have been only minimally acknowledged as legal rights by the courts. I have insisted that Japanese courts recognize that patient consent to medical deeds is critical, but medical experts seem to think that the explanation on which such consent is premised should be as limited as possible. However, courts have little by little accepted legal arguments about patients' rights. We will use this way of thinking as the basis for creating a legal structure for patients' rights.[39]

Recent efforts to bring about the enactment of a patients' rights law were preceded by several developments. In 1984, a group domin-ated by attorneys and led by Suzuki Toshihiro formed the National Reformation Committee for a Declaration of Patients' Rights (*Kanja no Kenri Sengen Zenkoku Kaikaku Iinkai*).[40] The Declaration is organ-ized into six sections: individual dignity, right to equality in receiving medical treatment, right to receive the best possible medical treat-ment, right to know, right to self-determination, and right to privacy. These rights are claimed to be grounded in three articles of the post-war constitution – Articles 13, 14, and 25:[41]

> Article 13: All people shall be respected as individuals. Their rights to life, liberty, and the pursuit of happiness shall, to the extent that it does not interfere with the public welfare, be the supreme considera-tion in legislation and in other governmental affairs.

> Article 14: All of the people are equal under the law and there shall be no discrimination in political, economic or social relations because of race, creed, sex, social status, or family origin . . .

> Article 25: All people shall have the right to maintain the minimum standards of wholesome and cultured living. In all spheres of life, the State shall use its endeavors for the promotion and extension of social welfare and security, and of public health.

The 1980 Japan Federation of Bar Associations' Declaration of a Right to Health (*Kenkō Ken Sengen*) offered additional support to the rights cited by the committee.

The latter half of the 1980s witnessed a recognition of the importance of patients' rights by several other groups. The Union of National Health Insurance Medical Groups (*Zenkoku Hoken Idantai Rengō Kai*) issued a Declaration on Private Practice Physicians (*Kaigyōi Sengen*), in which it addressed issues of patients' rights. A publication of the Japan Medical Association's Life Ethics Study Group, "A Report on 'Explanation and Consent'" (*Setsumei to Dōi ni Tsuite no Hōkoku* (the term informed consent is sometimes used in Japanese, and sometimes translated as "explanation and consent")), explained in detail how physicians could obtain consent, and offered a model consent form.[42] The Japanese Life Cooperative Union (*Nihon Seikatsu Kyōdō Kumiai Rengō Kai*) issued a Code of Patient's Rights (*Kanja no Kenri Shōten*). In 1991, two new groups pressing for patients' rights were formed.

One group, based in Nagano and called the Medical Malpractice Plaintiffs' Organization, consists of alleged victims of medical malpractice and their families. Founded by a father whose son has been bedridden for more than a decade because of an accident related to the administration of anesthesia, the organization is raising money to aid other malpractice plaintiffs and to study malpractice victims nationwide.[43]

The other group consists of medical professionals, attorneys, alleged malpractice victims, and their families. Called the Organization to Establish a Patients' Rights Law (*Kanja no Kenrihō o Tsukuru Kai*), it was started in 1991 with the explicit goal of enacting patients' rights legislation, as well as implementing a system to reduce and review malpractice cases. In March 1993, the group submitted a patients' rights bill to the Minister of Health and Welfare.

The bill submitted by the organization includes the right to self-determination (*jiki kettei ken*), the right to receive explanations and reports (*setsumei oyobi hōkoku o ukeru kenri*), rights to an informed consent process (*infōmudo konsento no hōshiki, tetsuzuki*), the right to the protection of personal information (*kojin jyōhō o hogosareru kenri*), and the right to inspect and copy medical records (*iryō kiroku no etsuran tōsha seikyū ken*), among more general rights such as access to medical care, not being forced to leave the hospital, and not being subject to mistreatment.[44] It also specifies a procedure for notifying the public about patients' rights, and suggests that a committee for the protection of patients' rights be formed. The Health and Welfare minister declared that the Ministry would convene a study group to discuss the implementation of informed consent at medical institutions when he received the bill in 1993, but, five years later, there was not yet national legislation on patients' rights or informed consent.[45]

To maintain and increase its political pressure, the Organization to Establish a Patients' Rights Law publishes a regular newsletter, *Rights Law News* (*Kenrihō News*), holds periodic meetings, and editorializes in national newspapers. The Japan Federation of Bar Associations has announced its support for the organization's proposed patients' rights legislation. More significantly, the Japan Hospital Association and other medical associations have implemented rules regarding patients' rights, specifically informed consent, access to medical records, and self-determination.[46]

None of the foregoing should be interpreted as suggesting that the explicit meaning of patients' rights in Japan mirrors that in the United States. Concepts central to the Western liberal political tradition, like autonomy and paternalism, have loomed large in the American debate. With regard to informed consent, they have been resolved, perhaps only temporarily, by emphasizing individual patient autonomy. In Japan, however, it is likely that a doctrine of informed consent will preserve a greater role for family decision making than for individual decision making, in keeping with traditions of family responsibility, and consonant with a perspective that diminishes the overriding importance of self-determination. Nonetheless, the use of the rhetoric of rights by critics of the Japanese medical system signals a fundamental challenge to the sovereignty of the medical profession. The prevalence of rights talk in debates over medical care, moreover, does not represent a sudden break with tradition. Instead, it exemplifies the way in which rights are used as political resources by those seeking social change.

LAW, RIGHTS, AND POLICY IN CONTEMPORARY JAPAN: TWO NARRATIVES

Two concrete narratives of policy conflicts that revolve around the assertion of rights are presented in the following chapters. AIDS policy is the subject of Chapter 4. The background of HIV spread and transmission is well known, so I have not included a generic public health description. In the years from 1982 until well into the 1990s, AIDS was transformed in Japan from "their problem" to "our problem," new interest groups were formed, discrete policy objectives were identified, and claims to rights became increasingly vocal. Indeed, demands for compensation by HIV-infected hemophiliacs led to one of the most volatile medical and political scandals of the postwar period (see Chapter 6).

Controversy over brain death and organ transplantation, the subject of Chapter 5, has spanned almost three decades. It is the story of a technical judgment – when is a person biologically dead – that has become a national obsession, much as the abortion debate in the United States has traversed scientific, moral, legal, religious, sociological, and political terrain. Brain death is unseverable from the question of organ transplantation, since without a brain death standard certain organs, such as hearts, cannot be transplanted. What is most interesting about the conflict is that both proponents and opponents have framed their arguments in the language of rights. While the account will cover many aspects of the policy debate, it is the rights claims that provide the unifying thread.

In the studies on AIDS and the definition of death that follow, rights were brought to the forefront by those trying to influence policy. While courts play an important role in these stories, and are discussed at length in Chapter 6, looking only at litigation would cause one to miss some of the most interesting ways in which rights have been part of the policy process. Rather than concentrating on courts and litigation, therefore, the studies take a broad view of law and conflict. Much of the attention is on the symbolic power of rights assertion, how it is used to marshal public support and reach the ears of the media, and how it affects bureaucratic and legislative behavior. In contrast to the popular wisdom that rights have no salience in Japanese law or society, the opposite turns out to be true. Because of the strong impact of rights talk, it is used cautiously and strategically.

What the following narratives show is that rights talk, rights claims, and rights assertion are legitimate and legitimating ways to express dissent. They can serve to unify people and attract publicity from the media and policy makers. They can lead relatively small groups of marginalized people to have an important impact on political decisions and legal outcomes. They can become a rallying cry for social protest. As the discussion of patients' rights reveals, and the following studies illustrate, rights play a critical role in the unfolding of contemporary policy in Japan. To ignore them is to overlook a key element in Japanese law, politics, and society.

CHAPTER FOUR

AIDS POLICY AND THE POLITICS OF RIGHTS

AIDS, PUBLIC HEALTH, AND INDIVIDUAL RIGHTS

In contrast to the emphasis upon the primacy of public health over the protection of individual rights in nineteenth-century America, AIDS exemplifies the shift toward rights in twentieth-century public health policy. "Rights-based concern has limited what American governments may do under the banner of promoting public health," write David L. Kirp and Ronald Bayer, arguing that "reliance on the idea of civil rights [with regard to AIDS] has been an American exceptionalism."[1] As Ronald Bayer further explains:

> The ethos of public health and that of civil liberties are radically distinct. At the most fundamental level, the ethos of public health takes the well-being of the community as its highest good and . . . would, to the extent deemed necessary, limit freedom or place restrictions on the realm of privacy in order to prevent morbidity from taking its toll.[2]

The volume and impact of court decisions related to AIDS and rights in the United States is surely significant, as is the frequency of AIDS-related rights assertion and its impact on AIDS policy. Unnoticed in the din about "American exceptionalism" is that the language of Japan's AIDS debate has come increasingly to resemble that in the United States.

In Japan, the balance between the personal and the social, respect for individual rights versus protection of public health, has been explicitly debated in the process of formulating AIDS policy. To some extent, the centrality of rights rhetoric in the AIDS debate is, like in the United States, a consequence of other rights-related discussions, such as the patients' rights movement (see Chapter 3) and the definition of death (see Chapter 5). As law professor Ebashi Takashi has written:

> In the 1970s in the U.S., there was a basic tendency to think about human rights issues in medicine, and patients' rights increased. In Japan, at first, we tried to ignore such problems, but because of euthanasia, organ transplants, and other issues, such discussion slowly entered Japan. It was on the groundwork of patients' rights in Japan that AIDS appeared . . . If there had been no such foundation, and the AIDS problem had appeared earlier . . . we could have had a policy of isolating AIDS patients, and a policy that most definitely would have infringed on rights.[3]

Moreover, views like Bayer's have been expressed with regard to Japan. Rikkyō University's health law expert Hatakeyama Takemichi observes that one aspect of Japanese AIDS policy "is that in order to protect public health, there are restrictions on the rights of HIV patients."[4] A Japanese member of the World Health Organization believes that "[T]hose countries that respect the rights and privacy [of HIV patients and carriers] succeed in prevention."[5]

While tension between individuals and the state is an aspect of AIDS policy worldwide, how it is voiced and resolved varies greatly. Differences in institutions, organizations, legal systems, cultures, and politics are all important factors that shape a nation's dialogue and policy response to AIDS. At the same time, AIDS-related controversies have themselves exposed and transformed the elements that shape AIDS policy.[6] AIDS-based conflicts in Japan cannot be explained by stereotypes of a nation with an all-encompassing public sphere, or a citizenry repelled by controversy, unfamiliar with law, or culturally repelled by rights. Instead, in the political, legal, and social conflicts concerning AIDS in Japan, demands that individual rights be acknowledged and protected, both legally and extralegally, are forcefully asserted and defended. Debate over the privacy of HIV-positive persons, the anonymity of those wishing to obtain HIV tests, the compensation of hemophiliacs infected through blood transfusions (see Chapter 6), and the array of discriminatory behavior against those who are HIV-positive reveals an unwillingness by affected parties to accept what they believe is unfair treatment, and the use of a variety of tactics to assert their rights. Even in comparison to the

United States, they have had a significant impact on the state's exercise of power to protect public health. It is the context and substance of rights talk in Japan's AIDS-related controversies that is the theme of this chapter.[7]

AN EPIDEMIOLOGICAL VIEW

In comparison to the United States, most of Europe, Africa, and other nations in Asia, the number of reported AIDS cases in Japan has been modest.[8] As of August 31, 1997, 1,657 cases had been diagnosed. Of those, 689 were hemophiliacs, 250 were gay men, 416 were heterosexuals, and 282 were listed as other/unclear because the etiology of their infection was not determined.[9] The number of people who have tested HIV-positive is also low. Also as of August 31, 1997, there were 4,144 identified HIV carriers in Japan. Out of that total, 1,808 were hemophiliacs, 523 were gay men, and 1,144 were heterosexuals.[10]

The epidemiological profile of Japan's HIV population is in sharp contrast to that in the West. AIDS in Japan is not characterized by a high incidence of infection among the gay population; it is not a disease of the urban poor; it is not spreading rapidly among injection drug users.[11] Instead, the majority of those who are HIV-positive or have AIDS are hemophiliacs.

Among those with AIDS or who are HIV-positive, there is a clear delineation between those perceived as "innocent" and "guilty" victims. Whereas hemophiliacs are seen as the passive recipients of others' tainted blood, gay men are viewed as putting themselves at risk by their own behavior. A comment of Shiokawa Yōichi, chairman of the Ministry of Health and Welfare's (MHW) AIDS Surveillance Committee, puts the matter starkly: "[Y]ou don't get infected [by HIV] if you live a sound life."[12] Abe Takeshi, a hematologist and former MHW official, holds a similar view: "Hemophiliacs keep their lives very nice."[13] This division (present not only in Japan) has contributed to the activist posture hemophilia groups have taken toward criticizing AIDS policy, while it inhibited, at least initially, an already muted gay voice. Indeed, until late 1988, there was no formal cooperation between hemophilia and gay groups. When a bridge was finally built, it was (and remains) tenuous. The most substantial elements were the individuals who formed the HIV–Human Rights Information Center, a group that has promoted AIDS education and attacked the perceived insensitivity to rights of government AIDS policy.

HEMOPHILIACS AND GAY MEN: RIGHTS, RISKS, AND REPRESSION

Hemophiliacs

The central role of hemophiliacs as rigorous rights asserters in Japan's AIDS policy conflict was cemented in 1983, when reports from the United States indicated that AIDS could be contracted from contaminated blood products. The hemophilia associations demanded that the MHW stop importing United States blood parts, which accounted for 90 percent of Japan's supply. They feared that imported (mostly American) blood concentrates might be tainted by HIV, and wanted blood products produced from domestic supplies. The MHW, falsely encouraged by the fact that no AIDS cases had yet been reported in Japan, took no action.[14]

By the fall of 1984, several laboratories in the United States had announced new procedures that allowed blood plasma to be heat treated, and thereby purified, without destroying its effectiveness. The Japanese MHW adopted these procedures for hemophilia A patients in July 1985, and for hemophilia B patients in December 1985. But for Japanese hemophiliacs, it was already too late.

Of a hemophiliac population estimated to number about 5,000, approximately 40 percent became HIV-positive. One study, testing 1,747 hemophiliacs in 1987, found 678 to be HIV-positive, a rate of 38.8 percent.[15] In contrast to the 1 percent of total AIDS cases traced to hemophiliacs in the United States (though there, too, almost half of hemophiliacs became HIV-infected), about 50 percent of Japan's total number of AIDS cases are hemophilia-related, and the number was once as high at 90 percent.[16] Litigation brought by hemophiliacs over HIV-tainted blood, in which they asserted their rights to an apology and to financial compensation, is discussed in Chapter 6.

Along with the stigma of being the only group with a high rate of HIV infection, hemophiliacs also consider themselves to be victims of a general Japanese prejudice against those with genetic disorders. Prior to AIDS, for example, hemophiliacs were on occasion excluded from schools, had difficulty finding jobs, and were treated as unable to function as "normal" people in other aspects of daily life. Since AIDS has become identified with hemophilia, however, the violation of individual rights has become more common and insidious.[17]

One family has reported, for example, that the teacher of their hemophiliac child demanded that the student bring evidence to school that he was not HIV-positive. When the child did so, the teacher posted the report at the entrance to the school. Other hemophiliac children have had "AIDS" written on their belongings, or have been greeted with chants of, "You are an AIDS patient."[18] Adult hemophiliacs have been required by employers to show copies of HIV test results, have had to change jobs, and have been shunned by neighbors.[19] Moreover, a survey of its members undertaken in late 1988 by the Japanese Society of Friends of Hemophiliacs, Kyoto Chapter, found that hemophiliacs are routinely turned away by dentists, internal medicine specialists, surgeons, and pediatricians.[20]

These difficulties have served as a unifying factor; hemophiliacs have highlighted their history as "victims" of rights violations as support for their general criticisms of AIDS policy. As a result, despite the stigma of hemophilia and the personal tragedies many hemophiliacs have had to endure as a result of HIV, hemophilia associations have been remarkably vocal and successful at organizing their members in opposition to aspects of the government's AIDS policy. The language of rights they have consistently invoked has helped shape the conflict over AIDS in Japan.

Gay men

Kūkai, founder of Shingon (True Word) Buddhism, is believed to have introduced the idea of a connection between male homosexuality and spiritual enlightenment from China to Japan in the ninth century. Ihara Saikaku, 800 years later, solidified his popularity as a novelist by writing about the ideals of "boy love."[21] Whether samurai connoisseurship of homosexuality, relations between priests and acolytes, male prostitution in urban centers, or affairs between Kabuki actors and their patrons, gay male relations were once a highly visible part of Japanese social life. In contemporary Japan, however, tolerance and acceptance of these relationships has lost ground. Although legal prohibitions do not exist against either homosexuality or sodomy, no legal protections are explicitly afforded to gay men, and rights violations are only starting to be challenged. Fear that gossip could harm their professional and personal relations leads many men to be covert about their sexual orientation. When jobs or housing are denied on the basis of sexual preference, a direct confrontation rarely occurs.

In fact, "homosexuality" is an ambiguous term in Japan, since many gay men, particularly those in their forties and older, have had to conform to social pressures. These men are what would be labeled bisexual in the West, living with wives and children but frequenting gay bars and saunas.[22] As it becomes more socially acceptable to marry later or not at all, this behavior may slowly be changing, but such a trend is too new to allow anything but speculation.

Despite the general ignorance about gay social practices, some interesting observations have been made about gay sexual behavior. Most significant, if anecdotal evidence is of any value, is that anal intercourse in Japan is far less common than it is in many Western nations. While a gay phone counseling service has reported that their calls indicate a trend towards more frequent anal sex,[23] it has been estimated that less than 25 percent of the patrons of gay saunas (nationwide there are approximately 2,000 gay venues and 50 bath-houses (called saunas in Japan)) engage in intercourse.[24] Among those who do, condom use has not become the norm. Bathhouse owners rarely distribute safe sex literature, and have refused to allow the free installation of condom machines. Gay prostitutes and massage parlor workers have also reported a lack of condom use. For many, safe sex has come to mean relations among Japanese only, and avoiding "unsafe" Westerners has substituted for a change in lifestyle. Thus, nine of the ten gay saunas in Tokyo's busiest gay entertainment district, Shinjuku 2-chōme, prohibit entry to foreigners.[25]

One reason for the lack of education and implementation of safe sexual practices is the absence of a sense of a gay community in Japan. During the past several years, however, there has been an increase in the number of groups concerned with gay issues, such as AIDS Action (part of the International Lesbian and Gay Association), the AIDS Care Project, OCCUR, Osaka Gay Community, and International Friends. Despite the potential risks posed by AIDS to Japan's gay population, gay groups played a surprisingly limited role in the initial development of a national AIDS policy or the creation of safe sex education programs. Only since the early 1990s have these groups begun to challenge the values and goals of Japan's AIDS policy and publicly assert their rights.

PROPOSAL, DEBATE, AND ENACTMENT OF THE AIDS PREVENTION LAW

A "foreign disease" enters Japan

AIDS attracted almost no attention in Japan until late 1986 and early 1987, when two women were diagnosed as having AIDS. The first

involved a Filipina working as a bar hostess/sex worker in Nagano Prefecture, who had gone to a clinic for a blood test. When HIV was discovered she was sent back to the Philippines on the pretext of a visa violation. Few details were reported in the press, and there was no protest
about potential violations of her civil rights, i.e., why and how her test
results reached the immigration authorities. The government conducted follow-up tests in the place she worked to ascertain whether she
had infected any of her customers. Not one was discovered.

The second case involved a Japanese woman who in January 1987
was discovered to be dying of AIDS. "Japan's First Female AIDS
Victim Is Kōbe Prostitute," announced an English-language daily.
Other papers ran similar stories, based on information provided by the
chairman of the Ministry of Health and Welfare's AIDS Surveillance
Committee, established in September 1984 to monitor HIV patients
and carriers in Japan. The victim was a 29-year-old sex worker who
had a Caucasian clientele, and who was allegedly exposed to AIDS
by a Greek sailor in the seaport city of Kōbe. The committee reported
that she had been a sex worker for several years after she had become
infected, but because she died on January 20, only two days after being
diagnosed, it was impossible to obtain details about her past behavior.

Because she was the first reported female Japanese AIDS patient,
and apparently was infected through heterosexual contact, this
woman's death triggered fears that all Japanese, not just those in
"high-risk" groups, were threatened. Soon after she died, *The Japan
Times* editorialized: "Rarely has the death of a single human, unfam-
ous and indeed anonymous, aroused so much concern among people
throughout our society."[26]

Between the announcement of her illness and her death, 2,487
people contacted the AIDS headquarters of Hyōgo Prefecture, where
Kōbe is located, inquiring about the disease. At public meetings,
people concerned about getting AIDS on local trains and in other
public places asked about the dangers of transmission. The Public
Health and Environment Committee of the Hyōgo Prefectural
Assembly held an emergency meeting to discuss measures to stop the
spread of AIDS. By mid-February, 200,000 handbills, pamphlets, and
posters had been printed by the Kōbe city government, in an effort
to both inform and calm the public. An AIDS hot line had received
over 100,000 calls, and almost 20,000 people had visited health consultation centers.[27] What the mass media dubbed Japan's "AIDS
Panic" had begun.

AIDS legislation: the first draft

The Nagano and Kōbe cases forced the government to develop a national AIDS policy. Since mid-January 1987, when the Kōbe case was reported, there had been official discussion about an AIDS law. The Ministry of Justice, particularly anxious for legislation, was pressing the MHW to implement a policy that would prevent foreigners with AIDS from entering Japan.[28] Just as the case of the pregnant AIDS patient in Kōchi Prefecture was making national headlines, the media reported on February 18 that the minister of health and welfare, Saitō Juro, was discussing the case with the Cabinet, and that the Cabinet had agreed on the necessity of legislation.[29] That day, Prime Minister Nakasone Yasuhiro ordered the Infectious Disease Department of the MHW to draft an AIDS bill.

Cabinet members disagreed about the stringency of potential AIDS legislation. MHW officials, led by the chief of the Department of Infectious Diseases, advocated a relatively moderate approach to legislation, recognizing the importance of maintaining good relations with groups whose cooperation was necessary for the control of AIDS. Other influential government officers, particularly conservative senior politicians of the ruling Liberal Democratic Party (LDP), insisted that the law impose stiff penalties on both physicians and patients, among other tough provisions. To gauge public reaction, the MHW leaked restrictively worded legislation to the press. Media and public reaction, if critical, could then be used as leverage in crafting permanent legislation.

Even before legislation was announced, hemophilia groups were on the offensive. One prominent hemophiliac opined in the *Asahi Shimbun*: "We must decisively stop the process of making legislation that disregards the human rights of hemophiliacs infected through a misfortune with pharmaceuticals."[30] But the legislative process was not to be derailed. On February 19, 1987, a MHW draft law was distributed to the press.[31] It included penalties of up to 300,000 yen or one year in prison for individuals with AIDS or HIV infection who engaged in unsafe sexual acts or donated blood, activities that could result in the transmission of HIV to others.[32] Individuals could be imprisoned for six months or fined as much as 200,000 yen for giving false replies when examined by medical authorities about HIV. Physicians could be fined up to 100,000 yen for failing to report an AIDS diagnosis to the prefectural government. The mandatory reporting to the prefectural government of the names of all AIDS patients and carriers,[33] the reporting of their names and addresses if they are sus-pected of disregarding their physician's advice and spreading the dis-ease, and an amendment to the Immigration Act aimed at the exclu-sion of foreigners were also included.[34]

Criticism was not long in coming, especially from the liberal fringes of the legal and medical establishments, hemophilia groups, and others concerned about individual rights and public health. A central issue raised by these groups was the right to privacy of AIDS victims, which they claimed required far more protection than the draft offered. The only law directly governing medical confidentiality, the "Doctors Law" (*Ishi Hō*), was enacted in 1948 to prohibit physicians from disclosing information obtained in the course of medical consul-tation. Doctors violating its provisions are subject to up to seven months in jail and a 10,000 yen fine; and a supplemental law that can increase these punishments. The law prevents laypersons from examining medical records, but does not limit physician access to the records of other physicians. Opponents of the AIDS bill believed that it was inadequate when applied to the testing and treatment of per-sons with HIV infection, for whom the violation of privacy or other rights could have severe consequences.

The Japanese Society of Friends of Hemophiliacs was the most vocal group in opposing the legislation. Hemophiliacs had long been closely allied with medical professionals because their treatment required regular visits to the examining room and close cooperation with physicians. They viewed such links as crucial to their physical health, and deeply valued the privacy of their interactions with the medical system. Consequently, they worried that in the political rush to create an AIDS policy, their privacy and individual rights would be sacrificed, with the sacrifice justified by appeals to the "greater good."[35] Such concerns were not unfounded.

At a press conference to discuss the proposed AIDS legislation, Ōhama Hōei, spokesperson for the LDP's AIDS Committee, made the following statement: "It is more important to prevent the spread of AIDS than to protect the privacy of high-risk groups. If we respect the human rights of one person, we are depriving ninety-nine others of their right to live."[36] To Ōhama, traditional coercive public health measures were the most desirable way to control AIDS. But others, particularly groups that fear they will be subject to coercive measures, argue differently. An advocate for the hemophiliac community retorted:

The problem with the AIDS Prevention Law is the protection of privacy. Mr. Ōhama of the Liberal Democratic Party said, "The lives of ninety-nine people are more important than one person's privacy." If AIDS were not a sexually transmitted disease, but people could be infected through casual contact, and ninety-nine people could unknowingly become infected, then that would have to be a consideration. But the facts are different.[37]

Such clashes served as a unifying factor, leading hemophiliacs to make use of their pre-existing social networks. Special camps operated for children. Newsletters provided information about health and recreation. Organizations like the Japanese Society of Friends of Hemophiliacs offered a friendly refuge from social prejudice. When hemophiliacs perceived the medical and social threat of AIDS, they were ready to fight. In selecting a strategy to voice their claims, they turned to the language of rights. Yasuda Yukuo, a prominent attorney and a chief organizer of the hemophiliac community, describes the situation faced by hemophiliacs before they united and adopted a language of rights:

> Even though there is absolutely nothing dangerous about AIDS infected persons, since there is excessive fear associated with AIDS, those infected, and those suspected of being infected, like hemophiliacs and their families, are ostracized, and their rights are seriously infringed. Moreover, the rights infringement is not settled, and there is a custom of somehow or other having no choice but to drop the matter.[38]

Engaged in what they considered to be a high stakes conflict with the state and large corporations, HIV-infected hemophiliacs did not simply "drop the matter." Instead, they mobilized and adopted a rights-based strategy to pursue their concerns.

It was not only hemophiliacs who criticized the draft legislation. Public health experts argued that strict punishments for patients would drive those in need of medical care away from care-giving institutions.[39] Pressure to reform the draft legislation may also have been exerted by Diet members sympathetic to the Japan Medical Association (JMA). While its influence has diminished in recent years, physician-Diet members tend to maintain strong ties to the JMA, serving as internal lobbyists for the association. Since physicians have traditionally enjoyed professional autonomy and remained relatively unregulated by the MHW, those sympathetic to the role of physicians would have found the proposed penalties against doctors objectionable. Nonetheless, the JMA itself did not actively lobby the Diet regarding the proposed AIDS legislation.

Predictably, the law was supported by the chairman of the AIDS Problem Countermeasure Subcommittee of the LDP (*AIDS Mondai Taisaku*), a physician who was also a former director of the Okinawa branch of the JMA. Without elaboration, he advocated three general points in a newspaper article of March 5: (1) better education regarding AIDS; (2) more strict immigration controls to prevent infected foreigners from entering Japan; and (3) strict government control of high-risk groups.

Public health and infectious disease laws

Under pressure from Prime Minister Nakasone to act quickly, the MHW had no time for conceptual creativity in constructing the draft legislation. Instead, it was forced to consult its archives of infectious disease laws in search of something quickly adaptable to the AIDS situation. Like such laws in most other countries, those in Japan were heavily weighted toward coercive measures and against respect for individual rights. As Kirp and Bayer write,

> it is necessary to recall that conventional approaches to public health threats were typically codified in the latter part of the nineteenth or the early part of the twentieth century. Even as public health laws have been revised in subsequent decades, they reflect the imprint of their genesis. They typically provide a warrant for mandatory compulsory examination and screening, breaching the confidentiality of the clinical relationship by reporting to public health registries the names of those with diagnoses of "dangerous diseases"; imposing treatment; and, in the most extreme cases, confining infected persons through the power of quarantine.[40]

The first law for the control of infectious diseases in Japan was enacted in 1895 as the Infectious Disease Prevention Law. Aimed at eleven different diseases, including cholera and dysentery, the law granted broad authority to public health officials. It permitted prefectural governors to isolate particular geographic areas, stop trains, and close roads. Physicians who diagnosed one of the controlled diseases were required to make a report to the prefectural government's health bureau. The official report indicated that a patient was diagnosed, described the symptoms, and discussed the results of the physician's attempt to trace the source of the infection. Unofficially there was a close relationship between physicians and government health officials, who could obtain detailed information about patients if they so desired. When those who believed that they had come into contact with an infectious disease failed to request a medical examination, physicians or officials would sometimes require them to submit to testing. Once diagnosed, people with one of the eleven infectious diseases were to be sent to an isolation hospital until they were either cured or died.

In reality, the powers granted to public health officials were rarely exercised, due to the limited incidence of controlled diseases since 1895.[41] Moreover, many of the documented cases of these diseases were said to have been traced to either foreign travelers in Japan or to Japanese who had contracted the disease while traveling overseas.

The 1948 Venereal Disease Prevention Law was aimed at preventing the spread of venereal disease through prostitution. It gave physicians who encountered victims of venereal disease the authority to "guide" (shidō) them through the medical system for the purpose of curing their illness. Physicians could require patients to submit to medical treatment, and were to either themselves pursue non-compliant patients or report them to the police. Each physician was required to file a report about the existence and general location of every venereal disease patient with the hokenjyo [district health office], and had to report the exact name and address of patients who could infect others to the chiji [prefectural governor]. Most reported patients were prostitutes, who were usually required (directly or through pressure on employers) to enter a different line of work. In the case of non-prostitute patients, physicians would generally provide treatment without making a report to government officials.[42]

In 1957, the Prostitution Prohibition Act was passed, making prostitution a criminal offense. Physicians stopped complying with the requirements of the Venereal Disease Prevention Law, despite a fine for non-reporting, because they believed that the 1948 law was superseded by the 1957 act. In addition, some physicians were concerned about patient privacy, and feared that the law's reporting requirements would dissuade patients from making medically necessary visits to physicians.[43] Physician non-compliance has continued to this day, the government is unable to maintain accurate records on the incidence of venereal disease, and as a result official figures are many times lower than actual prevalence.

Public health officials have rarely attempted to enforce the Venereal Disease Prevention Law since prostitution is outlawed and is therefore not supposed to exist. Yet, unsurprisingly, prostitution continued to thrive after it was banned, with little interference from the state. Today, many sex workers operate from what are known as "soaplands," establishments where male customers are invited to be bathed and massaged but where in fact a great deal more transpires. It was in the "soaplands" that the government feared an AIDS epidemic could begin, and when a legislative response was sought, the MHW used the 1948 Venereal Disease Prevention Law as a model for its legislation.

AIDS legislation: the second draft

Within three weeks of leaking the draft legislation, on March 6, 1987, the MHW submitted a new bill to the Social Affairs Subcommittee of the Liberal Democratic Party, which approved it the same day.[44] Among its provisions were the following:

Physicians must report the age, sex, and route of infection of all patients infected with the AIDS virus to the prefectural governor within seven days;

If a physician deems that a patient is not following the physician's advice and may be infecting others, the doctor must report the name and address of the patient to the prefectural governor;

If a physician believes a non-patient has transmitted AIDS to a patient, the doctor can give the name and address of the non-patient to the prefectural governor;

Prefectural governors can recommend that people suspected of being carriers and infecting other people be tested for the virus, and require a test for individuals who do not voluntarily comply.

Punishments included:

A fine of up to 300,000 yen or 1 year in jail for physicians or public officials who unjustifiably breach an AIDS patient's confidentiality;

A fine of up to 100,000 yen for persons who defy the prefectural governor's order to be tested, or who give false answers to questions about AIDS asked by the prefectural authorities.[45]

A proposed amendment to the Immigration Act of 1951 would have extended its reach to foreigners suspected of having AIDS "who it is feared could infect a number of other people with this virus."[46] This would have granted immigration authorities the power to deny entry to foreigners in a potentially arbitrary manner. Absent from the bill were the penalties to be leveled on physicians for failure to report AIDS patients to the government, as well as penalties for spreading the disease or withholding AIDS-related information from physicians.

In an attempt to stem anticipated conflict, the MHW included language that acknowledged the importance of protecting rights. Article Three of the proposed law states: "In addition to obtaining accurate knowledge concerning AIDS and endeavoring to take the necessary precautions for preventing it, the public shall ensure that the human rights of AIDS patients and the like will not be endangered." Nonetheless, like the earlier draft, this legislation was widely criticized. Foreigners, both residents and non-residents of Japan, complained about the potentially discriminatory immigration controls the bill would allow. Physicians questioned the ambiguity of sections aimed at the monitoring of patient care by public health authorities. An attorney who attacked the legislation argued that it would both infringe rights and be ineffective as a public health intervention: "The danger of infringing rights is very high. Furthermore, the more frequently forcible measures are undertaken, the more often people who need medical attention go underground, and surveillance becomes impossible. It is exactly the opposite of what is best."[47] Hemophiliacs, again the most vocal critics, echoed their earlier fears of rights violations. Ishida Yoshiaki stated:

> What we want is a medical system which will allow us to devote ourselves calmly to a medical treatment that will prevent the development or spread of AIDS. We must guarantee, not only for us, the adult patients, but more importantly for our young patients, who are unable to appeal against such law, that we can live in a society in which there is no threat to our basic human rights.[48]

Yasuda Yukuo, vice-chairman of the Japanese Society of Friends of Hemophiliacs, claimed: "The bill is extremely insensible [sic] to the human rights of carriers and those suspected to have been infected . . . [it] would fuel people's prejudice and discrimination against AIDS victims. It treats carriers as if they were socially dangerous."[49] His concern was echoed by Matsuda Jōzō, professor of medicine at Teikyō University: "I am afraid the legislation would be targeted 99.9 percent at hemophiliacs. In addition to the congenital handicap, they may even be ostracized from society."[50] Citing, in addition, the possibility of hemophiliac children being denied their right to attend schools and being shunned by other children, hemophiliac groups insisted that society react to AIDS with compassion and allow hemophiliacs to monitor themselves.[51]

The Japan Civil Liberties Union, a liberal group of attorneys similar to the ACLU but with far more limited resources, summed up the tenor of rights-based criticisms of the proposed AIDS legislation: "In comparison to prewar days, there has been great progress with respect to rights, but there are still many serious problems. With regard to AIDS policy, if we examine the AIDS legislation, there are many ways in which it does not give a thought to the human rights issues."[52] Gay groups, still poorly organized and informed, made no public comments about the legislation.

The proposed AIDS law, formally introduced in the Diet on March 31, 1987, was not discussed until the end of 1988, a delay of almost two years. This resulted in part from the presence of what were considered more urgent political issues, such as the prime minister's controversial sales tax proposal. More importantly, this long hiatus reflected the waning of the public panic sparked by the first reports of women with AIDS, and the high political costs associated with pressing for the enactment of legislation that had provoked heated controversy. During this long delay, the government attempted to mollify the group most vociferously opposed to the law by creating a financial relief scheme for hemophiliacs infected with HIV.

The hemophiliac relief fund

Persistent lobbying by the hemophilia associations helped them to create a close working relationship with MHW officials and others closely involved with the AIDS bill. Although they must have known that they would be unable to prevent the eventual passage of the legislation, hemophilia groups continued to assert their right to compensation, hoping that if they attracted enough media attention they could gain concessions from the government. In turn, the government was searching for a way to partially satisfy, and thus silence, the group most critical of the proposed law. What resulted was a system through which hemophiliacs affected by AIDS would be given financial relief as a way to lessen the sting if (or when) the AIDS bill became law, a method of compromise called *ame to muchi*, or "candy and a whip."

In fact, the government began discussing the establishment of a fund for hemophiliacs in early 1987, after hemophiliacs had made it clear that they considered the government's lax blood policy responsible for the high HIV-positive rate they suffered. In a confidential memo addressing the "principle for a total policy against AIDS," written by the minister of health and welfare for discussion at a 1987 Cabinet meeting, there was a hint that the government would attempt to obtain financial contributions from pharmaceutical companies that were in part responsible for the importation of HIV-positive products. Several months later, on May 15, 1987, newspapers reported that the MHW had started "informal negotiations with AIDS patients who were infected with the disease through transfusions of imported blood over compensation and relief measures for the disease."[53]

On April 16, 1988, the Ministry of Health and Welfare announced the establishment of a relief scheme (*HIV Kansen Higai Kyūsai Seido*) for hemophiliacs, to be implemented January 1, 1989. While the exact source and magnitude of the fund were unknown, the money was gathered by a MHW section called the Biological Management of Drugs (*Seibutsu Seizaika*), responsible for the management of blood clotting factor. Bureaucrats in that section approached the companies selling imported blood products in Japan and persuaded them to contribute. This was not difficult, given the close working relationship between the MHW and the pharmaceutical industry, and the possibility of multiple and costly litigation if the companies did not willingly pay.

The relief system did not drain general funds from the budget, obviating negotiations with the Ministry of Finance. It was modeled after a scheme designed to compensate those who suffered from iatrogenic diseases such as SMON (sub-acute myelo-optico neuropathy, a neurological disorder). After protracted conflict and litigation from 1971 into the 1980s, SMON's etiology was attributed to a stomach medication, and the courts found that the government and pharmaceutical companies had been negligent in permitting its use.[54] The Adverse Drug Reaction Fund was created as a result of the SMON conflict, and was the vehicle by which victims of thalidomide and other medically caused tragedies received compensation. Because the fund explicitly excluded payments for injuries caused by blood or blood products, however, the MHW was forced to establish a separate payment mechanism.

Under the relief system, beneficiaries were separated into two general groups: HIV-positive people who were infected by blood-clotting drugs, had AIDS-related symptoms, and had stayed in the hospital for more than eight days received 29,000 yen/month for an indefinite period of time; those who were diagnosed with AIDS received varying amounts. Those under eighteen years old received 85,600 yen/month, while those over eighteen got 208,900 yen monthly. Families who had lost a hemophiliac family member to AIDS received a flat sum of 5,648,400 if the victim was not the primary breadwinner, and 156,900 yen/month for up to ten years, minus the time the person received money as a patient, if the person was the primary bread-winner. Those who were asymptomatic HIV-positive received no compensation.

In late 1993, after a series of negotiations, the MHW agreed to begin paying a subsidy to HIV-positive spouses of people who were infected by imported, tainted blood products. Beginning in April 1994, the approximately thirty affected spouses who qualified for the program began receiving the same compensation as HIV-infected hemophiliacs with AIDS-related symptoms, which had been increased to 33,000 yen/month.[55]

Administratively, the program was under the auspices of the MHW section that was in charge of secondary drug effects compensation, with a special eight-member committee deciding whether those who applied should be granted relief. At the first meeting of this special committee, in February 1989, twenty-three applications were considered, thirteen of which were approved. By October 1990, 207 hemophiliacs were receiving relief, out of an undisclosed number of applications.[56] No rejected applicants had filed formal complaints with the ministry.

Although this scheme was a concession to the hemophilia groups, representing both a tacit acknowledgment by the government that it mishandled blood importation and a concrete attempt to remedy the mishap, hemophilia groups did not treat it as a major victory. Financial relief was viewed as small consolation for having been infected with HIV. At the same time, hemophiliacs argued that the level of payment should be significantly higher. More importantly, the groups rejected the government's attempt to sidestep responsibility for violating the rights of hemophiliacs by calling the payment scheme *relief* (*kyūsai*) rather than *compensation* (*isharyō, hoshō*), the latter implying both an acknowledgment of guilt and an apology. Hemophiliacs were split as to whether apology alone or apology coupled with a large payment would have been an acceptable government response. Since neither was forthcoming, some hemophiliacs refused to accept the relief system and instead went to court; their case is discussed in Chapter 6.

Final revision and passage of the aids prevention law

Discussion of the proposed AIDS bill resumed in late 1988. As with most legislation in Japan, it was first discussed by a Lower House committee, then voted on by the General Assembly, and finally sent to the Upper House. Typically, Lower House committees are critical in determining the success of legislation, and the General Assembly generally approves whatever is submitted for a vote. The Social and Labor committee (*Shakai Rōdō Iinkai*) of the Diet was responsible for the AIDS bill. It was both chaired and dominated by LDP members, as were all committees in the Lower House. Most prominent on the committee was Ozawa Tatsuo, a senior member of the Diet who had been the head of the AIDS Problem Sub-committee when it traveled to the United States in March 1987.

Those who testified before the committee during its consideration of the AIDS bill in October 1988 were essentially the same groups and individuals as had protested against the initial draft and the legislation that was introduced in the Diet. Members of the Japanese Society of Friends of Hemophiliacs, such as Ishida Yoshiaki and Yasuda Yukuo, argued that the law would infringe on the privacy rights of HIV-positive patients and would control their sexual lives. They insisted that the government accept complete responsibility for the importation and distribution of tainted blood, and more fully compensate HIV-positive hemophiliacs and the families of hemophiliacs who died from AIDS. Among other things, they demanded that the government pay for private hospital rooms, which some hospitals forced AIDS patients to occupy (supposedly to limit HIV transmission) but which were not covered by health insurance. Individual physicians also argued against the law, claiming that its failure to protect the confidentiality of patients would drive those at risk away from hospitals and physicians. Gay groups were characteristically uninvolved during these hearings.

After deliberating for several days, the Social and Labor committee of the Lower House incorporated four changes into the text. These were:

(i) The national and local government must educate the public correctly about AIDS;

70

(ii) The MHW and local governments must coordinate their education efforts;

(iii) Cases of HIV-positive persons infected through blood products (hemophiliacs) do not have to be reported to the government;

(iv) The prefectural governor (*chiji*) cannot question or control those who are suspected of being HIV-positive and dangerous to others based only upon government suspicion, but must limit contact to those who are reported by physicians as HIV-positive.

These changes, like so many other aspects of the creation of an AIDS policy, were the result of compromises brought about by the lobbying of the hemophiliac groups, a constant thorn in the side of the MHW since the beginning of the AIDS problem in Japan. They had formed a working relationship with the MHW bureaucrats largely responsible for the writing of the legislation, who were called in by the Social and Welfare Committee during its hearings to help make changes in the bill. Those bureaucrats made an effort to use their positions to reform the proposed AIDS law so that it was more palatable to the hemophilia groups but remained acceptable to the government. Despite the change to the bill that exempted hemophiliacs from the reporting requirements, however, hemophiliacs did not feel victorious. During the years before the bill was passed, most HIV-positive hemophiliacs had already received medical care, when their identities became known to the care giving hospitals and were reported to prefectural health authorities. For them, exclusion represented little more than a hollow gesture, which failed to address their demand for financial compensation, better medical care, and freedom from discrimination.

The AIDS bill, with its changes, was approved by the General Assembly of the Lower House on November 1, 1988, and sent for consideration to the Social and Labor Committee of the Upper House. After less than two days of testimony and discussion, the Upper House Committee appended (*futai ketsugi*) six additional provisions to the bill. They were:

The government should take proper measures in regard to the following:

(i) For HIV-positive persons, the government should prepare a counseling system; the government should also try to find a way to prevent HIV-positive persons from developing AIDS, and create drugs that prevent and cure AIDS;

(ii)   Medical reports concerning HIV-positive persons that are mandated by the AIDS law should be kept secret by the local government;

(iii) AIDS testing and counseling should be done confidentially, and a special effort should be made to protect privacy;

(iv)   The government should try to create a total prevention program for infectious and sexual diseases;

(v)   The government should try to establish a system of blood collection within Japan, especially with regard to hemophiliacs' clotting factor. For AIDS patients who were infected by blood drugs, the government should think about paying for their care, and making life easier for them;

(vi)   After three years, the government should review the policy concerning AIDS in light of the number of AIDS patients and HIV-positive people.

While a relief fund for hemophiliac patients had already been engineered, the fifth provision was a way for the lawmakers to indicate that they supported the MHW scheme. The bill was put to a vote by the entire Upper House, which quickly approved it on November 23, 1988, to be effective beginning in February 1989. In contrast to the controversy surrounding earlier drafts of the legislation, and the public panic over the death of Japan's first female AIDS patient, the final passage of the bill was scarcely noticed. Beyond small newspaper stories reporting the fact that the bill had been passed, there was virtually no public discussion about the law or its implications. This may be due to the fact that the media was preoccupied at the time by revelations concerning the Recruit political corruption scandal – Finance Minister Miyazawa was about to resign, and Recruit President Ezoe was on trial. Just as important was the way in which AIDS had ceased to be of concern to the average Japanese, who was no longer preoccupied with the possible dangers of contagious foreigners and had returned to the concerns of daily life. Yet passage of the AIDS Prevention Law also stimulated further criticism of the infringement of the rights of HIV carriers and AIDS patients.

AIDS, ACTIVISM, AND ACCOMMODATION

After the 1987 AIDS panic subsided, less time was devoted to AIDS by scholars, bureaucrats, and the media in Japan. Government officials, encouraged by the silence, took credit for having acted decisively in implementing a truly effective AIDS policy. But the number of individuals suffering from AIDS gradually grew, and they became increasingly outspoken. By the early 1990s, AIDS had returned. Newspapers, widely read weekly magazines like *Spa*, *Shūkan Playboy*, *Fōcus*, and *Jyosei Sebun*, and more serious publications like *Aera* and *Sekai* regularly featured stories on safe sex, HIV transmission, AIDS and prostitution, and other AIDS-related topics. Celebrity faces showed up on subway walls, over messages about AIDS, discrimination, and safe sex. Television shows and movies with AIDS-related themes were aired.

The most significant change in the complexion of AIDS activists was the increasing presence of gay groups, such as OCCUR, devoted to the opposition of discrimination and government indifference toward gay men. This caused a split in the gay community between those willing to remain marginalized and others who insisted that gays be more outspoken. Criticizing the heterosexual publisher of the gay publication *Barazoku*, for example, the leader of OCCUR states: "He doesn't talk about AIDS, discrimination, safe sex and other matters. He still views homosexuality as a form of recreation and not a lifestyle."[57]

As part of the effort to better educate the public about AIDS, a group of activists and concerned citizens brought a section of the NAMES Project's quilt on a tour of Japan's major cities. In each city where the quilt was displayed, people of all ages and backgrounds came to learn about HIV. Japanese panels were also included, the earliest ones containing no names because of fears about discrimination. Later panels displayed initials, and a particularly poignant contribution from a recently deceased hemophiliac AIDS patient was written in his own blood.

On October 17, 1990, a group of AIDS activists visited the offices of Diet members and MHW officials responsible for AIDS policy. Men and women, HIV-positive and negative, gay and hemophiliac, they shared an interest in persuading the government to improve public health strategies related to AIDS. To show that their interests were widely shared, they presented an "appeal" signed by 16,830 Japanese. It read, in part:

> In Japan, only a few medical institutions are positively engaged in treatment of HIV patients. It is not an overstatement to say that even the few medical facilities we have, that are positively helping HIV patients, receive meager support and depend on the dedication of a limited number of physicians.

> Japan is said to be a major economic power. We must not continue to ignore the pitiable condition of HIV patients and carriers. Victims are increasing throughout the world. It is time for Japan to take an international stance with regard to a policy on HIV.

The document went on to demand accessible medical facilities for HIV-positive people, a more generous compensation system for hemophiliacs, free anonymous HIV testing, HIV education programs, the elimination of discrimination against HIV patients and carriers, and a larger budget for HIV research, among other things. Letters from AIDS experts in the West were also displayed to show international support for the reform of Japan's AIDS policy.

Other general appeals for the greater protection of rights related to AIDS have also been made. The HIV–Human Rights Information Center, advocating the "protection of the rights of HIV patients and carriers," "the establishment of an HIV test that is free and where privacy is protected," and "HIV treatment that respects rights, and is free . . .,"[58] submitted a petition in 1991 to the minister of health and welfare. It stated:

> In Japan, compared to many other countries, discrimination is strong, and the protection of human rights is not well established . . . The idea of isolating HIV patients has been abandoned, and we believe that the foundation of a policy toward HIV must be a medical system that fully respects human rights.[59]

For its part, the Ministry both defends current policy, and promises change. In an official government publication that explains Japan's AIDS policy, the MHW contends:

> The [AIDS] law emphasizes the protection of the privacy and human rights of HIV-infected persons. Regulatory involvement is minimized;

instead, emphasis is placed on the voluntary contributions of citizens and the commitment of health workers to fighting the disease.[60]

At the same time, a document circulated at the Ministry that reviews the goals and operation of its AIDS policy states that "we must pay attention to the adequate protection of privacy and human rights."[61] Similarly, at a 1992 Cabinet ministers' meeting about AIDS policy, it was said that further efforts would be made to protect the privacy and human rights of those with HIV/AIDS.[62]

While the general discussion about AIDS policy and rights has continued, numerous specific issues have surfaced that concern rights assertion, infringement, and protection. A brief examination of them provides a more detailed picture of the substance and rhetoric of AIDS policy in Japan.

IMMIGRATION CONTROLS

As early as 1985, it was reported in the international press that the Japanese government planned to deny entry to foreigners suspected of being HIV-positive.[63] Those reports were supported by the first draft of the AIDS legislation, which called for amendment of the Immigration Act, a provision included in the final law. This aspect of AIDS policy initially attracted vigorous criticism, but the controversy disappeared as it became increasingly clear that the government had no intention of screening foreigners entering the country.

One factor that influenced the government to not exercise the border control powers incorporated in the AIDS law was the 1988 World Health Ministers AIDS Conference in England. At that conference, there was a general discussion of immigration controls, and the Japanese press reported that the idea of HIV border checks was strongly criticized by most attendees. Japanese policy makers were aware of this criticism, and realized that international censure would be strong if a restrictive immigration policy were implemented. Public Health and immigration authorities therefore decided that they would only use the powers granted by the law as a way of denying entry to women who planned to work in the sex trade and were suspected of being HIV-positive. Since prostitution is formally illegal, however, the law could not be explicit about the intent to ensure that only healthy prostitutes enter the country.

While individuals have not been denied entry to Japan on the basis of the AIDS law, there was an outcry about immigration restrictions with regard to Japan hosting the Tenth International Conference on AIDS, held in Yokohama in August 1994. The meetings traditionally attract at least 10,000 participants, about 10 percent of whom are AIDS patients or HIV-positive. Some are also sex workers and intravenous drug users, groups with high rates of HIV infection internationally, who have attended past meetings and pressed for the protection of certain rights. Aware that they could be refused admission to Japan, potential participants demanded that the Japanese government revise its immigration laws or that the meetings be relocated.

Japanese immigration authorities initially clashed with the MHW, refusing to suspend their power to deny entry to HIV-positive people, AIDS patients, sex workers, or drug offenders.[64] The MHW threatened to withdraw as sponsor of the meetings, an event that MHW officials said would be an international embarrassment to Japan. Eventually, a compromise was reached. The Ministry of Justice, which controls immigration, announced that HIV carriers and AIDS patients could enter the country in order to attend the Conference, but known sex workers and drug users could not.[65] The meeting was convened without incident.

Discrimination

AIDS patients, those who are HIV-positive, and members of groups associated with HIV have suffered various forms of discrimination. Professor Takeda Bin of Chiba University believes that the best way to halt discrimination is through education. He writes: "because it is easy to react [toward HIV patients] by excluding or discriminating, we must teach about rights in school – the right to exist, right to live, right to health, privacy – it is fundamental to make sure that students understand about their protection, and other things."[66] But for those who are currently victimized, the long time-frame required by education fails to address their immediate problems. Most outspoken against AIDS-related discrimination in Japan have been hemophiliacs, whose claims and assertions of rights are fully discussed in Chapter 6. Other groups, particularly gay men, have encountered similar problems but have only recently begun to speak out.[67]

Japanese gay men have been both perpetrators and victims of discrimination. Rather than identifying themselves as having common interests and concerns with homosexuals from other nations, many Japanese gay men, and the saunas they frequent, have adopted a posture of exclusion toward Western homosexuals. Whereas Western men were once actively pursued, since the late 1980s they have come to be treated as infectious, high risk, and dangerous. Almost all gay saunas (as well as many heterosexual sex clubs) post "Japanese Only" signs at their entrance ways. In bars and other social settings, except for those intentionally designed to attract a mixed clientele, Westerners are avoided. Like many others in Japan, gay men view AIDS as a "foreign" phenomenon.

But Japanese gay men are also victims of discrimination. One revealing incident concerns a study by a researcher studying sexual practices among Japanese gay men to learn about high-risk behavior related to HIV transmission. The researcher initially discussed his methodology and goals with gay groups, received their backing, and placed a notice soliciting respondents in a gay magazine. After extensive interviewing and data collection, however, a controversy arose as to whether data about gay sexual practices would lead to discrimination and persecution of gay men. Perhaps, they reasoned, it was best for such information to remain unknown. Enthusiasm for the research turned to contempt, and the researcher, who felt that the support of gay groups was essential, indefinitely delayed the announcement of his findings.[68]

There is, in fact, reason for concern in the gay community. The perception among gays that hemophiliacs have been the beneficiaries of government largesse, while gay men have been ignored or mistreated, to some extent reflects a bias within the MHW and the nation generally. In interviews with staff of the MHW's AIDS section, staff members spoke of former Minister of Health and Welfare Yamashita Tokuo as sympathetic to hemophiliacs but someone who "hated gays" and did not object to them being discriminated against.[69] Gay rights activist Minami Teishirō, in a belief that has come to be widely accepted, claims that the first diagnosed case of AIDS in Japan was in a hemophiliac, but that information about it was suppressed until cases of HIV-positive women and gays were officially reported. He describes this as "obviously discrimination against gays."[70] Minami says that the Tokyo Metropolitan Government gives money to gay rights organizations to keep them under control, and that such groups are only now beginning to emerge as independent entities.

The first case regarding gay rights in Japan was taken to court in 1990. It resulted from an incident in which a gay group was prohibited from renting a meeting hall managed by the Tokyo Metropolitan

Government. Yet such cases are rare, indicating that there remains a significant divide between the willingness of gay-oriented groups in Japan and the United States to engage in the important rituals of rights that would bring visibility to their concerns.

Medical treatment, testing, and patients' rights

For all people affected by AIDS in Japan, it remains difficult to find a physician willing to provide care. According to the Japan Institute of People With AIDS,

> Denial of treatment for HIV patients and carriers is prominent in Japan, and, in addition, since the enactment of the "AIDS Prevention Bill," there has been a decrease in the number of people receiving the HIV antibody test. In the midst of such unreasonable prejudice and spread of discriminatory acts, HIV victims are being deprived of their basic human right of health, which is tantamount to denying them the right to live.[71]

Akase Yasunori, the first Japanese hemophiliac to publicly reveal that he had AIDS, claims: "There exists a terrible discrimination against us among doctors and hospital authorities. They make a lot of excuses [to avoid treating those with HIV/AIDS at their hospitals], such as being short of facilities or staff."[72] While there has been no systematic research on this problem, many AIDS patients report that they have been turned away by private hospitals. Hospital administrators generally justify their actions by claiming that they do not have the facilities or expertise to care for AIDS patients, an excuse that critics interpret to mean that the presence of AIDS patients is bad for business. AIDS patients therefore seek treatment at national hospitals, but even that may not succeed. According to a newspaper account, an HIV-positive woman was taken for surgery at a public hospital after an accident injured her spine. Surgeons refused to operate, and the lower part of her body was paralyzed.[73]

The care of hemophiliacs has been particularly problematic. Adhering to the ethos of non-disclosure that pervades cancer treatment, many doctors of hemophiliac patients do not disclose information about HIV test results. Out of 454 hemophiliacs who responded to a survey in 1988, 106 were not informed of the results of their HIV tests.[74] Abe Takeshi, a prominent hematologist who once treated almost one hundred hemophiliac patients at Teikyō University (and will be discussed in Chapter 6), provides the following justification: "Until we can have a procedure to conquer AIDS, we prefer to hide the real data from the HIV test . . . We injected the contaminated blood preparation, and they got the infection . . . I am a criminal."[75] Abe, and other physicians who treat hemophiliacs, say they fear that if hemophiliacs are told they are HIV-positive, they might commit suicide or become irresponsible and intentionally infect others. They also claim that many hemophiliacs do not want to know their test results. Despite evidence that indicates 87 percent would prefer to know the truth, less than one half of tested hemophiliacs are given their test results.[76] One hemophiliac, for example, says that he was worried about exposure to HIV beginning in 1983. Although his doctor assured him that he was healthy, in 1989 he discovered that he was HIV-positive, the result of self-injection of blood products used according to his physician's instructions.[77]

As a result of similar misinformation, many hemophiliacs do not know that they are HIV-positive, and so continue to have unprotected sexual relations. Dr. Abe does not worry about HIV transmission to spouses. "I have all the information on their [HIV-positive hemophiliacs'] behavior," he says. "They have no opportunity to give the infection to other persons in most cases."[78] Despite his confidence, spouses have been infected, and are now plaintiffs in the litigation by hemophiliacs.

Other rights-based disputes over AIDS-related medical care have also emerged. The Public Health Bureau of the Tokyo Metropolitan Government, in an epidemiological research report, published data on AIDS patients that included their initials, gender, age, appointment dates, source of infection, and the names of the hospitals where they were treated. Yashiki Kyōichi of AIDS Action exclaimed: "A government must consider patients' rights when it plans any kind of publication. There was no need to disclose the initials."[79] In response, the director of the Bureau stated: "At present, initials are commonly used in medical data reports. We will now consider whether this violates patients' rights to privacy and act accordingly."[80]

Another aspect of the assertion of rights in the medical setting is the recent request of the Japan Hospital Association, representing one quarter of Japan's hospitals, that the MHW permit hospitals to ask patients to take an HIV test before surgery. According to Kawakita Hirobumi, vice-chairman of the association,

> The association . . . considers an AIDS test before surgery a necessary step to protect the human rights of the medical personnel . . . medical

doctors and nurses also have the right to choose whether or not they will participate in surgery on an AIDS patient.[81]

But he continues:

Medical doctors should bear in mind that so long as they insist on their right to know about a patient's infection with AIDS, they have the duty to provide medical treatment to the patient once they know that he or she is infected.[82]

HIV testing has also been a contentious issue because there is distrust of government testing centers that are claimed to be anonymous and confidential. The HIV–Human Rights Information Center has conducted research on a sample of HIV test sites, and determined that some of them are overly lax about protecting the identity of clients. Stories about individuals who have traveled to the United States for an HIV test suggest that skepticism about claims to anonymity is widespread. The MHW has cautioned prefectural testing centers to be careful about protecting privacy when conducting HIV tests, and to guard the human rights of those being tested.[83] A directive sent from the MHW to regional government centers advised: "With regard to the execution of HIV tests, from the perspective of the protection of rights, we must obtain the consent of the person taking a test. Also, we must adequately consider the protection of privacy when handling test results."[84]

Even if testing centers provided anonymous testing, however, problems would remain. Most significantly, laws regarding the use of blood and patient data in Japan are minimal, and blood samples are generously taken. Consequently, it is alleged that much blood is tested for HIV without patient consent, and those who fear they could be HIV-positive avoid the health care system entirely.[85]

The extent, if any, to which the MHW decides to revamp the current strategy for confronting HIV is likely to depend as much on its future spread in Japan as on the pressure exerted by particular groups and individuals. Yet it is clear that those most affected by HIV have united, publicly speaking out on the needs of HIV-positive people, the shortcomings of government policy, and the failures of the medical system. They have used the language of rights to press their claims, have directly criticized political and bureaucratic elites, and have become involved in the policy-making process. What is striking in the AIDS controversy, like the debate over brain death discussed in Chapter 5, is that contrary to the notion that rights are irrelevant in Japan, they have been frequently at issue in the shaping of AIDS policy. While not identical to the way in which they function in American law and politics, rights have had a profound impact on the AIDS policy debate in contemporary Japan.

CHAPTER FIVE

ASSERTING RIGHTS, LEGISLATING DEATH

RIGHTS, BRAIN DEATH, AND ORGAN TRANSPLANTATION

Since Japan's controversial first heart transplant in 1968, conflict about the definition of death has been joined by a diverse group of individuals and organizations.[1] Physicians, attorneys, journalists, philosophers, and political activists have all clashed in the battle over brain death. No single group, and there are many, has been able to attract widespread support for its particular view of what standard of death ought to be applied in Japan's hospitals.[2] Former Prime Minister Kaifu's administration tried to decide the matter through a high-level panel of experts it assembled in 1989, but failed. A transplant bill that was to be introduced in the 1993 Diet session was delayed; when it was introduced in April 1994, it too failed. Finally, after years of struggle, the 1997 Diet passed a law aimed at increasing the number of organ transplants in Japan. But even that legislation did not articulate a uniform definition of death. Fierce opposition to the bill resulted in feeble legislation promoting organ transplantation without endorsing brain death criteria.

Why is it that defining death as brain death remains controversial in Japan? Whether or not a brain death standard is accepted, the vast majority of people will experience death in its conventional form, the termination of heartbeat and breath. For them, death will result from the biological limits of vital functions, whether expedited by disease or the natural result of age. Only in cases such as cerebral hemorrhage or severe head injury, conditions that are present in less than 1 percent of deaths, are brain death criteria utilized.[3]

An analysis of the extensive media coverage and reports issued by professional and political groups uncovers three commonly provided explanations for Japan's brain death gridlock. First is the legacy of Japan's first heart transplant, the 1968 Wada case, and the way in which it has become a symbol of public mistrust of the medical profession. Second is what can roughly be described as Japanese culture, a catch-all to explain the tension between traditional Japanese views of death and the body and the mechanistic orientation of high-technology medicine. Third is the claimed need for, but current lack of broad public consensus in Japan before a policy can be adopted.

Each of these explanations has some validity. More importantly, all three share a common element. Each incorporates arguments that rely to some extent on the assertion of rights. Whether it is the rights of organ donors and recipients, the rights of families to control the treatment of their members, or the rights of the public at large to have a voice in the controversy, the language of rights is pervasive. In the context of a society that allegedly has no rights tradition and little understanding of or interest in rights, the centrality of rights claims in the brain death debate merits attention.

Those asserting rights with regard to brain death in Japan include politicians, philosophers, legal scholars, and people involved in personal human dramas about life, death, loss, and power. They fall squarely into Japan's tradition of conflict, where those who feel aggrieved complain, cajole, attack, and appeal in whatever measure and combination they think is most likely to lead to a desirable resolution.

There are, of course, certain differences between the brain death issue and traditional social protest, discussed in Chapter 2. Opponents of brain death are not united in a mass movement. Claims to rights in the brain death controversy do not pose a fundamental threat to the Japanese state. The government has not enacted repressive legislation on brain death. Nonetheless, the participants, contrary to the received wisdom that rights are alien to Japan, have cast their arguments in the language of rights. They have done so in order, perhaps not consciously, to endow them with power and legitimacy. Both opponents and advocates of brain death have used rights arguments because they understand that they attract attention and concern from the public, the media, and policy makers. Thus has the brain death debate escalated.

To a great extent, the evolution of the brain death controversy has occurred at the same time as the movement for patients' rights and debates over informed consent. Indeed, many of the founders and central figures in the patients' rights movement, particularly those who are active in the Organization to Establish a Patients' Rights Law (*Kanja no Kenrihō Tsukurukai*), were originally involved in the brain death debate. From the Wada and Tsukuba cases (discussed in Chapter 6), through the recent legislative deliberations over the transplant law, brain death has been a galvanizing issue in Japanese health policy and politics. Whether the brain death issue has inspired the assertion of patients' rights and concern about informed consent, or whether the controversy over brain death is a result rather than a cause, is impossible to say. But there is a strong link between brain death and patients' rights, and that link is solidified by the mistrust of physicians, a reaction to the medical world that is as prominent as deference to professional authority.

The Patients' Rights Conference (PRC), for example, is a group of physicians, hospital workers, and others who have been at the forefront of attacks on attempts to make brain death a legitimate definition of death. Despite the professional orientation of its membership, the PRC consistently criticizes the untrustworthiness of physicians, and their cavalier disregard for patients' rights. In the wake of a controversial transplant, for example, the PRC wrote:

> the case included the absolute negligence of both donor and recipient patient's rights. As for the donor, we can note the discrimination against psychiatric patients regarding consent, and the abandonment of her basic treatment, which consequently led to her death through the taking of her organs. As for the recipient, the essence of human experimentation was demonstrated by the forced consent, recipient selection, [and] the fact that this was the first combined pancreas/kidney transplant . . .[4]

The PRC has positioned itself as representing the interests of organ donors and recipients, equating them with the handicapped and mentally incompetent. Doing so has led to an alliance between the PRC and radical patient-centered groups. They amplify legitimate suspicion of physician authority – the fear that the combination of Japanese authoritarianism and deference to authority could lead to coercion and worse by doctors who want to increase the supply of organs – into a belief that doctors who promote brain death are bent on full-scale eugenics – the elimination of social "undesirables" and the quest for "perfect" people. While such a degree of physician mistrust is unusual, it does underscore the connection between mistrust, rights, and brain death that is so frequently voiced.

Less radical assessments of the brain death debate also point to its connection with mistrust and rights. Medical sociologist Nudeshima Jirō, for example, argues that a primary reason for the longevity of the brain death controversy is the institutional incapacity of the medical profession, particularly the lack of procedures and standards for respecting the rights of patients and obtaining informed consent.[5] As the following discussion will illustrate, the brain death controversy, and discussion of a transplant system, revolve around, and are animated by, notions of patients' rights and informed consent. In short, conflict over defining death in Japan implicates a range of issues, including religious traditions, professional norms, and institutional design. In the realm of politics and policy, these have all been expressed in a similar way. Each has been voiced in the language of rights. For thirty years, fueled by vocal rights assertion, the definition of death has been contested.[6]

DEATH, CULTURE, AND BODY PARTS

The bulk of literature about the brain death and organ transplantation debate suggests that it is intimately connected to custom, religion, and tradition rather than to rights. Typical of such a perspective is the writing of Umehara Takeshi, who treats Japan as a monolithic society dominated by the values and traditions of its feudal past. A philosopher and member of Prime Minister Kaifu's most recent government committee to address the brain death issue, Umehara writes: "Despite our seemingly boundless enthusiasm for things Western, we Japanese are unable to emulate the West in this one matter [organ transplants] because something in our basic ethical system resists the idea of organ transplants."[7] The absence of Cartesian dualism is also cited as a critical factor in the failure to accept brain death, as are social customs governing the management of the dead and the lack of a tradition of altruistic giving.[8]

The idea that brain death and organ transplants are fundamentally incompatible with Japanese culture is promoted as well by Western academic anthropologists. They have used the debate over brain death and transplants as support for the thesis that medical science is value-laden and strongly influenced by culture. Margaret Lock, for example, has sought to show that the locus of the self in Japan, unlike the mind-centered West, is in a part of the body that might help explain the ambivalence toward brain death and transplantation.[9] While there is some merit to this approach, different anthropologists have been unable to agree as to where the elusive Japanese self resides. Lock claims that the heart is its home, which explains why heart transplants are taboo; Ohnuki-Tierney believes that the stomach is critical, accounting for the reluctance to donate kidneys.[10]

To evaluate the power of the cultural perspective, it is necessary to examine certain Japanese traditions and to explore the ways in which they may influence contemporary attitudes toward death.

Religious/traditional views of death

Like people in most cultures, the Japanese have distinctive beliefs and practices that surround the phenomenon of death. Takie Lebra, for example, claims that "in Japan a heroic, romantic, aesthetic, and moral aura surrounds death in general . . .,"[11] and Lafcadio Hearn exclaims "that in all matters the dead, rather than the living, have been the rulers of the nation and the shapers of its destinies."[12] The earliest information about the treatment of death and dead bodies in Japan comes from Jōmon (until 200 BC) and Yayoi (200 BC–400 AD) archeological evidence. Burial mounds uncovered from Jomon days suggest that the dead were buried in such a way as to prevent them from returning after death to cause mischief to the living. Varying accounts describe corpses as buried with arms and legs folded, or with bones broken and buried holding a large rock.[13] Some of this fear of the dead appears to have been conquered during the Yayoi period, when the dead were buried in coffins with limbs outstretched.

Basil Hall Chamberlain describes the Japanese custom of placing the dead body in a mourning house, where the survivors would hold a feast with food that may have been meant as an offering to the dead. The corpse would be interred in a wooden bier, and buried with clothes and ornaments.[14] During the Kofun period (3–7AD), when Shintō beliefs were prevalent, coffins were sometimes shaped like boats, suggesting that the dead body would go on a voyage to another life.[15]

In his *History of Japanese Religion*, Anesaki Masaharu argues that spirits were the basis of Shintō belief. Although there was only a vague idea about the human soul and what happened to it after death, there seem to have been two lands where the dead were thought to go. One, the Land of Gloom (*Yomotsu-kuni*) or Bottom Land (*Sokotsu-kuni*), is a Hades-like place in the subterranean world. The other, the Plain of High Heaven (*Takama-no-hara*), is a heavenly land. Most legends spoke about the afterlife only in connection with great men, and it is not clear whether the souls of common mortals also went to these lands or simply vanished. It does appear that after death the soul was believed to stay among its fellow beings for an indefinite period.[16]

Lafcadio Hearn says that all people became gods upon their deaths, but retained the characteristics they had when living.[17] Thus, "good" people became "good" gods and "bad" people "bad" ones. The dead were seen as haunting their tombs and former homes, sharing in the lives of their descendants and having a constant presence in this world. These spirits required food, drink, and light – if they were well taken care of it would assure the living of continued happiness, but if they were neglected the living would suffer (though it does seem that the spirits performed far more benevolent than malevolent deeds).[18] Hearn also notes the appearance of two other Shintō beliefs – that every event in the world, good or bad, is the work of the dead, and that all human actions are controlled by the dead. He believes that traditional ideas about death and spirits have survived 2,000 years, and were still prevalent at the time of his writing (in 1904).

The "freshly dead" seem to have presented a special threat to the early Japanese. The dead were regarded as a great source of pollution and sin, and the freshly dead "hovered at the margin of nature and culture," inhabiting neither the world of the living nor the world of the ancestors.[19] The soul was polluted by its own death, and in this potentially dangerous state wandered through the world. To purify the freshly dead and make them into one of the truly dead with whom communication could be established, a series of rites and rituals were performed.

Traditions of ancestor worship have also been important in Japan. When the Meiji Constitution was promulgated in 1889, it was infused with references to the Imperial Ancestors, from whom sovereign power was a "sacred inheritance."[20] In fact, when the American army issued its directive aimed at "disestablishing" Shintō as the state religion after World War II, one of the targets was the shelves where tablets honoring the dead were kept: "God-shelves . . . supported wholly or in part by public funds are prohibited and will be removed immediately."[21] Still, Hozumi concluded that ancestor worship was the

> primeval religion of the country from the earliest times of our history and is universally practiced by the people at the present moment . . . neither the introduction of Chinese civilization, the spread of Buddhism nor the influence of European civilization has done anything to shake the firm rooted custom of the people.[22]

More recently, Picken has hyperbolically asserted that "the idea of death enshrined in Shintō mythology remains the fountainhead of the Japanese tradition. It influenced and transformed the Buddhist outlook when Buddhism came to Japan, and if one looks carefully, it can be seen to be an element present in uniquely Japanese attitudes to many issues."[23]

In addition to Shintō, scholars claiming that the contemporary brain death debate is shaped by traditional Japanese views of death can point to the impact of Buddhism on the rituals of death in Japan. Since its introduction into Japan in the sixth century, Buddhism has always been actively engaged in perfecting its funeral rites. Buddhism may have originally needed the income from funerals to support itself in Japan. Its connection with funerals was solidified when the Edo Shogunate ordered Buddhist temples to keep the census registers of the population.[24] As caretakers of the funeral, the Buddhists introduced a variety of new customs, such as the kindling of 108 fires for the return of the dead, supplying spirits with figures made of straw or vegetables to serve as oxen or horses, and preparing ships on which ancestors could return to the underworld.[25]

Although Shintō was concerned with the practice of honoring one's ancestors, its focus was not the actual life that would be led after death. Buddhism, in contrast, explicitly addressed what happened to the soul of the deceased.[26] The Buddhist idea of impermanence (mujyō), which says that all things in nature and culture are constantly changing, tended to relativize the importance of both death and life, and stressed instead the idea of reincarnation and the attainment of Buddhahood. Whereas Shintō emphasized death as a sort of journey, with welcomes and leave-takings,[27] Buddhism saw it as the opportunity to take leave of one world in hopes of attaining a new state of being.

Finally, the method by which dead bodies were disposed of was significantly altered as a result of Buddhist practices. Prior to the seventh century, the Japanese tended toward extravagant funeral arrangements. Fueled by a belief in ancestor worship and a desire to please the dead, huge burial tombs were erected and many objects were buried along with the corpse. As Buddhism spread throughout the country and began to exert a strong influence on governmental affairs, a decree was issued in 645 that put a limitation on the size of the mounds and the worth of buried objects.[28] It was during this same period that the Buddhist scholar Dōshō pioneered the practice of cremation in Japan. It did not take long for cremation to become the predominant method of interment. Yet in spite of the decree of 645 and other laws regulating death, all aimed at paring down funeral arrangements, it seems that the "tendency to extravagance in the matter of funerals [is] a tendency so strong that, in spite of centuries of sumptuary legislation, it remains today a social danger."[29] Itami Jūzō's 1984 movie "The Funeral" is a vivid illustration of the complexities a modern Japanese family encounters before cremating the dead, and a reminder that the sense of having a duty to the deceased is sufficiently strong to sustain a feature-length parody.

Brain death and tradition in Japan

Two aspects of Japanese tradition are particularly relevant to contemporary debates about brain death. First is the Shintō notion of ancestor worship. A central tenet of ancestor worship is the conviction that the welfare of the living is dependent upon paying appropriate homage to the dead. So long as the deceased is given the proper offerings and honored by suitable funeral arrangements, then the living should suffer no ill. But declaring a person dead based on a brain death criterion may not be the most respectful way in which to treat one's future ancestors, and cutting up their bodies in order to harvest their organs would seem to clearly violate the respect that is their due.

Despite the traditional role of the family in controlling the disposal of corpses, the language of rights has surfaced in this area. One manifestation of the historic role of the family in disposing of its dead can be found in the law controlling the donation of kidneys and corneas, which gives a great deal of power to surviving relatives. Family consent is necessary for organ removal, even if the deceased has consented in writing. Without regard to a donor's desires, relatives may consent to organ removal if they are so inclined. Professor Bai Kōichi, a noted legal scholar, states that the family of the deceased has "a certain voice in the disposal of any part of his body even during his life, although their voice is secondary to his own while he is alive. After his death, their voice becomes predominant."[30] He calls the principle on which this law is based the right of self-determination, although it reflects a somewhat unusual understanding of "self." According to Bai:

> We would recognize a right of self-determination on the part of a surviving relative in order to explain these situations [that the bereaved has a right of consent or refusal to the removal against a decedent's desire]. The bereaved has the same right to determine freely how to live as a decedent. As far as the cadaver has effects on the life of a surviving family, the later should be entitled to dispose it in accordance with his lifestyle.[31]

The family's power to determine whether a deceased member will donate organs was affirmed by guidelines drafted by the Ministry of Health and Welfare in January 1994 to supplement a draft brain death bill.[32] Even when a potential donor does not express a willingness to donate, the MHW guidelines say that families can decide whether to donate the deceased's organs based upon the person's history of blood donation, registration at an eye or kidney bank, inquiries about donor cards, expressed desire to further medical science, and other evidence.[33] The guidelines were immediately criticized by those who questioned whether the family ought to have such decision-making power. Hori Toshikatsu, a member of the Diet's Upper House, worries that families will be subjected to undue physician pressure:

> In our experience, there is no equal relationship between the doctors and patients in this country. If a doctor recommends that families donate the organs of their loved ones who have become brain dead, the families can hardly refuse. Therefore, establishment of patients' rights and a thorough practice of informed consent at medical institutions must come before the passage of the bill.[34]

Nakajima Michi, a journalist well known for her book *Mienai Shi* (Invisible Death) and for her active campaign against a brain death standard, has similarly written:

> I have been appealing to the public about how badly the human rights of patients have been treated in medical circles. If a bill that equates

brain death with death itself becomes law, it would be a foregone conclusion that the lives of those in weak positions, both in physical and
social terms, would be dealt with without due respect.[35]

The traditional role of the family in disposing of the remains of its
members, which Bai has formulated as the right of self-determination,
is thus pitted against and is threatened by physician coercion that
could force families to act against their own wishes and/or the perceived wishes of the dead member. That such a formulation has
emerged hints at the continued power of tradition, and indicates that
rights assertion has crept into the core of even the most traditional
practices.

A different aspect of Japanese culture, as tenacious as ideas about
traditional religious beliefs, has also influenced the brain death debate.
The need for consensus, an oft-cited element of Japan's political and
legal culture, has become a dominant theme in both public and private discussion. As one Western scholar has stated: "Every discussion
on the subject of brain death in Japan, even when presented by doctors eager to facilitate organ transplants, is based on the premise that
any changes in medical or legal practice in this area can only come
after a consensus has been established among the Japanese people as
a whole."[36] But the search for consensus has so far been unsuccessful,
for two general reasons.

On the one hand, beyond the ideological invocation of consensus
as a standard description by Japanese policy makers of how Japanese
policy is created, the breadth and depth of the agreement that consensus requires is vague. Those involved in trying to define death are
unclear as to who must agree, how deep their agreement must run, or
how long it must last. Consequently, when some are prepared to
declare consensus and move on, others argue that divisiveness is rife,
depending upon their views of the desirability of settling on a particular policy.

This is directly related to the second stumbling block of consensus –
that it supposedly entails some degree of *public* agreement. Given the
moral and psychological dimensions of defining death, it has been a
topic consistently prone to disagreement, both in Japan and in every
other jurisdiction that has considered it. If public consensus is
required before a brain death definition is implemented, then brain
death is not likely ever to be officially recognized.

Despite the democratic overtones of the rhetoric about consensus
in the brain death debate, on other issues public consensus has rarely

been of concern to the medical or political elite, who are not ordinarily reluctant to railroad through a policy without dwelling on public approval. Their insistence on consensus should instead be understood as a method by which policy makers have shifted attention away from the indecision and conflict plaguing experts' attempts to define death. By stating that consensus is an indispensable element in the official recognition of brain death, they have avoided the creation of a controversial policy until the true consensus makers agree – the individuals and organizations involved in the conflict at the highest medical, legal, and political levels.

Active opponents of the recognition of brain death – the Japan Federation of Bar Associations, the Patients' Rights Conference, and others – also championed the importance of consensus. While they may have believed that public opinion was important, they also understood that public agreement on the definition of death was exceedingly unlikely. By insisting on "true" consensus, they have been able to indefinitely delay, if not defeat, a legislative definition of brain death, thereby inhibiting the development of an active organ transplant program.

In the absence of general agreement among experts on how death should be defined, and paralyzed by the need for consensus, the brain death debate entered a stalemate. Even those organizations that could have been expected to fully support brain death often split into factions and were unable to develop a unified public position. Still, there was a steady flow of proposals, reports, and studies.

SCIENTIFIC, LEGAL, MEDICAL, AND POLITICAL ATTEMPTS TO DEFINE DEATH

One of the first attempts to introduce a brain death definition in Japan was made by the Japan Electroencephalography Association (JEA) (Nihon Nōha Gakkai) in 1974. A professional group consisting exclusively of physicians, the JEA drew up Japan's first medical criteria for determining brain death: (1) a coma in which patients exhibit no reactions; (2) dilated pupils; (3) lack of spontaneous breathing; (4) a rapid drop in blood pressure, succeeded by continuous low blood pressure; (5) flat brain waves; and (6) a continuation of conditions 1–5 for six hours. Tsukamoto Yasushi, a physician who has studied the brain death controversy, argues that the JEA criteria were meant to serve two purposes; to create standards for the treatment of patients in irreversible comas, and "to protect the donor's personal rights as a human being in organ transplantation."[37]

In early 1985, twenty-eight Diet members and forty-five other professionals and officials formed the Life Ethics Problem Study Parliamentarians League. Leading the group was a physician and Liberal Democratic Party Diet member, Nakayama Tarō, who would in 1988 be a key player in the formation of Prime Minister Kaifu's brain death committee, and later became minister of foreign affairs. The League set as its mission the determination of whether the Diet ought to enact legislation recognizing brain death, and after one year of monthly meetings endorsed the idea of brain death.

Speaking several months after its inauguration, Upper House member Takagi Kentarō, secretary general of the group, said: "There should be a law to recognize brain death as death. Otherwise, each hospital would diagnose brain death according to its own criteria ... There is fear among some patients who distrust doctors that their organs would be removed while they are still alive. We should have some kind of standards."[38] Despite the endorsement of brain death by a group including politicians from the ruling Liberal Democratic Party, no legislation was forthcoming.

As the Life Ethics Problem Study Parliamentarians League was in the midst of its policy deliberations, the Ministry of Health and Welfare (MHW), recognizing that the Japan Electroencephalography Association criteria were already outmoded, decided to reconsider the scientific guidelines for declaring brain death. The urgency of this task was highlighted by the release of a MHW study in May, 1985. Examining over 1,000 hospital cases in which patients in Japan were declared brain dead, the study concluded that in most situations the standards set by the JEA were violated.[39] Even though the study claimed that the JEA criteria were overly rigid, current medical practice appeared to be inadequate even when measured by less stringent guidelines.

Some reports of this study took a matter-of-fact tone and simply announced that the MHW would begin drafting clearer brain death criteria.[40] Others were less sanguine, citing the laxity in declaring brain death as a sign that patients' rights were being violated by transplant-happy surgeons. In a newspaper story titled "Brain Death Criteria Vary Case to Case," for example, the author states: "[T]he findings [of the MHW study] show that hospitals and other first-aid stations obviously adopt their own standards to facilitate the process of transplantation of organs."[41] In the absence of official recognition of brain death, and in an atmosphere where transplants from brain dead bodies were considered taboo, the belief that physicians operated more out of self-interest than in the interest of patients was frequently voiced.

In an effort to combat suspicion of the medical community, the MHW launched the Brain Death Advisory Council.[42] Headed by neurosurgeon Takeuchi Kazuo, former dean of Kyoto University's Faculty of Medicine (and later president of Kyōrin University), the council's seven other members were also physicians, primarily from the discipline of neurology. The Brain Death Advisory Council's final report, issued on December 6, 1985, was billed upon its release by the MHW as an official non-binding reference for physicians. Its criteria for determining brain death, based on the cessation of brain function, are: (1) deep coma; (2) cessation of spontaneous breathing; (3) fixed and enlarged pupils; (4) loss of brain stem reflexes; (5) flat brain waves; (6) 1–5 must continue for at least six hours.[43] Children under six are not subject to the criteria, and the presence of two physicians with no interest in the use of the patient's organs, in addition to the attending physician, is required when brain death is declared. In contrast to the guidelines of the JEA, the new criteria do not mention blood pressure and include reflex tests.

Emanating from an elite group of physicians, what have become known as "Takeuchi's criteria" continue to serve as the scientific backbone of brain death, and are alternately praised and damned as medically pristine or scientifically imprecise. Yet embedded in the guidelines is a deep ambiguity about the relationship between brain death and death. Despite the professional bias of Takeuchi's group toward viewing brain death as death, and the argument that if brain death can be precisely determined then an individual is dead, the Brain Death Advisory Council defined brain death without declaring it death. In fact, it did the opposite, declaring that "death cannot be judged by brain death." Takeuchi himself later proved equivocal, stating: "[A]ll the doctors in our hospital, myself included, feel that we should wait for the heartbeat to stop. There is no question about it."[44]

This ambivalence was reflected in the extensive media coverage of the report. One article, for example, while opining that the new criteria would "take Japan a significant step towards the recognition of brain death," reported: "[T]he team was adamant in stating that the brain death of a patient under their definition does not classify the patient as 'dead.' "[45] An editorial, summing up its view of the report, confusingly stated: "[W]e believe that the most likely choice at the moment is to conditionally accept brain death, based on the principle that the suspension of the heart beat is the very basis of the standard."[46] And another editorial warned that while "the team contends that the definition has nothing to do with the final judgment of death, it defines one death. Now, control over death has begun."[47]

A more cogent view was put forward in an editorial that saw the ambiguity of Takeuchi's Council report as a signal of the need to include non-medical criteria in the determination of death. It stated:

> The six medical conditions of brain death set out in the ministry's report represent an advance over previous formulations. Just the same, caution must be the watchword in applying the new criterion.
>
> Despite the report's assertion that the new standards should eliminate error in deciding when brain death has occurred, the report authors concede that the standards of judgment in determining when brain death means the end of a human life reaches beyond mere technical or medical considerations.
>
> Our supreme need is for a broadly based but informed moral consensus on what it means for a human being to die.[48]

What had emerged from the MHW was a medical definition of brain death authored by eight nationally known physicians who defined the state of brain death but did not consider it equal to death. This odd conclusion presaged a number of future reports that were also stymied by internal contradictions and an inability to present a unified, logical public face.

Within a year following the announcement of the Takeuchi criteria, the Medico-Legal Society of Japan, the Japan Transplantation Society, the Japan Medical Association, the Heart Transplant Study Society, and numerous university ethics committees had already begun to consider brain death, and several of them issued reports of their deliberations.[49] Most important were the opinions of the Life Ethics Deliberative Council of the Japan Medical Association (JMA), which managed to retain consistency between a March 1987 interim report and a January 12, 1988 final report.[50] The JMA group, chaired by Katō Ichirō, president of Seijō Gakuen University, former civil law professor of Tokyo University and author of a book and numerous articles on brain death, recommended that a whole-brain (as opposed to brain stem) definition of death be recognized.[51] According to the report, brain death could be diagnosed with reference to the Takeuchi criteria if a patient or representative consented to brain death being used as the measure of death. In addition, "organ transplants may be carried out, according to policies determined by the Japan Transplant Association, as long as donor and recipient have been given full explanations and permission is freely given by the donor or the donor's family." The JMA based the importance of consent to brain death on the right to self-determination:

> The opinion of people who refuse to approve determination of final cessation of life on the basis of brain death should be recognized. This should in no way interfere with determination of cessation of life on the basis of brain death from the viewpoint of people who approve this criterion. Such an approach reflects a certain right of self-determination in that it allows the individual to decide for himself while respecting the determinations of others insofar as doing so imposes no inconvenience.

Mr. Katō emphasized that the JMA report was intended to define the biological death of human beings, not their social or legal death. While he admitted that they were closely related and claimed that social and legal thought would follow the biological definition, he indicated that the consent procedures recommended by the report were designed to accommodate the time lag between the acceptance of these different aspects of death.[52]

The JMA report was influential, but it had no legal force and was not the final word.[53] Bai Kōichi, for example, attacked the distinction between biological and legal/social death as specious, criticized the report's notion of consent as ambiguous, and rejected the view that brain death could be applied to consenting individuals before it was accepted by the general public.[54]

In June 1988, the Japan Society of Psychiatry and Neurology issued a report that opposed recognizing a brain death definition. It said: "A system has not yet been established in Japan to prevent pressure on donors and to preserve the rights of the weak, such as patients with mental disorders, at the time of transplantation."[55]

Most powerful among the critics of the JMA's conclusions was the Japan Federation of Bar Associations (JFBA). Nishioka Yoshiki, speaking unofficially for the JFBA, argued immediately upon release of the final report: "[C]onsensus on this issue has not been established.

We urge medical doctors not to consider today's report as a green light for organ transplant operations."[56] In June 1987, after its Human Rights and Medicine Committee held a series of meetings, the JFBA formally opposed the JMA's interim report, and on July 15, 1988 that committee released a detailed criticism of the final JMA guidelines.

The JFBA's opposition to the JMA is rooted in a concern over human rights. The committee's report states:

> From the standpoint of the Japan Federation of Bar Associations, the basic attitude to both brain death and organ transplants must be determination to protect the patient's fundamental human rights completely in order to prevent the recurrence of anything like the Wada heart-transplant case.

> On the basis of this organization's opinion of the final report, human-rights problems are involved in transplanting organs from brain death individuals. Consequently, it is unwise to perform such operations without the most serious consideration. Taking this final report as an opportunity to express its opinion, the organization urges the necessity of extensive specialist and nonspecialist discussion to ensure protection of patients' fundamental human rights in relation to the many problems inherent in brain death determination and organ transplants.[57]

The Report emphasizes the importance of obtaining the informed consent of both donors and recipients before organ transplant operations. It stresses the importance of determining death without regard to the will of particular individuals or families, in contrast to the JMA position that individuals and families ought to have a say in the method used to declare death. And it states that legislation and a social consensus are necessary before brain death can be sanctioned in the same way as cardiac death.

The JMA report thus served both as a symbol of the increasing willingness of the medical establishment to support brain death, and a stimulant to those opposed to approval of brain death and transplantation. Nonetheless, no brain death policy was forthcoming, and no organ transplants relying on brain death criteria were legally performed.

In addition to the formal organizations that have been involved in the debate over brain death, one journalist has also played a particularly significant role. Tachibana Takashi, who established his reputation by helping to expose the Lockheed scandal that brought down the government of Prime Minister Tanaka Kakuei, has become an important influence on both expert and public opinion. He is critical of brain death and the pressure that the medical establishment is exerting to have it officially recognized. While he is not against the recognition of brain death *per se*, Tachibana is skeptical of "expert" opinion and feels that all aspects of the issue must continue to be widely debated and understood, and a "consensus" reached, before it is formally legislated.

Tachibana wrote a well-regarded book on brain death in 1985, in which he challenged the idea of brain death as a loss of brain function, and instead argued that it should entail the death of brain cells themselves.[58] Concerned that some people could be declared brain dead who still retain living brain cells and cognitive power, he argued for a brain death definition based on tests that confirm the absence of all brain cell life and brainstem responses. Tachibana has also authored numerous articles related to brain death, was an early critic of the 1968 Wada case, and has hosted a variety of television specials, the most recent of which formed the basis for his second brain death book.[59] His television shows, always aired during prime time on a national station, have addressed the current status of brain death and organ transplants abroad, with vivid footage of transplant operations, brain dead individuals, and organ banks. In addition, he has brought together experts of differing opinions for in-depth television debate. Tachibana's fame and media access have made him an important shaper of public opinion, and a powerful influence on national policy.

POWER POLITICS AND BODY POLITICS: THE AD-HOC COMMITTEE FOR THE STUDY OF BRAIN DEATH AND ORGAN TRANSPLANTATION

After two decades of controversy over brain death and transplantation in Japan, by 1988 no resolution was yet in sight. The confusion over the Wada case, the ambivalence of Takeuchi's Ministry of Health and Welfare Group, the opposition of the Japan Federation of Bar Associations (JFBA), the objections of Tachibana, and the activism of the PRC had all served to stimulate discussion and debate, but no agreement. Pressure was building from many medical schools for a brain death definition, as hospital ethics committees approved transplant operations in principle but surgeons were unable to proceed because of the lack of a brain death definition.[60] Physicians who felt their hands tied by the lack of a policy on brain death began to widely publicize the occurrence of kidney transplants, explicitly allowed by law, and liver transplants from live donors. Neither of these operations were dependent upon brain dead donors, and physicians hoped that drawing attention to them would lend a positive image to organ transplantation and help promote the further benefits to be derived from the implementation of a brain death definition.

Adding to the confusion was the fact that some Japanese were going abroad for transplants that were unavailable at home because of the lack of a brain death standard (heart) or the inadequate supply of donated organs (kidney). In July 1990, for example, of sixteen people waiting for kidney transplants in Queensland, Australia, five were Japanese. They were given lower priority than locals despite the large sums they were willing to pay for the procedure.[61] A similar situation existed in certain large transplant centers in the United States and Europe, where the insufficient number of available organs required ranking recipients on the basis of age, illness, ability to pay, and sometimes nationality. Pressure from the medical establishment, and growing concern from abroad, were factors leading to overseas trips by a number of high-powered groups in Japan – a Liberal Democratic Party (LDP) investigative team, a group from the Japan Medical Association, a party sponsored by the Ministry of Health and Welfare – to learn how other nations were coping with brain death and to determine whether there were any lessons for Japan.

Most influential among these was the LDP's Investigative Panel on Brain Death and Life Ethics and the Problem of Organ Transplants, which in September 1988 set off to visit five Western nations. The panel was led by Dr. Nakayama Tarō, who had in 1985 chaired the Life Ethics Problem Study Parliamentarians League, and whose interest in foreign affairs led him to his post as minister of foreign affairs. Upon returning to Japan, he sponsored a bill to establish a consulting body to advise the prime minister on defining death and transplanting organs.[62] Opposed only by the Communist Party, the bill created the *Nōshi Rinchō*, or Ad-Hoc Committee on Brain Death and Organ Transplantation (AHC). The committee was chartered to meet regularly for two years under the direction of Nagai Michio, former minister of education and a well-known elder statesman in Japanese politics. Its fifteen full members and five affiliated experts included a number of prominent transplant surgeons, the head of the Japan Federation of Bar Association's Human Rights and Medicine Committee, a scholar of the history of medicine, and a former president of Tokyo

University, as well as a philosopher, a novelist, and other well-known figures.

In addition to meeting as a group more than once each month, the AHC also held a number of public meetings, where approximately 300 individuals who expressed prior interest were invited to a gathering to hear presentations by non-AHC experts about brain death and to ask questions. The AHC invited an array of individuals to present their views before the committee, including journalist Tachibana Takashi and legal scholar Katō Ichirō. To enhance their understanding of the ways in which the definition of brain death and organ transplantation has been handled by other nations, members of the AHC went abroad in three separate groups – one to the United States, one to Europe, and one to Australia and Thailand, and each trip culminated in a lengthy report.

In Japanese politics and policy making, the formation of a blue-ribbon advisory group to the prime minister is a clear signal that new policy initiatives have already been determined and a formal seal-of-approval is on the way.[63] It thus came as a shock when on June 14, 1991 the AHC's interim report was released in two sections because of a split within the group. Unable to convince the four dissenters to come into the fold, and unwilling to censor them outright, Nagai took the unusual step of releasing a report that included both a majority and minority view.[64]

The majority opinion contained few surprises. It reviewed the Wada case, touched on the mistrust of the medical profession that resulted from it, outlined the relationship between brain death and organ transplantation, and acknowledged the importance of patients' rights. It then made clear its goal:

> This group will not argue in favor of or against brain death with the aim of promoting organ transplants. Without doing that, and acknowledging that the donation of organs is based on individual will, we shall from the standpoint of humanity explore whether there are adequate medical and social grounds for the recognition of brain death as the death of a person.[65]

Addressing the medical aspects of brain death, the report turned to an examination of scientific criteria and endorsed the view of brain death as the irreversible loss of brain function and the Takeuchi criteria as an acceptable means of determining such a condition. With regard to social issues, it noted the general agreement abroad regarding brain death, mentioned the importance of consensus in Japan, and outlined six reasons why brain death is so controversial there: (1) in a state of brain death, a person's heart beats and the body remains warm, so it is hard to positively say the person is dead; (2) traditional cultural beliefs; (3) the fear that physicians will prematurely declare death in order to harvest organs; (4) uneasiness of individuals and families who will be confused about when a person is dead; (5) mistrust of physicians; and (6) physicians will take organs from brain dead individuals without their consent.[66] But the majority report claimed that a social consensus was gradually being formed in favor of brain death, and it endorsed the removal of organs from brain dead individuals:

> When the brain dies, the sense, the feeling, and all the functions to coordinate different parts of the body are permanently lost. If that happens, it is no longer considered life even though some organs may still be working individually. Regarding brain death as the termination of human life, legally and socially, is the most logical, and goes along with internationally accepted norms . . . It is our unanimous view that organ transplants be allowed as long as there are those whose only chance at survival is the transplant operation and those who are willing to donate their organs.[67]

In contrast, the minority opinion shattered the hope that the AHC would make a blanket endorsement of brain death and transplants. In the minority were four people of widely differing backgrounds – Umehara Takeshi, a philosopher known for his close ideological connection to the former government of Prime Minister Nakasone Yasuhiro; Yonemoto Shōhei, an historian of science and liberal critic of the government; Mitsuishi Tadahiro, head of the JFBA's Committee on Human Rights and Medicine; and Hara Hideo, an attorney. Of these, Umehara and Hara were full committee members, Mitsuishi and Yonemoto affiliated experts. Despite their divergent social and political perspectives, all four agreed that the majority view made public opinion into the cart drawn by the medical profession, while they believed that it should be the horse behind which medical professionals followed.

At a press conference held separately from the one at which the majority discussed its views, Hara explained that the minority did not necessarily oppose transplants, but thought that equating brain death with death was premature. The majority's view of life as requiring a brain that maintains the existence of an integrated organism is not a scientific truth, claimed the minority, but a biological theory based on values and beliefs. While the minority also pointed out that transplantation techniques are imperfect, they nonetheless approved of transplants if four conditions were met: (1) there is prior intent of donor to give organs; (2) brain death is clearly ascertained; (3) donor and recipient informed consent is unambiguous; and (4) medical facilities performing transplants must respect the rights of patients in all aspects of care.[68]

Finally, the last section of the minority report, titled "Flexible Law" (*yawarakai hō*), suggested that a system be developed whereby transplants could be undertaken but brain death criteria would not have to be officially approved.

Announcement of the AHC's interim report prompted a torrent of responses from experts and the media. Over forty newspaper editorials discussed the document, with some criticizing the fact that all meetings were not open to the public and that possible human rights violations were inadequately addressed. One paper stated: "It is particularly important to note the rights of the organ donor. The will of both the patient receiving the organ and the donor should be confirmed. There should be informed consent."[69] Other editorials discussed distrust of the medical profession, the laxness of the Takeuchi criteria, and cultural aspects of death and the body.

Because of the minority's willingness to at least nod in favor of organ transplantation, some experts tried to minimize the split within the committee. Katō Ichirō, for example, stated:

> [A]lthough the interim report attached two members' opinions denying that brain death is human death, the two members agree to transplanting organs from people pronounced brain dead. It seems that all members of the panel agree on organ transplants.[70]

Chairman Nagai echoed these sentiments when he said:

> People do have different views on death. The minority opinion in the report is not an objection as much as it is a reflection of this diversity. Every member of the Commission accepts organ transplants, and we would like to use the time remaining before January to work out specifics.[71]

But others seized upon the minority report as evidence that even at the highest echelons of government agreement on brain death was elusive, and that arguing against defining death as brain death was not hopeless. Again, opposition came forcefully from the legal community in the form of concern about individual rights. Just five days after the interim report of the AHC was announced, Tanabe Nobuyoshi of the Kyoto District Public Prosecutor's Office said:

> The definition of a human being's death should be objective and unanimously recognizable by people because it is closely connected with legitimacy of rights in civil law and with factors defining such crimes as murder and abandonment of a dead body. Doctors have various views concerning the standard of confirming brain death. The report lacks objectivity on the standard.[72]

The JFBA also entered the fray, though this time it was not the Committee on Medicine and Human Rights, but the section devoted to criminal law that objected to brain death.[73] According to the criminal law section, no consensus yet existed on the question of brain death, and accepting it as a definition of death would cause judicial problems regarding inheritance. Brain death could also lead to the use of brain dead individuals for medical experimentation. Caution was urged in the pursuit of organ transplants, particularly with respect to obtaining consent from donors.

Some strongly emphasized the incomplete and unofficial nature of the June 14 report's conclusions and the fact that current policy remained unchanged. On July 4, 1991, the deputy chief of the Osaka Prefectural Police phoned the Senri Lifesaving Center when he heard that a liver transplant was going to be performed from a brain dead donor by a transplant team from Osaka University hospital. He informed the Center that in his jurisdiction death requires termination of the heartbeat, that a police autopsy would be performed on the donor with this in mind, and that evidence of a "premature" operation might be construed as a crime. As police kept watch at the hospital, the doctors waited for the heart to stop, and were then unable to proceed with the operation.[74]

An equally tense situation developed in front of the Ministry of Health and Welfare on the afternoon of August 9, as the AHC held its first public meeting since the release of its interim report. Outraged by what it described as the beginning of a state eugenics policy that would pit doctors and the government against all handicapped or otherwise undesirable individuals by using brain death as a way to systematically violate their rights and kill them off, the Chūkaku-ha, long known for its violent protest against the construction of Narita International Airport, entered the brain death debate. It made physical threats against Nagai and other members of the AHC, and said it would disrupt the public meeting within the Ministry.

In anticipation of the release of the Ad-Hoc Committee's final report in January 1992, a number of groups began meeting in the hope of influencing the outcome. The Patients' Rights Conference held intensive meetings to clarify its position in light of the interim report. The Life Ethics Study Group, including such influential journalists as Tachibana Takashi and Nakajima Michi, as well as more than a dozen surgeons, attorneys, and other prominent intellectuals, released a model law that avoided defining death as brain death but permitted transplants from brain dead donors.[75]

On January 22, 1992, the final report of the Ad Hoc Committee was presented to Prime Minister Miyazawa.[76] The *Yomiuri Shimbun*, Japan's largest circulation daily, proclaimed, "Final Report Recognizes Brain Death and Organ Transplantation,"[77] while the *Asahi Shimbun* announced "Report Says that Brain Death is Death."[78] But the simple, declarative headlines could not mask what became obvious upon reading the first few paragraphs of either article. The blue-ribbon government panel had failed to reach a consensus.

As expected by those following the brain death debate, there was little in the final report that had not been suggested by the interim report. Structurally, the most significant change was that the separate minority opinion of the former was incorporated into the body of the latter. This gave the impression of a reconciliation between the two sides, though in reality deep ideological divisions remained.

The majority opinion of the final report can be summarized as follows: (1) brain death, defined as the loss of the ability to integrate the body's functions and determined by the Takeuchi criteria, is a valid definition of death; (2) social consensus has been reached that brain death is death; (3) an organ transplantation program ought to be established; (4) donor intent is critical for the performance of organ transplants, and when donor intent is unclear, a third party will be appointed to insure that the family is not agreeing to donate organs because of undue pressure from medical professionals; (5) it is important to secure informed consent before a transplant is undertaken; (6) laws should be enacted making the buying and selling of organs illegal, establishing an organ network and donor cards, and legalizing organ transplants from brain dead donors; and (7) organ recipients must be

selected systematically and fairly. The committee was aware that pass-
ing a transplant law would involve myriad difficulties, so as a tempor-
ary measure it declared that even in the absence of a law transplants
could be legally performed.

The minority opinion argued that the acceptance of brain death
would necessitate a new way of understanding life and death and
would lead to social and legal confusion. Further, it claimed that no
social consensus was yet established. Still, the minority was willing to
approve of organ transplants where the consent of a donor was clearly
and openly determined.

Discordance between the majority and minority of the AHC gave
resonance to outside criticisms of the report. Just prior to its release,
member Umehara Takeshi, well aware of the contents of the final
version, once again assailed the idea of brain death. He argued that it
was promoted by an arrogant medical profession, reflected a Western,
Cartesian view of the body, lacked a profound understanding of the
meaning of death, and posed a threat to the rights of the powerless.[79]
"As long as the conception of death remains ambiguous," wrote Umehara, "if organ transplantation is unconditionally permitted, we will
see the severe infringement of the rights of patients."

Tachibana Takashi agreed that the AHC had only a superficial
grasp of the meaning of death, and argued that it is almost impossible
to state when a patient is beyond a medical "point of no return." As a
result, he feared that under the AHC guidelines some arguably living
patients would be treated as corpses, having their organs removed
when they could still be considered alive.[80] Tachibana's guiding principle, one he claims was ignored by the AHC, is that it is preferable
to treat the dead as living than the living as dead.

Beyond these relatively academic objections, a number of more
practical problems remained. The majority of the AHC advocated the
creation of a law legalizing transplants from brain dead donors, and
said that as it was being written transplants should be allowed. But
the Criminal Law Academy sided with the minority and other outside
groups in saying that transplants could be made legal without a law
concerning brain death.[81] The necessity and scope of transplant-
related legislation thus continued to be an unsolved question despite
the strong recommendations of the AHC.

Related to this was the persistent disagreement between government agencies as to whether they should recognize brain death as
death. As the institutional base of the AHC, the Ministry of Health

and Welfare could be expected to support the thrust of its findings. In contrast, the Ministry of Justice, National Police Agency, and Office of the Public Prosecutor all indicated on the day following the announcement of the final report that they would continue to rely on the traditional definition of death.[82] Just one week after the AHC announcement, doctors at the Mishima Emergency and Lifesaving Medical Center in Osaka declared a teenage motorcycle accident victim brain dead. The boy had previously indicated his desire to donate his organs, and his family consented at the hospital. But the local police refused to consider the victim dead until his heart stopped, thwarting plans for the transplantation of several vital organs.[83]

A great deal of confusion also continued to surround the question of who makes the decision to donate organs. Both the majority and minority opinions strongly emphasized that the intention of donors themselves was the most important criterion. In the absence of a clear and unambiguous written statement, however, this would be difficult to ascertain. So the AHC majority suggested that physicians confirm the person's intention by speaking to the family, and that a third party be appointed to insure that this conversation is free from pressure or coercion. How much credence should be placed on the word of the family, who should appoint the third party, the type of people who could serve as third parties, and under what guidelines a third party would operate were all left vague. The minority was less willing to entertain evidence of donor consent beyond the donor's expressed wishes, and proposed setting up a system that would hasten its determination.

Underlying this disagreement, and many other reservations about the AHC report, was an acknowledgment that an open and fair system of organ transplantation would require a style of medical care currently unavailable in Japan. The full AHC encouraged the adoption of informed consent, for example, as part of the process of protecting the rights of organ recipients.

> Regarding the concept of informed consent . . . it must include the notion of adequate explanation by the physician in order to insure that patients make appropriate decisions. Informed consent is necessary not only to expand patients' consciousness of their rights, but also because it would entail the explanation of increasingly complex medical conditions.[84]

Yet, as discussed in Chapter 3, no tradition of informed consent exists in Japan, and it is unlikely that physicians will suddenly acquire the inclination or skill to adequately inform their patients of the risks of medical treatment.

In contrast to the nuance of the majority opinion, which viewed rights as a tangential problem solvable by informed consent, the minority treated rights as a central problem of a brain death standard: "We fear that the recognition of brain death as death would lead to the infringement of the rights of patients. At the moment that 'brain death' is declared, humans become objects, and objects have no rights."[85]

Nishioka Yoshiki, an attorney representing the Patients' Rights Conference in its murder complaints against several transplant physicians (see Chapter 6), highlighted the need to consider patients' rights, notwithstanding the majority opinion's claim that social consensus on brain death has been achieved. "We have not been able to build a consensus around brain death . . . But if eventually an agreement to recognize brain death is reached, we must still confront such problems as drafting a transplant law and protecting patients' rights."[86]

Other concerns about the AHC majority's opinion also revolved around patients' rights. Not only the donor's right to self-determination and the recipient's right to be fully informed of the risks and benefits of an operation, but the right of access to medical records, the right to receive reimbursement for the costs of a transplant, and the rights of family members to act in each other's interests have all come under scrutiny in the aftermath of the AHC announcement.[87] The rights of potential organ recipients have also been championed. As Dr. Ōta Kazuo, a prominent transplant surgeon, has argued: "In Japan, since we do not recognize brain death as death, we cannot perform organ transplants, and are therefore unable to protect the rights of those who may need life-saving operations."[88] Similarly, Katō Ichirō, who chaired the 1980 JMA committee, stated: "While there has been a good deal of emphasis on organ donors, how to protect their rights, and how to avoid exerting undue pressure on them, there has been insufficient attention to the importance of these issues as they affect recipients."[89]

More general comments about rights appeared in various newspaper accounts. One paper opined that "the time for the medical world to take action with regard to respecting the rights of patients is now approaching,"[90] while another wrote that "how to protect the rights of brain dead people is a big problem, for they are the weakest of the weak, and can make no demands."[91]

Finally, an academic group opposed to brain death expressed its concern in this way: "Brain death occurs in a closed medical environment, and is difficult to observe for anyone outside the medical profession. In the event that brain death is legislated, we fear that it will be difficult to protect patients who are physically or socially vulnerable."[92] Despite the strong recommendations of the AHC, therefore, concerns about patients' rights continued to thwart the passage of brain death/transplant legislation.[93]

A TENTATIVE TRUCE IN THE FIGHT OVER DEATH

Compromise legislation was finally passed by the Diet on June 17, 1997. Supported by clear majorities of 181 to 62 in the Upper House and 323 to 144 in the Lower House, longtime proponents of brain death and organ transplants were able to declare victory in their battle to legislate death. To the Japan Society of Transplantation, which had threatened to perform transplants even without a legal recognition of brain death, the new Organ Transplantation Act was welcome news. Yet it fell considerably short of the original legislation proposed by physician and Dietmember Nakayama Tarō.

Nakayama's version of the bill, which had been submitted to the Diet in April 1997, clearly declared that brain death is human death. But opponents succeeded in revamping the bill, so that the final version no longer established a uniform definition of death. Instead, potential organ donors must not only indicate their willingness to give their organs; they must also have consented to being diagnosed as brain dead, and their consent can be vetoed by family members. Heralded as a law in which the "rights of donors is the key issue," the new legislation failed to overcome the cleavages between brain death advocates and opponents.[94] Because it sidesteps the question of whether medically, ethically, or legally brain death is human death, it may well prove to be just another twist in the long battle over rights, death, and transplants in Japan.

Japan, the conventional wisdom holds, is a society built on duty, not rights, with a Western-style legal system out of step with the rest of society. But when specific political, legal, and social disputes are closely examined, a more complex picture emerges. In the battle over brain death and organ transplantation, contentious issues of medicine, morality, and power have been articulated and disputed through a rhetoric of rights. What began as a general discussion about physician power, Japanese traditions, and personal religious beliefs has become a battle over the rights of the dying, the rights of organ donors and their families, the rights of the handicapped, and the rights of potential organ recipients.

While the form of the brain death controversy has in good measure been shaped by the language of rights, such rights have neither been validated nor rejected by the legislature or the courts. Still, it is necessary to acknowledge and assess the concept, reality and influence of Japanese rights talk in order to dispel historical and sociological misunderstandings about the relationship between conflict, law, and policy in contemporary Japan. Examination of the brain death/organ transplantation controversy helps to reveal insights about how rights-based claims are used to garner support for particular viewpoints, the extent to which they force policy makers to pay attention to certain issues, the ways in which rights claims legitimize protest and justify conflict, and the behavior of policy makers in acknowledging or denying the importance of rights. In that regard, brain death is not an isolated example. The battle over AIDS policy, the subject of the previous chapter, also featured the rhetoric of rights. By deploying rights talk to frame their concerns about the Ministry of Health and Welfare's emerging AIDS policy, advocates used rights as a resource to attract the support of like-minded individuals. Eventually, they were able to have an impact on the AIDS Prevention Act, and as described in Chapter 6, achieved an historic victory in the courts.

CHAPTER SIX

LITIGATION AND THE COURTS: TALKING ABOUT RIGHTS

RIGHTS AND THE LEGAL PROCESS

The Japanese, we have long been told, go out of their way to avoid courts. Noda Yoshiyuki, a prominent member of the University of Tokyo's Faculty of Law for over three decades, describes the Japanese aversion to the courthouse in this way:

> To an honorable Japanese the law is something that is undesirable, even detestable, something to keep as far away from as possible. To never use the law, or be involved with the law, is the normal hope of honorable people. To take someone to court to guarantee the protection of one's own interests, or to be mentioned in court, even in a civil matter, is a shameful thing . . .[1]

Noda goes on to say that even when the Japanese have a right that they believe is "beyond dispute," the "good citizen" may well not enforce it because it "weighs on the conscience."[2] John Haley, a leading authority of Japanese law at the University of Washington, dismisses Noda's psychosocial explanation, and others like it, complaining that "[F]ew misconceptions about Japan have been more widespread or as pernicious as the myth of the special reluctance of the Japanese to litigate."[3] Instead, Haley explains low litigation rates by emphasizing what he calls "institutional" factors, such as limited remedies and the small number of judges and lawyers.

Whether or not "the Japanese," evaluated collectively, in fact have an aversion to courts and litigation has been a central theme of sociolegal scholarship about Japan for much of the postwar period. The central intellectual puzzle has been to explain *why* there is so little recourse to courts. As a result, too little attention has been focused on actual cases, and even less on the relationship between going to court and attempting to influence policy at the legislative and administrative levels.[4]

This chapter examines two areas where neither the cultural constraints emphasized by Noda, nor the institutional barriers detailed by Haley, have kept people away from the courts. Those areas are AIDS and the definition of death. Chapters 4 and 5 illustrated the extent to which contemporary conflicts over policy continue and extend a tradition of protest in which rights are invoked to frame arguments, attract attention, and generate sufficient pressure to influence policy. Here, it is demonstrated that rights assertion is not limited to the policy making arena, but that civil and criminal causes of action have been deployed by advocates in the AIDS and definition of death debates as part of a strategy of using the courts both to legitimize their political claims and to seek concrete judicial remedies. Rights assertion, in short, is the centerpiece of how advocates seek to bring about social change.

What is featured is litigation by HIV-positive hemophiliacs against pharmaceutical companies and the Ministry of Health and Welfare, alleging negligence for the distribution of HIV-tainted blood, and criminal complaints against transplant surgeons for murdering organ donors. Advocates in both cases understand the limitations placed on remedies, the slow pace of trials, the complexity of discovery, and the fact that many years will elapse before a judgment is rendered. And they use these factors well. Unlike reluctant litigants wary of disturbing community harmony, they are resolute in their determination to manipulate the courts in their best interests. In so doing, they benefit from what have been generally viewed as institutional barriers to litigation. Criminal procedure, prosecutorial discretion, and the relationship between the Ministry of Justice and the Office of the Prosecutor, for example – all of which may have been expected to discourage the filing of charges – resulted in confusion and delay over how to handle accusations about brain death. By casting a pall on surgeons who may otherwise have conducted transplants, such institutional features worked in the interests of advocates. In AIDS litigation, the "constraint" of the relatively small number of attorneys in Japan, and the absence of a public interest bar, was a factor in the formation of a large lawyers' group in which attorneys each donated a small amount of time, leading to a lawyers' network, frequent publicity, and new plaintiffs. There are also strong connections between the AIDS and brain death cases, and the patients' rights movement. One of the leading attorneys in the litigation over AIDS, Suzuki Toshihiro, was an architect of the proposed Patients' Rights Law, and the group most active in seeking brain death prosecutions has been prominent in litigating other patients' rights issues.

The legal battles discussed in this chapter have antecedents like the Big Four pollution cases, SMON, thalidomide, PCB, and other lawsuits over environmental and social issues. All of those past cases involved groups of people who claimed that their interests were injured by corporate or government actions. They united, hired lawyers, and initiated legal proceedings. While such cases have been analyzed from the perspective of the sociology and politics of social movements, as attempts to institutionalize "new rights," and as a way to understand their impact on social change in Japan, they have rarely been studied with an eye toward how they reflect and influence the role and importance of rights talk in contemporary Japan.[5] It is through that additional lens that the AIDS and brain death cases are presented.[6]

AIDS: CRISIS, COMPENSATION, AND THE COURTS

The background
Hemophiliacs, almost all men, suffer from a condition in which their blood does not spontaneously clot. For centuries, hemophiliacs were severely hindered in their daily activities, forced to limit their lives to avoid the possibility of excessive blood loss and death. The burden of hemophilia was greatly lightened when medical science isolated clotting factors, coagulant proteins, from donated blood.[7]

The first medical advance, cryoprecipitate, is the third step in a process where whole blood is first collected, plasma and red blood cells are then separated, and cryoprecipitate (cryo), a mixture of various blood clotting elements, is finally extracted. A more complex procedure in which individual clotting elements such as factor 8 and factor 9 can be isolated and concentrated (hence the name concentrates) from blood plasma was developed some years later. Concentrates are the most effective way to treat hemophilia, and minimized certain side effects caused by cryoprecipitate. Both of these technological advances caused a revolution in the lives of hemophiliacs, particularly those with severe forms of the disease. By receiving regular treatment, first with cryoprecipitate and later with concentrates, they were able to go to school, to work, and to live in a fundamentally unencumbered way.

Japan's Ministry of Health and Welfare (MHW) approved the use of cryoprecipitate in 1970, and the use of concentrates in 1978. The source of the blood from which they were taken, however, was different. While US Occupation authorities had redesigned Japan's blood collection system to make it exclusively donated (as opposed to sold) and entirely domestic, the quantity of blood donated in Japan was only sufficient for use in whole blood transfusions and in the production of a small amount of cryoprecipitate. Concentrates, on the other hand, were isolated from plasma collected primarily in the United States, where a commercial blood market ensured a supply.

Unlike whole blood, which is exclusively under the control of the Japanese Red Cross Society, concentrates are treated like all other pharmaceutical products. That means the price at which physicians and hospitals are reimbursed for using them is set by the MHW. Reimbursement levels are determined with reference to the cost of manufacturing blood concentrates in Japan, where the small domestic production is more expensive than imported products. Since a large percentage of the operating funds and profits of health care providers comes from their ability to reap the difference between the price of pharmaceutical products reimbursed by the government, and the amount providers actually pay for drugs once they negotiate a discount price with pharmaceutical companies,[8] prescribing imported blood concentrate was a lucrative business. Blood products are consequently both a critical component of hemophiliacs' lives, and a financial boon to physicians and hospitals.[9]

Each of these elements – the efficacy of blood concentrate in comparison to cryoprecipitate; the approval of blood products by the MHW; the division between domestic and foreign blood; and the pecuniary interests of pharmaceutical companies and medical institutions – came to the fore in litigation filed by HIV-positive hemophiliacs.

The claim
On October 27, 1989, a group of HIV-positive hemophiliacs and family members of hemophiliacs who died of AIDS filed a lawsuit in the Tokyo District Court. Over the next several years additional

plaintiffs were added, and a similar case was presented to the Osaka District Court.[10] Japanese hemophiliacs, like their counterparts in the United States, France, Germany, the United Kingdom, and other industrialized nations, went to court because they were exposed to HIV through their use of medications made from blood products. Of the estimated 5,000 hemophiliacs in Japan, at least 40 percent, or 2,000 became HIV-positive.[11] As described in Chapter 4, this common tragedy unified hemophiliacs; they first emerged as a force in the debate over the AIDS Prevention Law, and their legal claims were facilitated by a close-knit organizational structure that enabled them to overcome barriers to collective action.

Plaintiffs were organized into several associations (*HIV Soshō o Sasaeru Kai*, for example) modeled on Japanese citizens' movements of the 1970s. These organizations published newsletters, held symposia, and appeared in the media at every opportunity. When the Japanese Society of Friends of Hemophiliacs announced in 1988 that it was going to sue the government and five pharmaceutical companies it said that like SMON victims (see Chapter 4) its members had a right to compensation for drug-related accidents.[12] Emphasizing the importance of effective legal and political action, and of mobilizing a large citizens' movement, an attorney presenting oral arguments in the Tokyo District Court harkened back to SMON and stated, "I think that we have learned on other occasions that rights will not be bestowed from above if we are silent."[13]

Each plaintiff paid 100,000 yen annually to be represented by a group of almost sixty attorneys, about half in each city, most of whom donated their time. At the helm of the Tokyo attorneys' group was Suzuki Toshihiro, a central figure in the movement to legislate patients' rights. Defendants were five pharmaceutical companies – Green Cross Corporation, Cutter Japan, Baxter Corporation, Bayer, and Nippon Zōki Pharmaceutical Corporation – as well as the Ministry of Health and Welfare.[14]

At issue in the litigation was whether the defendants were negligent in importing and distributing blood concentrates that led to the seroconversion of almost half of Japan's hemophiliacs. Numerous dates were highlighted by the plaintiffs: July 1982, when three cases of hemophiliacs with AIDS were reported by the Centers for Disease Control and Prevention (CDC) in the *Morbidity and Mortality Weekly Report* (MMWR); February 1983, when the plaintiffs asserted (indeed, overstated) that the CDC had determined that HIV could be transmitted through blood; March 1983, when plaintiffs claimed that donor exclusion was recommended in the *MMWR*; July 1984, when it is asserted (incorrectly) that heat treating the blood supply was required in the United States; and the summer/fall of 1985, when heat treatment in Japan began. Plaintiffs indicated that companies received approval to sell heat-treated blood in the United States in March 1983 (only Baxter received such early approval), and they highlighted the long period during which they claimed there was technical knowledge in the United States about the connection between blood and HIV, yet in Japan unheated blood products continued to be used and imported.[15]

In July and November 1985, heat treated factors 8 and 9 concentrates were approved in Japan, but many hemophiliacs were already infected. While the MHW did agree to a compensation scheme (see Chapter 4), hemophiliacs were not satisfied. One member of the first plaintiffs' group, a thirteen-year-old boy, stated, "I don't want to die until I see the government and pharmaceutical companies take responsibility for causing this hell."[16] Another member declared, "The government is still neglecting to take sufficient care of hemophiliacs with HIV. It's an unimaginable infringement of fundamental human rights."[17] A supporter of the plaintiffs said, "The issue of HIV infection for hemophiliacs is a political problem rather than a medical one."[18] And an attorney for the plaintiffs emphasized the primacy of justice over money: "The purpose of this lawsuit is not money. They [the plaintiffs] want to know who is to be blamed, and to clear the issue up. So I would say that the hemophiliac litigation is about human rights. That is the most important part of the litigation."[19] Nonetheless, the damages requested by the plaintiffs were no small sum. Each person demanded 115 million yen, almost $1 million after the 15 million yen attorney's fee is subtracted. Specifically, damages were sought for being infected with HIV, suffering from AIDS, and being a victim of, or fearing, social discrimination.

There was no dispute in the case over the importation of HIV-tainted blood concentrate from the United States, the date when the MHW approved heat-treated products, or the fact that many hemophiliacs are infected. Nor was the fact that many hemophiliacs self-medicate an important issue. But several major elements of the negligence claim — causality, foreseeability, and avoidability — were vigorously argued.

Causality

The skeleton of the plaintiff's claim was: (1) there was a high risk of HIV infection from imported US blood products; (2) the injured parties used those products; and (3) after using them, plaintiffs became infected.[20] Unfortunately for the plaintiffs, however, their claim was complicated by the existence of five corporate defendants, each of which sold almost identical blood concentrates. Most plaintiffs used the products of different companies at different times. The defendants thus claimed, for example, that if the products of companies y and z were used in 1979 and 1980, and those of company x were used in 1983, since the first AIDS case was reported in 1981, only company x is responsible for the HIV infection.

In response, plaintiffs argued that the HIV virus is complex and unpredictable, but that should not absolve y and z of responsibility. Although AIDS was not recognized until 1981, the virus was surely present in the late 1970s. They pressed the court to accept a theory of multiple infection, or alternative liability, under which all companies supplying blood concentrates from the late 1970s would be held responsible for any subsequent infection. Plaintiffs also wanted the burden of proving when infection occurred placed on the defendants, and they asked that the court presume HIV infection in March 1983 in the absence of other compelling evidence. One important question before the courts, therefore, was how to handle the possibility of multiple infection, and how to parcel out fault, at a time when AIDS was not yet a known disease.

Foreseeability

The most enigmatic issue in the litigation was whether the defendants could have foreseen the injury caused to the plaintiffs. Even the plaintiffs concede that in the 1970s no one could have foreseen the possibility of HIV infection, since HIV was unknown. Instead, they argued that factors inherent in the collection and distribution of foreign (American) blood products made it foreseeable that some disease-causing virus would be transmitted.[21] At the very least, they asserted that "with regard to HIV contamination specifically, they [drug companies and the MHW] could have forecasted in July 1982 the risk that the concentrates might have contained a new life-threatening pathogen, which was afterwards called HIV."[22]

An attorney for the plaintiffs portrayed the commercial blood market in the United States as dangerous, noting a blood collection center in San Francisco that is only a ten minute walk from the predominantly gay Castro district. It was described as a gathering place for "homos" where 10 percent of donors were gay, many others were black or Mexican, with a despondent, unsanitary atmosphere. Similarly, a Japan Broadcasting Corporation (NHK) report said that some of the blood plasma used to make concentrates in the United States came from centers in South and Central America, where different blood samples were combined in plastic bags, and left on dirty floors.

In addition, plaintiffs observed that in the United States donated blood is pooled. As a result, concentrates may be extracted from the blood of 1,000, or even 20,000 donors, greatly increasing the possibility that any single batch of concentrate was contaminated. Next, it was stated that imported blood is more infectious than local blood, because a virus that is dormant in one area can become infectious somewhere else. Finally, plaintiffs questioned whether those responsible for blood collection and distribution took adequate precautions to guard against hepatitis. Considering these four points together, plaintiffs argued that the spread of HIV through blood was foreseeable.

The arguments made by the plaintiffs illustrate the degree to which issues of race, xenophobia, and nationalism can permeate "legal" and "scientific" argument. Lest such concern about blood seem uniquely Japanese, it should be recalled that during World War II, and under the approval of the Red Cross, the secretaries of the war and the navy, and the surgeons general of the army and navy, plasma of white and black American soldiers was segregated.[23] In support of this racist policy, historian John Dower quotes John Rankin, Congressman of Mississippi, who decried mixing blood as a communist plot to "mongrelize America," and accused those who supported such action of wanting "to pump Negro or Japanese blood into the veins of our wounded white boys regardless of the dire effect it might have on their children."[24]

Avoidability

Even if HIV infection could have been foreseen, the question remains whether it could have been avoided. Here, the disagreement between plaintiffs and defendants was technical. All parties agreed that hemophiliacs required a steady supply of blood-based medication for their disease, so that defendants could not have stopped distributing all blood products. But there was disagreement about what constituted effective medication. Plaintiffs contended that cryoprecipitate, manufactured from Japanese blood supplies, was an adequate treatment, particularly because HIV infection and the death of many people was a foreseeable consequence of distributing concentrates made from imported blood. Medical experts were divided, though several testified on the plaintiffs' behalf.[25] Plaintiffs argued that the MHW should have stopped importing and using concentrates at the latest by July 1982, and instead should have utilized domestic cryoprecipitate supplies.

In fact, both houses of the Diet passed Resolutions calling for domestic self-sufficiency in blood products in 1988, and the MHW started the New Committee for the Study of the Promotion of the Blood Program in 1989. One result of the Ministry investigation was its directive to the Japan Hospital Association and two other hospital organizations to give priority to blood products manufactured domestically, despite the greater profits from using foreign-made blood. The Japanese Red Cross itself concluded that "this dependence on importation for plasma derivatives presents problems from the standpoints of ethics, safety, and stability of supply . . ."[26] Still, in 1991, only 24.4 percent of plasma derivatives used in Japan came from domestic blood. The remainder continued to be imported from the United States until the mid-1990s.

The response
Defendants in the litigation, joined by a common human tragedy, had deeply divided interests. There were tensions between foreign and domestic pharmaceutical companies; between the pharmaceutical companies and the Ministry of Health and Welfare; and between companies that had heat-treated blood products available at different times. Competition between these companies did not cease with the onset of litigation. Linked by the lawsuit, however, they presented a unified defense. In doing so, they relied on two general arguments. They claimed that scientific knowledge of the as-yet-unidentified etiological agent that caused AIDS was inadequate in the early 1980s, making it impossible for them to know what course of action was best for hemophiliacs. Since the use of blood products was the favored treatment for hemophilia, and other therapeutic drugs like cryoprecipitate were unavailable in sufficient quantities and had undesirable side-effects, there was no choice but to continue to import and distribute foreign blood products. They also highlighted aspects of the regulatory system designed to safeguard the Japanese public from dangerous products, and claimed that the delays caused by the system were necessary to ensure the safety of heated products.[27]

With regard to limited scientific knowledge, what can be called the "official" view emphasized that in July 1982, when the first cases of hemophiliacs with a new and deadly disease were reported to the US Centers for Disease Control, no one, that is no one anywhere in the world, knew how the disease was spread, whether or not it was a virus, whether it was always deadly, or how to detect it. It was not until April 1984 that the HIV virus was identified; only in March 1985 was a test developed that could detect HIV in blood; and it took until 1989 for the US Food and Drug Administration officially to ban the use of non-heat-treated blood products.[28] In that view, a high degree of scientific uncertainty about whether blood could spread the etiological agent responsible for AIDS continued well into the 1980s.

It was therefore argued by the defendants that the Ministry of Health and Welfare, and pharmaceutical companies, all acted appropriately. They kept apprized of, and participated in, the work of the international scientific community with regard to identifying HIV and developing techniques to secure the safety of blood products. When they were convinced of their safety, they began using them in Japan.[29] As explained by a Ministry official:

> With regard to the danger posed by imported blood products, there was really nothing else that could be used for the medical treatment of hemophiliacs. If we stopped importing and using it, there was the possibility of a real disaster ... AIDS was discovered in America in 1981. Before that, even in Japan, there was the AIDS virus. We didn't know that blood products were a cause of AIDS, we didn't even know about AIDS.[30]

From this perspective, the distribution of tainted blood products to Japan's hemophiliacs was an unavoidable tragedy, given the state of scientific knowledge.

In addition to knowledge limitations, defendants also highlighted the legal and regulatory system as presenting barriers to Ministry action. In the early 1980s, as evidence accumulated in the United States of a new disease, possibly a virus, possibly spread through blood and blood products, responsibility for blood in Japan was divided. The Japanese Red Cross collected and distributed whole blood in Japan, while blood products were under the control of the Green Cross and other pharmaceutical companies. Since pharmaceutical companies were importing and distributing blood products purchased from donors in the United States, responsibility fell to the MHW to oversee and license their activities.

Even when it was known in Japan that the US FDA had approved the sale of heat-treated blood products, Japanese regulators remained cautious. Ministry officials claimed that research on the heat-treating of blood in the United States was inadequate. They analogized blood factors, which are proteins, to eggs, also proteins. After an egg is boiled, according to a bureaucrat in the Pharmaceutical Affairs Research Bureau, the outside retains a shape identical to a raw egg, even though the inside has changed. Concern that blood could go through a similar transformation was said to have led the Ministry to conduct its own extensive tests before approving heat-treated products.[31]

What would be described by some as the Ministry's excessive caution emanates from its legal responsibility to ensure the safety of all drugs it approves for distribution, sale, and use, and the too numerous accusations that Japan leads the industrialized world in "drug-induced tragedies."[32] The SMON incident, for example, (see Chapter 4) contributed to a general distrust of the Ministry of Health and Welfare, and the Ministry's awareness of its public relations troubles. One plaintiff stated that he joined the HIV litigation because of the hypocrisy of the MHW, which claimed it would keep AIDS out of Japan with the AIDS Prevention Law but in fact imported tainted blood.[33] Like swine flu in the United States, which contributed to the CDC's cautious actions toward HIV and the blood supply,[34] SMON and other iatrogenic diseases in Japan may have been in part responsible for the hesitancy of the MHW to move quickly in approving heated blood products.

Plaintiffs countered that the MHW delayed the approval of heated blood products in Japan for reasons that had nothing to do with ambiguous information about HIV transmission through blood, or with a regulatory process designed to protect the public. Rather, they claimed that the delay resulted from a set of factors that pre-dated the existence of blood products by many decades. The Ministry and the private sector negligently distributed contaminated blood, they argued, because of a corrupt relationship between MHW officials and the companies they were entrusted to regulate. That relationship featured a reliance on advisory committees (shingikai) dominated by individuals who had a financial interest in the outcome of Ministry decisions; employment patterns that led many former government officials to accept lucrative positions in the pharmaceutical industry; and bureaucratic norms that encouraged the MHW to consider the market share of domestic companies a relevant factor in regulatory decisions. In short, plaintiffs contended that corporations and regulators had blindly ignored the risks of blood products to hemophiliacs in order to satisfy their narrow individual and institutional interests. Persistently and publicly asserting that regulators had ridden rough-shod over their rights, hemophiliacs pressed their claims in court.

The settlement

The first court proposal
The institutional framework of litigation in Japan, particularly the protracted court process, made it unlikely that the 1989 HIV lawsuits would be settled in less than a decade. As the legal process continued, strains and tensions began to take a toll; bickering between the Osaka and Tokyo plaintiffs over strategy and goals threatened to undermine the solidarity of the litigants. Many plaintiffs were HIV-positive, and could not endure a lengthy lawsuit; almost one third of the original plaintiffs had died by 1995. Arguments in the Tokyo and Osaka District Courts ended in May and July 1995; decisions were expected six months later. Few observers doubted that whatever opinion the court issued would be immediately appealed.

As the Tokyo District Court judges prepared their opinion, the activities of the plaintiffs' support group escalated. One year earlier, at the Tenth International Conference on AIDS in Yokohama, they had organized a demonstration and satellite meeting to publicize the case of Japanese hemophiliacs. Over 1,000 people participated, and membership ballooned. From several hundred early in the 1990s, the HIV Litigation Support Group could boast 4,000 members by 1996. Borrowing from the successful tactics of Japanese citizens' movements seeking "new rights" in the 1970s, they held sit-ins and rallies at the Ministry of Health and Welfare.[35] A focal point of the plaintiffs' activities was Kawada Ryūhei, a hemophiliac infected with HIV in his early teens who "went public" and became a central figure in the hemophiliac community. Explaining his decision to reveal his identity, Kawada stated: "I came out not because I am HIV-positive but because I am a victim of the drug-induced disaster. If we cannot change through our activities the current health administration system, in which people's right to health can be easily ignored, another drug-induced disaster will happen in the future."[36]

In the midst of this mobilization, shifts in national politics brought about by the Liberal Democratic Party's 1993 loss of a majority of seats in the Diet unexpectedly became a factor in the bad blood controversy. Until 1995, the government had maintained a hard line, saying that compromise was impossible because it was not responsible for the HIV infection of hemophiliacs. The entire HIV-tainted blood episode took place during the rule of the LDP, and politicians from that party were predictably wary of accepting responsibility for spreading HIV infection. But that position softened when a new health and welfare minister, Morii Chūryō, was appointed in August by Prime Minister Murayama of the Social Democratic Party of Japan (SDP), formerly the Socialist Party.

Morii wasted little time in announcing that he would consider a compromise solution to the litigation if it were recommended by the courts. Capitalizing on Morii's statement, plaintiffs filed a petition with the Tokyo District Court demanding that if the court were to suggest a settlement, it should contain an acknowledgment that the MHW and pharmaceutical companies were legally responsible, and should urge them to apologize. Soon after, in October 1995, what had appeared to be a typically lengthy legal battle took a turn. The Tokyo and Osaka courts jointly recommended an out-of-court settlement in which each plaintiff would receive 45 million yen, with payment divided 60/40 between the pharmaceutical companies and the government. In comparison to settlements in the SMON and thalidomide cases, when the government was ordered to pay one third and the drug companies two thirds, the allocation of payments suggested that the court considered the government particularly culpable. The payments would be the largest ever in a Japanese pharmaceutical-related case.[37]

The court justified its reason for urging a settlement by declaring its sympathy for infected hemophiliacs. As victims of discrimination, unable to receive care for HIV infection, fearful of disclosing their names and addresses, hemophiliacs were dying from a tragedy for which they carried no responsibility.[38] Conversely, under the Pharmaceutical Affairs Law, the Ministry of Health and Welfare was responsible for protecting Japanese citizens from drug side-effects, and the manufacturers of pharmaceuticals had the responsibility to sell safe products. Together, according to the court, they should have undertaken at least one of three possible interventions: provided information about the potential danger of unheated blood products; promoted alternative therapies, such as cryoprecipitate, imported heated products, or the emergency manufacture of domestic blood products; or stopped selling unheated products.[39] Knowing the risks posed by contaminated blood, but pursuing none of these options, the court suggested that the defendants accept responsibility and voluntarily settle the case.

In the aftermath of the proposed settlement, hemophiliacs continued to publicly make their case. Commemorating the December 1 World AIDS Day, 1,400 students assembled on the Waseda campus to show their support for HIV-infected hemophiliacs. Two weeks later, rallies were held in eight cities across the nation, with 2,000 people gathering at Tokyo's Ministry of Health and Welfare. One Waseda University student said of his interest in the issue: "I believe it is a good opportunity to think of the relationship between people and the state. We should change the current system of government, which decides things behind closed doors."[40] Another described her involvement by saying:

> We are surprised at what we have done during the past year to raise public awareness of the disaster caused by bureaucrats and medical experts. We are very happy to hear that many people say our activities have been effective in helping a wide segment of the public to understand the victims' plight, leading to pressure on the government to change its stance on the issue little by little.[41]

Students continued their protests, collecting hundreds of thousands of petition signatures and staging a sit-in at the ministry in frigid February conditions.[42]

It did not take long for each defendant to agree to participate in settlement negotiations. While the court had not rendered a specific opinion on the plaintiffs' negligence claim, the language of the court's proposal made clear its substantial agreement with the plaintiffs' position. Refusing to negotiate would have been unthinkable. Neither the plaintiffs, the defendants, nor the court, however, could have anticipated the extraordinary political developments that pushed the HIV-contaminated blood litigation into its final phase.

Politics, blood, and bureaucracy
When former Minister of Finance Hashimoto Ryūtaro became Japan's prime minister in 1995, his Liberal Democratic Party lacked a majority of seats in the Lower House of the Diet and was unable to form a single-party government. Hashimoto was consequently dependent

upon a coalition of three parties; the LDP, former Prime Minister Murayama's Social Democratic Party, and a recently formed party called New Party Sakigake.

The opportunities presented by the HIV/blood conflict were not lost on Prime Minister Hashimoto. It was Hashimoto who as minister of health and welfare in 1979 tearfully apologized on behalf of the Japanese government for the SMON incident. He promised that the government would prevent future drug-related disasters, and the Pharmaceutical Affairs Law was revised to make the ministry responsible for drug safety. Hashimoto used the affair to political advantage, taking credit for being more open than Ministry bureaucrats about the damage caused by the Ministry-approved drug. The controversy over HIV and blood was similarly volatile. Approached cautiously, it could be a political asset; but in the hands of a politician not dependent upon the largesse of the LDP, it could be used to embarrass the government and shame the MHW.

As Hashimoto configured the new Cabinet, his first choice for leading the Ministry of Health and Welfare unexpectedly pressed for a different appointment, and the post of minister of health and welfare became available. A Cabinet-level position for Sakigake was a condition of its participation in the coalition. In January 1996, Sakigake's Kan Naoto got the nod. Within weeks of taking control of the ministry, Kan transformed the conflict over contaminated blood. No longer was it hemophiliac plaintiffs against the MHW and pharmaceutical companies. Health and Welfare Minister Kan turned against the corps of career bureaucrats in his ministry, and elevated the dispute over HIV-tainted blood into one of the most violent scandals of the 1990s.

Kan's first public act in the HIV-contaminated blood conflict was to order bureaucrats in his ministry to produce the files long requested by the plaintiffs. If they were "missing," as was claimed, it was time to investigate and find them. He ordered the creation of an HIV Infection Investigation Project Team, and in only three days their search was rewarded. On February 9, 1996, Kan held a press conference to announce that nine long-missing files had been located. They included detailed meeting minutes and documents related to the 1983 discussions of the MHW's AIDS Task Force, and similar material from its Subcommittee on Blood Products. Kan stated:

> We now understand to a reasonable degree the details of the creation of the Task Force. Until now, the courts involved in the settlement have been concerned with the inability to securely place responsibility

on the Ministry of Health and Welfare. However, after seeing these documents, it is apparent that the government will broadly accept responsibility. This will have an impact on settlement procedures.[43]

Over the next months, Minister Kan continued to engage in a public battle with his ministry staff. As long-hidden information from the 1980s slowly emerged, attention focused on the new minister. On February 16, 1996, he met with 200 HIV-infected hemophiliacs and their families at the Ministry of Health and Welfare, and offered the apology that had for so long eluded them. "Representing the ministry, I make a heartfelt apology for inflicting heavy damage on the innocent patients. I also apologize for the belated recognition of the ministry's responsibility for the case. I understand that the delay has tormented the victims."[44] In what had become known in Japan as the Kan-kan war, a pun on the fight that developed over HIV and blood between Minister Kan and ministry bureaucrats, known as *kanryō*, the minister had won a decisive battle. He had apologized, but there was no confusion about the meaning of his apology. Kan had no link to the 1983 MHW, no influence on decisions about blood products, no responsibility to protect hemophiliacs from HIV. By apologizing, he simultaneously won the unanimous support of the public, declared the career bureaucrats in his ministry venal and corrupt, and showed himself to be a protector of the rights of ordinary citizens.

While political opportunism may have emboldened Kan to vigorously pursue the conflict over contaminated blood (as an opposition party leader with a strong "outsider" perspective, being the hero of the blood scandal would almost certainly add to his popularity), information that emerged from the first publicly released file fanned the flames of scandal. The file, turned over to the press on February 21, contained information about three Task Force meetings between June and August 1983. Named the "Gunji File" after the director of the Biologics and Antibiotics Division of the Pharmaceutical Affairs Bureau during that period, Dr. Gunji Atsuaki, the file consisted of material indicating that the Task Force had discussed the potential danger of imported, unheated blood products.

Most contentious were notes written by Gunji in preparation for a July 4, 1983 meeting of the AIDS Task Force. Titled "Handling of Blood Products and AIDS," the document outlined a possible MHW response to HIV and blood. First, it recommended the use of heated products; second, it encouraged foreign pharmaceutical companies developing heated products to seek approval from the ministry as soon as possible; third, it suggested using administrative guidance in instructing pharmaceutical companies not to use unheated blood products. The document also acknowledged that those actions could have an impact on the economic well-being of domestic pharmaceutical companies. None of the responses described in the document were discussed further at any subsequent meeting.

Whereas Gunji was vilified by the press for drafting the July memo but failing to act on its recommendations, Dr. Abe Takeshi, chair of the AIDS Task Force, was accused of pressuring the Task Force to allow the continued use of unheated products for his own financial gain. Plaintiffs had long asserted that Abe delayed the approval of heated blood products so Japan's largest pharmaceutical company, Green Cross, could better compete with rival firms. A delay would allow the Green Cross to make large profits on unheated, foreign blood products that it had purchased (or could obtain at a discount), while developing competitive heating technology. Abe is accused of accepting a bribe from Green Cross in exchange for the delay, and at the same time demanding money from rival firms in exchange for approving the clinical testing of heated blood products.[45]

The court's second proposal

Negotiations continued over the court-proposed settlement, and hemophiliacs insisted upon several conditions. With many litigants seriously ill from HIV, access to quality health care was a primary consideration. Despite Japan's system of health insurance, guaranteeing a basic level of coverage to all citizens at low cost, HIV-infected hemophiliacs found it difficult to locate hospitals that would care for them.[46] So they pressed the court to recommend the creation of better medical care for the plaintiffs. In addition, they sought financial benefits for the families of hemophiliacs who died from AIDS; demanded a thorough investigation of the contaminated blood incident; and sought the establishment of a system that would eliminate future drug-induced tragedies.[47]

On March 7, 1996, the Tokyo and Osaka District Courts announced a second version of their October proposed settlement. It did not increase the lump-sum payments from 45 to 60 million yen, as plaintiffs had demanded. But it did recommend that in addition to the payment, every hemophiliac with AIDS receive 150,000 yen monthly ($1,500), and the current MHW-administered compensation scheme continue. The court also suggested that a medical care system for victims of contaminated blood be established, whereby the government would pay for all medical care provided to HIV-positive hemophiliacs and 40 percent of the care provided to those with AIDS, with pharmaceutical companies paying the balance. As in the first recommendation, the court emphasized that the government and pharmaceutical companies were responsible for the distribution of tainted blood, and urged them to apologize. And it set a settlement deadline of March 29, leaving the parties only three weeks to settle differences that had simmered during six years of litigation.

Responding to the proposal, Kawada Ryūhei stated: "What we want to have most is the defendants' recognition of their responsibility and an expression of heartfelt apology to us based on the recognition."[48] Suzuki Toshihiro, lead attorney for the Tokyo plaintiffs, reiterated Kawada's concerns, emphasizing that payments from the defendants signaled their responsibility for the incident, not social welfare.

It did not take long for the remaining defendants to follow the example set by Minister Kan. The plaintiffs assembled into five groups on March 14, 1996, and visited the offices of the five pharmaceutical companies they held responsible for their HIV infection. At each location, presidents and top executives of the companies offered their apologies, emphasizing that hemophiliacs were "innocent" victims of HIV. In Tokyo, Bayer President Wolfgang Plischke stated: "We would like to apologize from the bottom of our heart for the suffering of hemophiliac patients and their family members, who are unwitting victims of a terrible tragedy."[49] At the Japanese headquarters of Baxter, President Bob Hurley announced:

> On behalf of Baxer employees worldwide, I would like to extend a sincere and deep apology to the HIV infected victims including the plaintiffs and their families. You are the innocent victims of a terrible disease and we deeply regret that the early versions of the therapies that were designed to save lives, carried the virus that causes AIDS.[50]

In Osaka, Green Cross President Kawano Takehiko read from a prepared statement, saying, "We deeply regret that our products created a serious situation that resulted in pain and grief." Those in the room became indignant, accusing him of offering superficial and insincere words. Kawano then made another statement, accepted responsibility on behalf of his company, got down on his hands and knees, and bowed so deeply that his forehead touched the floor. It was the defining moment of the conflict; a display of physical and psychological vulnerability from the president of Green Cross, a company that had its start in blood banking, dominated the domestic pharmaceutical industry, exerted influence on government policy, and was accused of infecting thousands of the most vulnerable Japanese citizens with a fatal disease. New revelations and further outrage would keep the nation focused on the blood scandal. But nothing could supplant the image of a rumpled President Kawano that flashed on every front page and television news in the nation.

One day later Minister Kan reiterated his apology, and signaled the government's intention to settle the HIV litigation. At a ceremony on March 29, all parties to the conflict signed a settlement agreement prepared by the court, which stated: "Each of the defendant government and pharmaceutical companies hereby apologizes from the bottom of its heart for the fact that enormous damage, physically and mentally, has been caused to the HIV infected victims including the Plaintiffs."[51] Hemophiliacs, who had first voiced their claims in the language of rights in order to oppose the AIDS Prevention Act, and went to court in 1989 to press what looked like a hopeless case, had scored a dramatic victory. Litigation over HIV-contaminated blood products came to a close.

The aftermath

With the formal settlement of the litigation, the Office of the Prosecutor abandoned its reticence to investigate charges filed against certain actors years earlier and started to sift through evidence of possible criminal wrongdoing.[52] One complaint that prosecutors explored was filed against Dr. Abe, who like many Japanese physicians failed to reveal to his patients their actual medical diagnoses. According to Abe and other physicians who treat hemophiliacs, they feared that if hemophiliacs were told that they were HIV-positive, they would commit suicide or intentionally infect others. They also claimed that many hemophiliacs did not want to know their test results, despite evidence indicating that 87 percent would prefer to know the truth.[53] As a result, a group of hemophiliacs accused Abe of criminal negligence, saying that he knew the blood products he administered to hemophiliacs could infect them with HIV. In August, 1996, the Tokyo police arrested the eighty-year-old Dr. Abe. According to the Prosecutor's Office, the hemophilia expert had ignored evidence of blood product contamination when designing the blood policy of Teikyō University Hospital, where he was once vice-president. Abe's failure, prosecutors claimed, caused hemophiliac patients treated with blood products at the hospital in the 1980s to become infected with HIV.[54] He was released on 100 million yen bail, and as of late 1999 his trail was still ongoing, adding new energy to the increasingly vigorous movement for patients' rights discussed in Chapter 3.

Criminal accusations were also filed against Matsushita Renzō, former director of the MHW's Pharmaceutical Affairs Bureau and later the president of the Green Cross Company. According to the relatives of the first non-hemophiliac adult to die from an HIV-tainted blood transfusion, the deceased was given HIV-tainted blood products in April 1986, long after the Green Cross knew about the danger of unheated products. Matsushita, as well as former Green Cross president, Kawano, who had apologized on his hands and knees to the hemophiliacs, were (along with a third former Green Cross president) arrested and are on trial for murder.

Pursuing the lawsuits against the MHW, the five pharmaceutical companies, and individual actors was a coming-out ritual for the hemophiliac community, a declaration that mistreatment, discrimination, and abuse would no longer be tolerated, and rights violations could no longer be ignored. As a consequence HIV-positive hemophiliacs and their families have spent what for some are their final days locked in a battle with corporate and government elites. However and whenever the criminal prosecutions are resolved, one salient point remains – hemophiliacs have strategically used a rhetoric of rights to press for recognition and recompense by the body politic. They have succeeded in influencing policy, improving their medical care, and establishing their status as "innocent" victims, effectively using the language of rights to frame and press their claims. It is an interesting irony that HIV-infected hemophiliacs in the United States look longingly in the direction of Japan when they think about what courts and legislatures can do to make them whole. The US government did not design a compensation package for hemophiliacs until 1998; their class action lawsuit against the pharmaceutical industry was decertified; an out-of-court settlement yielded only a fraction of the sum paid to those in Japan.

Given that medical science has yet to find a way to save the lives of people with HIV, infected hemophiliacs in Japan are a long way from rejoicing at their legal and political achievements. Engaging in the ritual of rights assertion, however, Japan's hemophiliacs scored a stunning legal, political, and moral victory, winning a public apology and massive financial compensation and humiliating the state.

BRAIN DEATH AND ORGAN TRANSPLANTATION: ACCUSATION AND DISCRETION

The oxymoron of Japanese criminal procedure

There are important procedural and doctrinal differences between hemophiliacs' claims against the MHW and pharmaceutical companies, and claims related to brain death and organ transplantation. Doctrinally, the most notable difference is that the HIV-tainted blood claims were brought under tort law, while those related to brain death were criminal complaints. This has a number of consequences, such as the type of evidence that must be presented, the length of time a case may take before it is resolved, and the possible remedies.

While the substantive differences between a tort and a criminal action – negligence and homicide, in AIDS and brain death respectively – are huge, they should not be overemphasized. The objective of appealing to the formal legal system in both cases was not primarily concrete victory based on the articulation of legal doctrine. The plaintiffs did not expect unambiguous victory, and may not even have desired it. In reality, the choice of a particular cause of action had more to do with convenience than conviction.

What is most important about the choice of a cause of action is that it has a profound impact upon the process through which a claim is adjudicated. Negligence as a civil (tort) claim (as opposed to possible administrative, criminal, or constitutional law claims, that were also considered) required that plaintiffs in the HIV litigation present their arguments within a particular legal framework, with contentions about causality, foreseeability, and avoidability supported by whatever evidence they could offer. But unlike civil claims, or "accusatorial" criminal claims in common law jurisdictions, Japanese criminal law follows a continental (primarily German) "inquisitorial" model.[55] Merryman characterizes criminal procedure in civil as opposed to common law jurisdictions as the substitution of public officials for private accusers, the shift in judges' functions from passive arbiters to active questioners, and the abandonment of bipolar party participation in favor of a contest between individuals and the state.[56]

These differences are critical to understanding the design and disposition of charges related to brain death. Those who accuse transplant surgeons of homicide are restricted in their ability to investigate the facts, charge the defendants, and go to court. Responsibility to do all three of those rests with prosecutors. While Japanese prosecutors are able to exercise some degree of autonomy in deciding which accusations to aggressively investigate and which to neglect, they are formally under the control of the Ministry of Justice. Measuring or in some way empirically evaluating the extent to which the ministry pressures prosecutors to act or not act in particular cases is difficult. Many participants in the brain death debate, however, were convinced that because accusations related to brain death raised questions implicating complex legal, political, and ethical issues, the strong arm of the state was being used to limit prosecutorial action. More particularly, activists believed that bureaucratic discretion and other exercises of state power would overwhelm their desire to use the criminal process as part of a strategy to assert and defend the rights of those who opposed brain death.

At the same time, as accusations challenging the behavior of transplant surgeons slowly accumulated, it became clear that inaction could be an extremely effective weapon in the brain death debate. Had prosecutors quickly pursued the cases, there is a strong likelihood that the defendants would have been acquitted. Inaction, on the other hand, allowed the accusers to point to the fact that a number of surgeons could, at least in theory, be found guilty of murder. Not until the Organ Transplantation Act was passed in 1997 did prosecutors consider the various accusations related to brain death; in March 1998, all of them were dismissed.

Each of the brain-death-related legal actions – and there were eight of them – followed the same course. The Japanese Code of Criminal Procedure has two provisions through which the public can inform authorities about an alleged criminal offense. The first, complaints (*kokuso*) lodged by victims, witnesses, their legal representatives, spouses, or relatives, are written or oral reports filed with the police or prosecutors. Second are accusations (*kokuhatsu*) that can be brought by anyone who believes there has been a criminal offense, even though the accuser was not the victim.[57] The legal actions over brain death fall into the latter category. Accusers are not family members or relatives, but are instead individuals not directly related to the incidents who are filing accusations for less immediately personal reasons.

One other aspect of the Code of Criminal Procedure has been critical to brain death opponents. Japanese criminal law, in providing that individuals not directly injured may notify the authorities that they would like a particular matter prosecuted, also directs officials, in this case public prosecutors, to investigate the alleged offense. After investigation and evaluation of the evidence, a decision is made as to whether a case will be prosecuted.[58] The Criminal Code does not include a time frame for such investigations, however, and nothing precludes prosecutors from declaring that an investigation is "ongoing," whether or not any action has been taken. The way in which prosecutors exercise their discretion in deciding how aggressively to investigate an accusation and whether the evidence warrants prosecution will, therefore, determine the outcome of a case.[59] Prosecutors only investigated and disposed of one accusation related to brain death, and they decided not to prosecute. Not until 1998 were the other cases dismissed. This cast a shadow of ambiguity over the brain death controversy, and significantly strengthened the position of brain death opponents. In essence, by turning to prosecutors and the courts, they seized control of the public debate and stalled efforts to legislate death in Japan.

The Wada case: operations and protestations
Like the unfolding of a Shakespearean tragedy, the drama of brain death and organ transplantation in Japan has been influenced by a single, random event. It began on August 8, 1968, when Yamaguchi Yoshimasa, an economics student living in Hokkaido, went down to the ocean for a swim. Something went wrong, and he had to be pulled from the water unconscious and rushed to Sapporo University Hospital. Two hours later he was declared dead from drowning. Early in the morning of the following day the heart was taken from his corpse and implanted into Miyazaki Nobuo, an eighteen-year-old suffering from chronic heart disease. Less than three months later Miyazaki died.

From a medical perspective, the fact that the recipient lived for eighty-three days was cause for pride. After all, the world's first heart transplant had been performed just one year earlier, by Dr. Christian Barnard in South Africa, and his patient lived for only eighteen days. But in Japan no policy sanctioned the determination of death based on brain criteria, the method by which Yamaguchi was declared dead. Without a policy, the distinction between caring for an organ recipient and killing a donor became dangerously murky. Had Dr. Wada

Jōrō, head of the transplant team, killed Yamaguchi Yoshimasa in order to try his hand at transplanting a heart into Miyazaki Nobuo? Did Miyazaki even need a new heart? Were the medical records describing the operation altered to mask the truth of the patients' conditions? Or had Wada performed a brilliant technical feat in order to save a waning life, only to be criticized by those unable to understand the benefits conferred by modern medical technology?[60]

This single operation is regularly credited with fomenting the entire debate over brain death and transplantation in Japan. More than the surgical procedure itself, however, the legal maneuvering that it stimulated has been a powerful deterrent to other ambitious transplant surgeons, and has become a model for subsequent criminal accusations directed at inhibiting organ transplantation.

Criticism of Dr. Wada Jūrō and his transplant team came from physicians within the medical community who were in principle neither opposed to a brain death standard nor to organ transplants. Many, in fact, believed that organ transplants would soon be performed in Japan, once the dual obstacles of the definition of death and the ability to suppress the body's rejection of organs were overcome.[61] Dr. Wada, however, had jumped the gun. He did not consult outside experts, and ignored the fact that a committee made up of members of the Japan Society of Transplantation, Ministry of Health and Welfare (MHW), and Ministry of Justice had convened in May 1967 to consider legislation related to organ transplants, and had not yet announced its findings.

With no generally accepted brain death criteria, no consensus about pursuing heart transplants within the medical community, and no guidance from the bureaucracy, it was an ideal opportunity for anyone opposing brain death and transplants to let themselves be heard. Just four months after the operation, and scarcely one month after the death of the organ recipient, an accusation was filed with the Office of the Public Prosecutor in Sapporo. The plaintiffs were six practitioners of traditional Chinese medicine in Osaka; they accused Dr. Wada of killing heart donor Yamaguchi.

The investigation pursuant to the accusation focused on three fundamental questions: Was Yamaguchi really brain dead when his heart was taken? Did Miyazaki need a new heart? Were medical records tampered with?[62] Other issues that were investigated included the consent of the donor, and Miyazaki's post-operative care.

Was Yamaguchi brain dead?

Concerns about whether Yamaguchi was actually dead at the time his heart was taken center on the events between the time he arrived at the hospital and the moment when his heart was extracted. Physicians at the hospital made contradictory statements about Yamaguchi's initial care, with some saying he received pressurized oxygen, and others claiming that he was not left in the treatment room long enough to receive the necessary oxygen therapy. There is also disagreement over why Yamaguchi was taken to Wada's surgery department, and the actual cause of death. Wada indicated in the charts that he died from water in the lungs, but other physicians who were present disagree.

More important are the accusations over the determination of death. According to Wada, Yamaguchi was declared brain dead at 10.10 p.m., and the transplant began about four hours later, at 2.05 a.m. The declaration of brain death, however, must be based on the measurement of brain function, an electroencephalogram, and it appears that no such equipment was available in Wada's department. Even if it were, it is contended that Wada should have been required to wait more than four hours before harvesting Miyazaki's heart, and should have gotten outside confirmation by a neurologist of his death, to comply with minimum standards of determining brain death. It is also claimed that Wada's operating room lacked the necessary technology to measure Yamaguchi's heart beat. If neither Yamaguchi's brain waves nor heart beat were adequately measured, then it is possible that his heart was seized while his brain was functioning and his heart was beating, making Wada a killer;[63] this is exactly what the accusers claimed, and what the prosecutors investigated.

Did Miyazaki need a new heart?

The treatment and death of Miyazaki was also the subject of dispute. Since transplantation technology was still in its infancy, problems of organ rejection had not yet been solved. Wada claimed at a press conference after Miyazaki's death that the heart transplanted into Miyazaki was in excellent condition, and his death resulted from other causes. In March 1969, Fujimoto Teruo, a physician from Sapporo University Hospital who performed a dissection on Miyazaki, wrote an article contradicting several claims that Dr. Wada made at that press conference.[64] He asserted that the heart transplanted into Miyazaki was not in good shape at the time of death, but was enlarged and had reacted badly to certain medications. In addition, he argued that the severity of Miyazaki's pre-transplant heart condition had been exaggerated by Wada, probably in order to justify the transplant.

Two months later, in a special issue of *Naika* (*Internal Medicine*), Professor Miyahara Mitsuo, an internist at Sapporo University Hospital who examined Miyazaki, wrote an article questioning the correctness of Dr. Wada's clinical judgment in deciding to perform a heart transplant.[65] Like Dr. Fujimoto, he claimed that the condition of the recipient was far less severe than portrayed by Wada, and argued that he could have benefited more from a heart valve replacement than a total heart transplant.

> If Miyazaki had just been left alone, and was not given any treatment, he wouldn't have had a long life. But with an artificial heart valve, he could have lived a perfectly normal life for around ten years. So I brought this up at the hospital, because it seemed that a transplant was not an appropriate treatment.[66]

What happened to Miyazaki's heart is a puzzle. After the autopsy it seems to have disappeared, and it was later alleged that Wada kept it in his office for several months. When he finally produced it the controversial valve had been cut out.[67]

Miyahara also highlighted the possible dangers from the imbalance of power between physicians and patients that could result in transplants, criticized the adequacy of treatment given to the donor, and questioned the procedure for obtaining the consent of the donor's family. Concerning the latter, it was alleged that by the time Yamaguchi's family was asked to consent to the transplant, his chest had already been split in preparation for the operation.[68]

Were medical records altered?

Finally, after the transplant was completed and controversy was ignited, investigations of the operation led to an examination of the patients' medical records. Despite the complex and innovative nature of the procedure, however, written records were minimal, and it was claimed that even those had been tampered with to mask wrongdoing and incompetence. There is no evidence or even anecdotal information to support this claim. But along with other assertions of wrongdoing, it added to the atmosphere of unease surrounding the operation.

Further investigation

Prosecutors investigating the above questions were not alone in attempting to recreate the events surrounding the 1968 heart transplant. In June 1979, they requested the assistance of a group of prominent surgeons and other medical professionals, and asked them to make a judgment about the propriety of Wada's operation. After many months of discussion this group was not able to offer a concrete opinion. In addition, a group was formed by two former health and welfare ministers, social critics, physicians, and others that went under the name "Study Group on the Wada Heart Transplant Indictment." This interdisciplinary team discussed the Sapporo transplant publicly as well as with the Judicial Affairs Committee of the Diet, a Ministry of Health and Welfare Deliberation Council, and the Human Rights section of the Japan Federation of Bar Associations (JFBA). They concluded that the controversy was at root a dispute over the balance of power between patients and physicians, and issued a "Declaration of the Rights of Hospitalized Patients" (Byōsha no tame no jinken sengen).

Ultimately, the prosecutor's office exercised its discretion in deciding that there was not enough evidence to prosecute Wada for homicide. Yonemoto Shōhei, a prominent commentator on Japanese politics, ascribes the failure to prosecute to the immense power of the medical profession, particularly those who ran university departments and were able to "ride out" the conflict and escape undue legal consequences. The accusation against Wada was dismissed for lack of material evidence, the JFBA sent him a warning, and the affair was formally settled. Dr. Wada moved his medical practice to Tokyo, having left his university position in Sapporo. But the Wada case itself has had a more turbulent legacy, as a series of other criminal accusations makes evident.

The Patients' Rights Conference: abiding accusations
In December 1984, a dramatic transplant was attempted when the kidneys, corneas, pancreas and liver were taken from the body of a woman who suffered a cerebral hemorrhage. Cornea and kidney transplants had in the past been successfully performed in Japan, but this was the first attempt at a simultaneous kidney/liver transplant. The doctors relied on the Takeuchi brain death criteria to make the determination of death, and were praised by the *Asahi Evening News*, which suggested that organ transplantation should be accelerated. Accolades did not come from all quarters. The following day, another newspaper published comments critical of the operation that were made by members of the Patients' Rights Conference (PRC) at Tokyo University.

The Patients' Rights Conference, affiliated with Tokyo University Hospital until a recent split (see Chapter 3), was started in the early 1980s by patients, hospital workers, and physicians, under the guidance of Dr. Honda Katsunori. Honda was active as a radical organizer of the Tokyo University Hospital medical staff during the student protests of the 1960s, and engaged in physical skirmishes with university officials at that time. For a quarter of a decade, he has retained an unsalaried position at the hospital in order to fight for reform of the medical profession from within an institution that he believes to represent strict hierarchy, elitism, and a lack of concern about patient rights. While the PRC has been involved in a variety of issues – informed consent, the use of medical technologies, in-vitro fertilization – its participation in the brain death controversy was the first time it had risen to national prominence.

After the 1984 simultaneous transplant in the city of Tsukuba, Dr. Honda and the PRC immediately questioned the possible infringement of the donor's and recipient's rights. Having studied the Wada heart transplant case carefully, they understood the attention and controversy generated by the accusation filed against Dr. Wada, and the taboo on recognizing brain death and performing heart transplants that it helped to create. Within ninety days of the Tsukuba operation the PRC filed two accusations against the head of the surgical team for killing the donor, damaging a corpse, and injury that resulted in the death of the recipient.

The accusation in the Tsukuba case focused on several issues. Like the Wada incident, it questioned the diagnosis of brain death, pointing out that the transplant was performed before the Takeuchi criteria were approved, and claiming that taking the donor's organs was tantamount to homicide. It ridiculed the procedure through which consent of the recipient was obtained, describing it as his being told to say in a loud voice, "yes, please perform the transplantation for me from the donor."[69] The lack of a medical indication for transplanting organs into the recipient, the negative result of an antigen test, and poor post-operative care, are all highlighted in the accusations as having caused his death.

The PRC also raised the issue of possible discrimination against psychiatric patients, since the donor had been admitted to a local mental hospital; it is not clear that she was able to give informed consent to donating her organs. In addition, while the transplant surgeons removed her corneas, kidneys, pancreas, liver, and spleen, only three of the organs were transplanted, and the others were used in medical research. The PRC accusation claims that this is a violation of Japanese law prohibiting the damage of a corpse.

In the years since Tsukuba, the PRC filed other criminal complaints about organ transplant operations. Twenty-four members of transplant teams, in eight separate incidents, were accused of homicide.[70] In addition to surgeons and hospital administrators, the accused included a university hospital ethics committee that approved a transplant operation, the first time such a group had been a named party in a criminal or civil legal action. These cases were brought throughout the nation, in areas including Tokyo, Osaka, Hiroshima, Niigata, and Okayama. Legal action was usually taken in collaboration with a local citizens' group, or nurses union, or those advocating handicapped rights. A well-publicized accusation in Osaka, for example, was brought by the Osaka University Hospital Brain Death and Organ Transplant Problem Support Group (*Handai Byōin Nōshi to Zōki Ishoku no Mondai o Sasaeru Kai*), the Osaka University Affiliated Hospital Nurses Labor Union (*Osaka Daigaku Fuzoku Byōin Kangofu Rōdō Kumiai*), and the PRC.

All eight of the accusations remained in a condition described by the accusers as *tōketsu*, literally meaning frozen. They were on file in various prosecutors' offices, but were neither investigated nor dismissed. While an outright victory would have been the most desired result of the accusers, ambiguity was also a powerful ally. The accusations remained viable though dormant, reminding surgeons of the possibility that a transplant could lead to negative publicity and criminal investigation. With the passage of legislation in 1997 allowing organ donors to consent to being declared brain dead (see Chapter 5), however, all eight cases were dismissed. Despite any evidence of consent in the cases, the presumption that brain death does not equal death has clearly been weakened. Those who have fought against a brain death standard thus find themselves in need of a new legal strategy.

For several decades, however, the PRC-inspired and other prosecutions had a chilling effect on the definition of death and promotion of organ transplants in Japan. Mitsuishi Tadahiro, an attorney and member of the Ad-Hoc Committee on Brain Death and Organ Transplantation, believes that without the accusations, former Prime Minister Kaifu would not have initiated that blue-ribbon committee (see Chapter 5).[71] Another member of the Ad-Hoc Committee, former president of the University of Tokyo, Hirano Ryūichi, attributes much of the stalemate over transplantation to the Wada incident and its progeny, and believes that the government should set up a panel to study controversial transplant cases.[72] The attorney for the PRC, Hironaka Junichirō (ironically, the attorney now defending Dr. Abe in his HIV/blood-related criminal prosecution), is forthright in explaining that while an average homicide case takes between three and six months to investigate, the long delay in investigating the PRC accusations permitted his client to intimidate physicians.[73] Ogata Tsuyoshi, an official in the Ministry of Health and Welfare section responsible for transplants and brain death, states that the accusations had a particularly strong effect on emergency room physicians who are on the front lines in identifying brain death.[74]

Inaction was an appealing alternative to the Office of the Prosecutor, which was loath to be too centrally involved in the decision about whether or not brain death was equivalent to death. Prosecutorial actions were constrained not only because of the close connection between prosecutors and the Ministry of Justice, which wanted the issue kept out of the courts. There was also extensive communication between prosecutors and the Ministry of Health and Welfare, which had actively pressed for the passage of a transplant bill in the Diet. All of these parties were acutely aware of the tension and indecision that characterized the brain death debate, and the lack of agreement on a policy solution at many levels of government, law, and the public. An official misstep, particularly one that would feed the mistrust and suspicion of medical and ministerial authority, was highly undesirable. Given the alternatives, inaction was the safest course of action.

The accusations, framed in the language of rights, thus succeeded in stalemating the controversy over the definition of death. The PRC and other parties were less interested in the technical merits of brain death than they were in standing up both *for* individual patient's rights and *against* a powerful professional and political coalition that they believed would create and interpret medical criteria counter to the interests of most citizens. Speaking on behalf of individuals declared brain dead, they claimed: "While healthy people may claim to accept patients' rights, living wills, and death with dignity, so-called brain dead patients can't communicate with the outside world. Who can secure the rights of patients, if the existence of the patients themselves is not accepted by their families or society?"[75] By arguing in favor of patients' rights, and formally accusing transplant surgeons of homicide, the PRC and others challenged those who were anxious to see Japan follow the West in the acceptance of brain death and transplantation. For many years, their accusations served as reminders to transplant surgeons that they were under close scrutiny, and any overzealousness could result in a criminal accusation. By invoking the language of rights in the debate over the definition of death, opponents of brain death for over a decade used the threat of prosecution and the possibility of court action as part of a strategy to postpone brain death legislation. They simultaneously ensured that the 1997 legislation made explicit reference to the primacy of patients' rights in the determination of death and the transplant of organs. For advocates, this may not have been considered a sweeping victory; brain death is now an accepted definition of death in Japan, albeit in limited circumstances. By invoking the language of rights in their long battle again brain death, however, they made effective use of a powerful rhetoric that has long animated social, political, and legal conflict.

CHAPTER SEVEN

A SOCIOLEGAL PERSPECTIVE ON RIGHTS IN JAPAN

RIGHTS, MODERNIZATION, AND THE "UNIQUENESS" OF THE JAPANESE LEGAL SYSTEM

Since the postwar period, the study of the Japanese legal system has been locked into a narrow paradigm. Among the central features of that paradigm are: a view of Japanese law as encumbered by elements of the "traditional" legal system; the idea that the Japanese legal system is changing, and developing in the direction of a "modern" system; an assumption that the Japanese legal system is unique; and a belief that fundamental characteristics of Japanese culture have shaped legal behavior. There have been challenges to this paradigm, such as those asserting the influence of institutional constraints on legal behavior, and rarely have all elements of the paradigm been evident in any one scholar or publication. As an overall orientation to the study of law in Japan, however, the paradigm has exerted a steady influence. Within it, the answer to almost every question about law in Japan contains a familiar refrain – in Japan, there is a lack of rights assertion and a reluctance to go to court.[1]

Several factors have helped to sustain the accepted paradigm that rights assertion, and resort to the law more generally, are particularly infrequent in Japan. Modernization theory has contributed to the paradigm by providing a framework within which Japanese law can be compared and contrasted to Western legal systems, and a perspective for thinking about how legal systems change. Literature focusing on the uniqueness of Japanese law and legal thinking, part of a larger body of work about Japanese uniqueness, extended the perspective of modernization by focusing on the characteristics of the Japanese legal system that differentiated it from other such systems. The paradigmatic thinking about law in Japan was also reinforced by the powerful image of legal transplants, which linked the possibility for legal change to the willingness and ability of the legal system to import foreign legal doctrines and practices.

Once the paradigmatic view of Japanese law is understood, it becomes easier to see its flaws. First, highlighting the distinctiveness of Japanese legal behavior depends upon simplifying and amplifying the features of other legal systems. In postwar scholarship, it is the legal system of the United States that has been most prominently positioned as the foil to Japan. Without significant reference to scholarly debate in the United States, particularly research in the past two decades, much writing on the Japanese legal system accepts as a "fact" the occurrence and vast dimensions of a litigation explosion in the United States; ignores the many personal or social inhibitions to litigation in the United States, and treats access to courts, lawyers, and legal judgments as unproblematic. In addition, it overlooks the fact that in Western law and language, not only in Japanese, the term "rights" is complex and ambiguous, and no single or simple definition is possible. Sociolegal research in the United States has addressed these issues, but that work has had little impact on sociolegal studies about Japan.

Second, perhaps as a consequence of dichotomous thinking about Asian and Western legal systems, cultural and structural explanations of Japanese legal behavior have been similarly divided. Many scholars who have written about law in Japan adopt cultural or structural approaches without specifying what "cultural" and "structural" represent, or analyzing what differentiates or unites such perspectives. The explanation of a complex, human institution like legal behavior is multicausal. As this chapter discusses, structure and culture do not stand in opposition – they are intertwined, interdependent, and interactive.

Third, too much empirical sociolegal research by Japanese law scholars has examined the frequency of court filings, and sought to determine if particular types of fact patterns would lead people to assert their rights. By presenting people with vignettes and asking how they would react to barking dogs, unpleasant neighbors, and unscrupulous shopkeepers, these researchers have concluded that the types of annoyances that might spark a lawsuit in New York will cause scarcely a ripple in Tokyo. Such research overly limits what counts as rights assertion, limiting it to something people do in court if they think that their concrete legal interests have been violated.

The most basic, and important, limitation of the postwar paradigm is that it canvasses too narrow a range of social interactions when seeking evidence of the importance of rights. By looking at the political use of rights rhetoric, and the strategic assertion of rights in the policy process, it turns out that rights-based conflict is not so anomalous in Japan. To recognize such conflict, however, requires that law is seen as encompassing more than what happens in court, and rights assertion is thought of more broadly than claims about legally cognizable interests.

The way rights talk animates policy disputes is shaped in part by Japanese culture; the sympathy shown to certain "victims" groups by the media and public, the power of group identities to facilitate rights assertion, and the power of apology as a remedy are important cultural forms. Equally important are structural elements, such as the slow pace with which legal actions move through the courts, hierarchical social relationships that may inhibit the expression of dissent and conflict, and limited access to attorneys. In the following pages, I suggest that neither scholarship on legal culture, nor that on structure, makes a persuasive case in explaining why rights are not asserted in Japan. While in part a failure of theory, this represents a basic empirical error. Rights are asserted in Japan, and the challenge for sociolegal scholarship is to understand who asserts them, for what purpose, and with what impact.

The impulse to explain why rights assertion is so uncommon in Japan, at the expense of understanding when, where, why, and by whom rights are asserted, is rooted in the powerful image of legal systems provided by modernization theory. The influential social scientist Reinhard Bendix, in his essay "Tradition and Modernity Reconsidered," presents a brilliant assessment of the goals and failures of research on modernization.[2] His goal is "to show that the invidious contrast between tradition and modernity is the master-theme which underlies a great diversity of topics and influences our understanding of modern society to this day."[3] Without intending to do so, Bendix provides a conceptual framework for understanding the intellectual paradigm that has shaped postwar thinking about Japanese law and rights.

Bendix does not conceive of modernization as following a uniform evolutionary path. He recognizes that each transition is unique,[4] but at the same time identifies the similar challenge modernization has posed to "backward" societies, which seek to close the gap created by England's early industrialization and France's early democratization. As political scientist Harry Eckstein points out:

> From the outset, development was, as stated, a norm-laden concept, distinguishing "us" from "them," Western achievements from non-Western aspirations . . . The difficulty here is . . . the tendency to conceive political development simplistically – as what exists in the West and had gone on in its history (especially its recent history), and what was sought to be replicated, or was bound to occur, in "backward" societies.[5]

All "backward" societies, in other words, attempt to determine the factors which were "conditions of development in the advanced countries," and seek to create or promote such factors. In addition, "backward" societies have a tendency to try and "reconcile the strength evidenced by the advanced society with the values inherent in native traditions."[6]

Some scholars who believed that the characteristics of the Japanese legal system might eventually come to resemble those of Western legal systems have sought to identify the "native traditions" of Japanese law. Many started from the premise that understanding Japan's "unique" legal culture was the first step in understanding the Japanese legal system.[7] Their perspective is linked to a genre of writings about Japanese culture and identity called Nihonjinron (theories of Japaneseness). Whether in its popular or academic form, Nihonjinron seeks to discover the core meaning of Japaneseness on both an individual and aggregate level. The least palatable of these writings declare Japanese intestines or snow or rice or emotions to be singularly unique. More subtle, and sometimes insightful works hone in on particular social norms, political arrangements, and economic practices.

Work influenced by Nihonjinron[8] is sprinkled with wareware Nihonjin and wagakuni, "we Japanese" and "our nation," implying that all individuals in Japan share a unitary and distinctive Japanese vision. There was (and sometimes still is) a reification of wa, or harmony, as an ultimate value and prime reason for the avoidance of conflict, infrequent use of courts, and preference for conciliation. Some legal scholars have even claimed that the vagueness inherent in the

Japanese language makes legal disputes unresolvable through words and rationality, but amenable to *haragei*, a non-verbal, emotional, abdomen-centered form of communication that only Japanese can understand.[9] The allegedly unique ambiguity of Japanese language makes it unable to accurately capture the "real" meaning of Western legal terms. In contrast to words in the Western legal tradition, which it is claimed have precise, fixed definitions, the Japanese language is like air, continually shifting and impossible to specify.[10] The gap between the perceived exactitude of Western law and language and Japanese ambiguity has colored the discussion of rights; it suggests that the word rights could never be adequately described by such an inherently ambiguous language, and that such a concept is therefore without "true" meaning in Japanese society.

The impulse to focus on national uniqueness, within and beyond the realm of law, is itself not unusual. Libraries are full of volumes describing the distinctive national character of the French, the British, the Dutch, and the Germans. What is special about Japanese legal sociology is its adaptation of a perspective and vocabulary of uniqueness that is harnessed to a particular reading of legal history. That reading sees the traditional roots of Japanese legal behavior as so deeply embedded in culture that they are able to persevere in the face of legal principles and practices imported from the West. Despite the developmental model Bendix describes, the ideology of uniqueness has permeated academic thinking, leading to a view that while Japanese law and legal behavior may become more like that in the West, it will remain unique. Legal scholarship thus becomes a search for difference; one way of theorizing about those differences is through the metaphor of legal transplants.[11]

RIGHTS AND THE METAPHOR OF LEGAL TRANSPLANTS

The metaphor of legal transplants emerged from insights about modernization and social change that conceptualized elements of political and legal systems as autonomous and portable.[12] Some comparativists treat legal transplants as the most important element of legal change. Ugo Mattei, for example, claims that "[I]n most cases changes in a legal system are due to legal transplants," and argues that one reason why law is transplanted and legal change occurs is related to the desire to emulate more efficient systems.[13]

The goal of efficiency is only the most recent way to express the aspiration of certain countries to reconfigure their legal systems in the image of those they imagine to be "better." Bendix suggests a conceptual map for such aspirations, describing the economic transformation of England in the eighteenth and nineteenth centuries as a model for France, and the political revolution of France as a model for England. With both nations having undergone an economic and political "breakthrough" by the end of the eighteenth century, they became what he calls "pioneering countries," and every other nation was thus "backward." "Ever since," he writes, "the world has been divided into advanced and follower societies."[14]

Which countries are advanced and which are followers has since that time repeatedly changed. But the desire of follower societies to close the gap between themselves and the advanced societies, while trying to preserve the character of their native culture, has been a constant. In a comment later echoed by the literature on legal transplants, Bendix writes: "All aspects of modernity are up for adoption simultaneously, and it depends upon available resources, the balance of forces in the 'follower' society, and the relative ease of transfer which aspects will be given priority."[15] Alan Watson's pioneering work on legal transplants picks up on the idea of advanced and follower nations by viewing legal change as a process of transplanting rules from donor to recipient jurisdictions. Viewing the shifting and sharing of legal rules and doctrines as transplants paints a colorful picture of the intimacy of exchange, the fundamental compatibility of donor and recipient, and the way different jurisdictions are united and divided by legal formulations. It allows us to think about the world's legal systems as similar in their essentials, but at different stages of evolution. Just as organ transplants only succeed between similar species (such as humans), or those in the same developmental line (like children and baboons), legal transplants provide hope to ailing members of the world community that their non-functioning (or absent) parts may be replaceable.

In describing the metaphor of transplants, Watson writes: "A successful legal transplant – like that of a human organ – will grow in its new body, and become part of that body, just as the rule or institution would have continued to develop in its parent system. Subsequent development in the host system should not be confused with rejection."[16] But he overlooks other aspects of the transplantation image that are equally central to a successful operation. Transplants in the physical body are substitutions. They include both removal and replacement, not the insertion of a previously absent organ. The patient is often in a critical state, victim of a malfunctioning organ, which is heroically seized and replaced by a new or donated body part. Donors are usually dead, and always thought of as altruistic; recipients are grateful, and will always be to some extent impaired.

Despite the fact that the metaphor of legal transplants draws on but does not explicitly imitate its medical model, the dual images of high technology medicine and the human body to a large extent condition the way in which we view transplants of law. Law is transplanted to, not from, Africa and Asia, from victors and conquerors in Europe to less fortunate neighbors. It is given by the strong, Westernized states, by those who are healthy and robust, benevolent and self-sacrificing, evolved and advanced, to nations in need of help, with diseased parts, far behind in the evolutionary order. With regard to the law, Japan consistently has been viewed as recipient rather than donor. First from China, then Europe, finally from the United States, the Japanese body politic has run a solid trade deficit in the exchange of legal parts.

Watson's use of the transplant metaphor was originally quite restricted. His stated intention was simply to examine the way legal rules were moved between jurisdictions, and whether they were altered when they were introduced:

> When a legal rule is transplanted from Germany to Japan it will interest us whether it can be moved unaltered, or whether and to what extent it undergoes changes in its formulation. Whether, how, when and how far the effect is altered though the formulation is the same, are different and more difficult matters and will not be considered here.[17]

But the power of the transplant image has come to cloud Watson's initial goal; the "more difficult matters" he carefully circumscribed, because they are also the more interesting matters, are now routinely included in evaluations of the shifting and sharing of law in different locations.

Other metaphors may more accurately describe the process of legal exchange, depending upon the context. Grafting, which can mean both the process of fusing the lives of two different living organisms or the covering of one by the other, better captures many aspects of the exchange. The Japanese translation and enactment of Western legal codes in the late nineteenth century can be thought of as grafts rather than transplants, for example. In order to be judged as a successful transplant, Western law must lodge itself firmly in Japan, be accepted, and grow. But thought of as a graft, it fits well into the important distinction made in Japanese between *honne* (reality, practice) and *tatemae* (formality, pretense). Western law can then be understood not as a new, living, and vital addition, but as a superficial coating, a decoration (*kazarimono*) masking actual practice. Given the unequal treaties imposed on Japan, as Chalmers Johnson writes, there was "a practical interest in causing Westerners to see in Japan Western-type legal codes, parliamentary bodies, and commercial practices, regardless of how Japanese actually did things."[18]

Applied to rights, modernization's emphasis on advanced and follower nations, echoed in the transplant metaphor, suggests that prior to the Meiji Restoration and the vocabulary of *kenri*, there was neither a word for nor a concept of rights in Japan. Japan was a backward nation, with a traditional legal system. One aspect of Japanese modernization was therefore the importation of rights, thought to be a necessary element of modern law, which is in turn an important feature of a developed society. Consequently, it is not surprising that a foundational issue of legal sociology in Japan is to study the modernization of Japanese law, measured by its importation and operationalization of Western legal doctrines, norms, and practices. Only occasionally is Japan examined on its own terms. Whether rights-like ideas and practices existed before Western influence, and have continued, is a question overshadowed by assumptions that rights were absent, and that the continued lack of rights claims and consciousness evidences the persistence of both backwardness and uniqueness. Japan's undeniable economic strength, however, challenges the conclusion that it is a "follower." Japanese legal sociologists thus illustrate Bendix's contention that developing societies will seek to integrate "values inherent in native tradition" into advanced society.

LEGAL CULTURE, LEGAL INSTITUTIONS, AND JAPANESE LAW

Uniqueness, modernization, and legal transplants are each ways to understand and explain the nature of legal change. By asking to what extent Japanese legal norms and practices have and will continue to develop and evolve from traditional to modern, from Eastern to Western, legal scholars put the study of legal culture and legal change at the center of their agenda. Lawrence Friedman, in a pioneering work, defines legal culture as "the network of values and attitudes relating to law, which determine when and why and where people turn to law or government, or turn away."[19] Friedman's conception of legal culture as people's attitudes, values and opinions about law has been accepted by many scholars. Austin Sarat embraced it in his study of American legal culture.[20] Henry Ehrmann, in his volume *Comparative Legal Cultures*, uses a similar definition, calling legal culture the "attitudes, beliefs, and emotions of the operators as well as the users (and victims) of the legal system. . ."[21] In his study of the civil law, the legal comparativist John Henry Merryman proposes the category of "legal tradition" rather than "legal culture," but his definition remains close to Friedman's:

> A legal tradition . . . is a set of deeply rooted, historically conditioned attitudes about the nature of law, about the role of law in the society and the polity, about the proper organization and operation of a legal system, and about the way law is or should be made, applied, studied, perfected, and taught. The legal tradition relates the legal system to the culture of which it is a partial expression. It puts the legal system into cultural perspective.[22]

Until recently, most studies of legal culture focused on entire nations, or even groups of nations. Merryman and Ehrmann, for example, concentrate on transnational groupings;[23] Sarat and Friedman stay within national borders, concentrating on the legal culture of the United States, although they do occasionally mention the multiplicity of different legal cultures within the country.[24] Gibson and Caldeira investigate the legal cultures of countries that are part of the European Union.[25] Sanders and Hamilton compare Japanese, Russian, and US legal culture; Bierbrauer looks at the legal culture of Kurds, Lebanese, and Germans.[26] Some recent studies in the United States have narrowed their focus to the legal culture of specified social groups, small towns, and single institutions. Thomas Church, for example, has looked at what he calls the "local legal culture" of several criminal trial courts; Ewick and Silbey focus on the experience of one person to gain an understanding of the broader legal consciousness.[27] This trend, however, has not yet infused scholarship on legal culture and rights in Japan.

Scholars of legal culture largely consider it to be built upon individual attitudes, by which they mean thought and behavior, not "general dispositions of actors to act in certain ways in sets of situations."[28]

149

For the most part, legal scholars have muted predictive aspirations. Friedman, for example, is suspicious of prediction, saying that "only one thing is certain about the future, and that is uncertainty."[29] Others are equally disinclined to treat prediction as a reachable or desirable goal. As a consequence, legal culture scholarship has, perhaps inadvertently, avoided the frustration of being unable to satisfy predictive goals by largely avoiding predictive aspirations. Aaron Wildavsky's desire to use "inches of facts" to generate "miles of preferences" about politics has given way to the collection of facts, period.

A consequence of the focus on describing attitudes is a heavy reliance on the methodology of survey research, without an adequate acknowledgment of the drawbacks of such a method. This is well illustrated by Sarat's 1977 assessment of survey research on American legal culture. He identifies two benefits of survey research on legal culture; it can illustrate public thinking about law and the legal system; and it facilitates explaining and evaluating how the legal system performs.[30] These are balanced, in Sarat's view, by two difficulties; inadequate attention to the actual meaning and measurement of legal attitudes, and the challenge of understanding how attitudes and opinions influence the structure and substance of the legal system.[31] In addition to these issues is the "epistemic gap" Harry Eckstein describes between the ability to observe behavior and the inability to observe what underlies that behavior.

Recent assessments of scholarship on legal culture have been sharply critical, frequently citing the extent to which the concept of "legal culture" itself remains foggy.[32] In his article "The Concept of Legal Culture," for example, Roger Cotterrell critiques Friedman's work on legal culture, which he takes to be the most sustained effort to explore the concept in the sociology of law. According to Cotterrell, "the concept [of legal culture], as developed and applied in Friedman's work, lacks rigor and appears – in certain crucial respects – ultimately theoretically incoherent."[33] In an insightful review article of scholarship on legal culture, David Nelken acknowledges that "the sociological task of understanding and mapping the differences among legal cultures bristles with theoretical and methodological difficulties."[34] Both Cotterrell and Nelken think it important for research on legal culture to continue (Cotterrell suggests calling it legal ideology, though it is unlikely that such a change in terminology will lead to more conceptual clarity); neither has proposed a workable way to surmount the conceptual difficulties that have hindered study of legal culture.

It was during the peak of interest in legal culture in the United States, a peak that coincided with an era of social turbulence in the 1960s and 1970s, that the paradigm surrounding Japanese law and legal behavior took root. Academics within and outside of Japan were quick to realize that the Japanese case was conducive to the theories and methods of research on legal culture. Japan, at least in the United States, could be too easily stereotyped and overgeneralized. The impact of Ruth Benedict's *The Chrysanthemum and the Sword: Patterns of Japanese Culture* shows clearly how ready Americans were to accept overstated claims about Japanese culture.[35] Many Japanese were themselves receptive to broad-based cultural arguments, as postwar devastation yielded to an "economic miracle" that demanded an explanation. In that climate, a paradigmatic view of Japanese legal behavior emerged that has continued to form the borders of sociolegal research on Japan.

The claim that the Japanese are oriented toward groups and away from the individual, a central feature of the paradigm, is regularly asserted in both academic and popular writings. In his 1965 essay, "Japan: The Continuity of Modernization,"[36] Robert Ward claims that Japanese political culture is characterized by a strong sense of national unity, a preference of group over individual action, an emphasis on consensual decision making, and an expectation that the government will contribute to individual well-being. Harvard University's Susan Pharr, in her 1990 study of Japanese conflict, highlights the importance of deference to authority, hierarchy of social relations, avoidance of conflict, preference for consensus, compromise, social harmony, and a dislike of protest.[37] According to legal expert Koga Masayoshi, current Japanese law is premised on an ethic of individualism that lacks roots in Japanese society. "Even now," he wrote in 1977, "the ethos that impeded the appearance of individualism infiltrates our society."[38] A Western journalist encapsulates these stereotypes about individualism, writing that "it would be easier to get the entire population of Tokyo to wear matching outfits than to get any two randomly selected Americans to agree on pizza toppings."[39] Almost every primer on Japanese society, and even some on Japanese law and legal sociology, highlight the absence of individualism as an important fact of Japanese life and a key explanation of political and legal norms and practice.[40]

The perceived absence of individualism in Japan leads directly to a theory of rights that is shared by scholars of political and legal culture. Stated crudely, the theory holds that Japanese traditional values are hostile to individualism, and hostility to individualism translates into an inability to understand the meaning of individual "rights." Because rights are not understood or accepted they are infrequently asserted.[41] Pharr, for example, treats rights and rights assertion as a concept and behavior that does not conform to the ethos of Japanese political culture. She suggests that Japan's "particular traditions" have created a preference for renegotiation over appeals to rights. According to Pharr, while an "'official ideology' of egalitarianism" has begun to take hold, she concludes that in Japan, in contrast to the United States, "calls for individual rights . . . run contrary to prevailing norms, even today."[42] Her belief that "particular traditions" explain contemporary attitudes and behavior concerning law is consonant with the analysis of Japanese legal behavior provided by many scholars of legal culture.

First among Japanese sociologists of law to have devoted himself to the study of legal culture is Kawashima Takeyoshi, the most influential figure in postwar Japanese legal sociology.[43] Kawashima questioned the connection between the advanced capitalism of Western Europe, the system of modern law Japan imported from it during the Meiji era, and the lifestyle of contemporary Japanese.[44] He sought to account for a perceived anomaly of Japan's modernization, "the apparently contradictory combination of rapid industrialization and extremely few litigated cases and lawyers,"[45] by invoking traditional legal culture, which he said discouraged utilization of the legal system and would wither away as Japan came increasingly to resemble the West. Kawashima thus links contemporary legal attitudes and behavior to Japanese tradition and culture, and claims that the development of Japanese society will lead to a convergence with Western legal attitudes and behavior. According to Kawashima, "it is clear that the Japanese attitude toward law, right, and social order will continue to undergo changes in the direction of the patterns of Western society . . . when the traditional social structure becomes disorganized as the process of industrialization proceeds."[46]

Kawashima's work on Japanese legal culture and rights played a critical role in shaping the postwar paradigm about rights assertion as an unimportant and invisible element in Japan. The power of his analysis came from his use of modernization theory to explain the basis of Japanese legal behavior and to predict how it would change. In Japanese society, traditional and contemporary, Kawashima contends that people are obligated to perform many acts, and these are regarded as duties. A word for duty exists in Japanese (*gimu*), and it has been in use for many centuries. But there was no word for "rights" until the Meiji Restoration, Kawashima claims, because there was no demand – as he puts it, something like rights was never felt or understood. Even after the word *kenri* was introduced, he says that people did not like it because it was not proper Japanese. He cites with approval the words of Japanese history scholar George Sansom:

> So unfamiliar was the concept of the rights of the individual subject that in purely Japanese legal writings there is no term that closely corresponds to the word "rights" as expressing something that is due to a person and that he can claim; nor indeed did familiar speech include such a word in its vocabulary.[47]

According to Kawashima, Japan's development will be accompanied by the increasing importance of rights, as well as other elements of "modern" law, as the traditional legal culture is transformed. But that process will take time, and at the time of his writing there were only a few signs that it had started.

Still, during the Tokugawa period (1603–1868), well before he thinks the process of modernization had begun, Kawashima acknowledges that people possessed private land and houses, and therefore had a concept similar to rights. "In any society there exists some kind of property," he wrote, "and the notion of right existed in that sense and to that extent."[48] While Kawashima recognizes that the rules and legal procedures that control property required a rights-like concept, he denies that there was a general concept of rights in Japan.

His discussions of employment and finance posit a similar sense of rights. Kawashima claims that traditionally employers had control over employees, and employees had no power to assert rights. Nonetheless, without thinking about rights, workers believed that they could demand wages and appropriate work.[49] Much the same situation existed with regard to the borrowing and lending of money, in which he says there was no consciousness of rights but a sense of one's interests.

How can these seeming contradictions be reconciled? Clearly there cannot both be, and not be, a Japanese concept of rights. Most scholarship on rights in Japan has accepted Kawashima's basic claim about the lack of rights assertion in traditional Japan, and started from the premise that it is the central feature of legal culture and should be studied and explained. There has been some disagreement about the speed of change in the Japanese legal system, and some debate about to what extent, and whether, rights would ever become as prominent as in the West. But the bulk of work on Japanese legal culture has started from Kawashima's claim about the absence of rights, and sought to explain why it is so.

Such an approach fails to appreciate a different, and more sympathetic, reading of Kawashima. Kawashima uses a Western term "rights" (actually, the Japanese translation of that term, *kenri*) to evaluate Japanese legal culture. Although he concludes that both the word and the concept for rights are absent, in doing so he implicitly accepts rights as a legitimate measure of Japanese legal culture. Without examining the meaning of "rights" in Western European legal systems, Kawashima assumes there is a uniform and coherent conception of rights, one that does not (and could not) accurately describe Japan. If that is so, his argument can be reconceptualized as saying that there is a concept of rights in Japan different from the concept in the West, and the two must be distinguished. Given Japanese law's 2,000 year history, it would be remarkable if the rituals and rhetoric of rights were conceptually the same as Western legal systems. Kawashima may thus have been calling attention to the difference between rights in Japan and in what he considers "the West," rather than rejecting the possibility that there are rights-like concepts and attitudes in Japan. He is uncomfortable with referring to "rights" in Japan, because rights in Japan are not identical to rights elsewhere. Indeed, Kawashima's evidence could be inverted and turned into a description of Japanese rights. Identification with groups, the infrequency (compared to "the West") with which individuals *as* individuals formally assert themselves against the collectivity, the propensity to informally resolve disputes, and the power of apology as a remedy to the infringement of rights could then in part be understood as saying something about the nature of Japanese rights assertion – that rights in Japan often adhere to groups and are frequently asserted and resolved outside the formal legal system. Why this is so – in other words, saying something about what is distinctive and important about rights in Japan – would then become a central scholarly concern.

Kawashima instead denied that there was a concept of rights in

Japan before the influence of Western law, and posited an evolutionary model of the development of rights. Had he described rights-like concepts in Japan, hypothesized about their meaning, and focused his analysis on the sorts of factors that generate legal behavior, he may have avoided some of the ambiguity that characterizes his work, and subsequent interpretations of it. Instead, Kawashima's claim that there was no general concept of rights in Japan, and his developmental perspective on rights and the legal system have influenced a generation of Japanese legal sociologists.

The impact of Kawashima's approach is apparent in the work of Japan's most prominent sociolegal scholars. Rokumoto Kahei, Kawashima's student and successor to the legal sociology professorship at the University of Tokyo, attempts to stem what he perceives as a misunderstanding of Kawashima by analyzing the meaning of legal consciousness, *hō ishiki*, and its use as the standard by which to measure the "legal-ness" of Japanese society. In his influential treatise on legal sociology, Rokumoto devotes a lengthy chapter to the discussion of legal consciousness, where he defines and distinguishes between legal attitudes, legal knowledge, legal ideas, legal consciousness, and legal conceptions.[50] Rokumoto's central contention is that Kawashima was referring not to legal or rights consciousness, but to legal and rights conception (*hō kannen*), which he defined as follows: "The former [consciousness] refers to the knowledge, opinions, and evaluation of the existing legal system under specific conditions, while the latter [conception] refers to a conception of law 'as an abstract, ideal image.'"[51] According to Miyazawa Setsuo, a leading legal sociologist at Kōbe University, Rokumoto is suggesting that researchers should measure the general normative framework underlying opinions about contracts or litigiousness.[52] That goal, if successfully pursued, could generate insights about law and legal culture in Japan. But Rokumoto appears to have a somewhat different idea in mind. Rather than moving from the measure of opinions themselves, he appears to be suggesting that we pay attention to a different group of opinions; those about law as an ideal type rather than law in practice.

In one of Rokumoto's articles, for example, he uses a famous story about a Japanese judge to inquire about peoples' attitudes toward the law. After World War II, the story goes, there was not enough rice for the population. It was therefore rationed, and a black market quickly developed. As someone with influence and money, a certain Judge

Yamaguchi could have supplemented his ration. But the judge refused to break the law he was sworn to uphold. He ate only his fair share, his weight steadily declined, and he eventually starved.

The judge's travails were used by Rokumoto as a tool for studying Japanese legal culture. He surveyed 1,500 people and asked whether they thought the judge had acted correctly, what they would have done in his situation, and other questions. Based on that data, Rokumoto concluded that the legal character of the Japanese could be classified into three categories; indifferent, flexible, and strict.[53] The same case was used by Toshitani Nobuyoshi of Tokyo University's Institute of Social Science as evidence that Japanese legal culture has remained constant since Meiji, because surveys from 1947 and 1978 show that people consistently were critical of Judge Yamaguchi's behavior.[54]

In another study, Rokumoto interviewed eighty-five residents living near the University of Tokyo who had been involved in either a housing dispute or a car accident.[55] Few of the cases ended up in court; most were handled informally by people who specialized in settling such disputes. His conclusion, as summarized by Miyazawa, was that access to lawyers and legal specialists, "and hence to mobilize the formal legal system to one's advantage is unevenly distributed in society."[56]

Miyazawa Setsuo, in an insightful review of the literature on Japanese legal culture, concludes that "[S]ince Kawashima's works appeared, the dominant form of analysis of Japanese legal consciousness has been anecdotal," and points out that Kawashima's own analysis of legal culture was circular.[57] Miyazawa describes the most important forays into Japanese legal culture, and finds little of value. He calls the large, national surveys conducted in the 1970s and 1980s by the *Nippon Bunka Kaigi*, *Nihon Bengoshi Rengōkai*, and others "ambiguous" and "contradictory." Of Wada Yasuhiro's survey on dispute resolution in daily life,[58] he concludes that the research design was flawed and shed no light on "individual attitudes as explanatory variables for individual dispute behavior . . ."[59] Miyazawa finds the surveys on legal culture contain poor questions, obtain unreliable answers, and fail to explore what he thinks Rokumoto meant by "legal conceptions."[60]

Miyazawa's approach to research on Japanese legal culture comes from the work of Lawrence Friedman. He believes that legal culture should be analyzed at the individual and aggregate levels, which he distinguishes by calling the former "attitudes," the latter "culture." According to Miyazawa, "[T]he impact of culture on individual behavior has to be ascertained through analysis at the individual level." He seeks to do this by framing questions that address these different levels: "[W]hat would you do if you had problems with your neighbor," is a question included in a survey that Miyazawa says focuses on the aggregate level, whereas, "[I]s it acceptable for you to use the court to solve civil disputes," comes from a survey of individual attitudes.[61] It is impossible to distinguish between these levels, however, without starting from a set of assumptions, or at least hypotheses, about the meaning of culture. Is culture, for example, merely an aggregate of individuals, or is it something more? By accepting Friedman's problematic definition of legal culture, and not clarifying his own definition of culture, Miyazawa's analysis stalls. His interest in the question of how research on the individual level can be generalized to say something about the society is well placed, but he has not suggested a resolution or an escape.

Part of the problem with the study of Japanese legal culture is that it has been conducted primarily through opinion polls, questionnaires, and surveys.[62] Research focuses on what people think, or more accurately what they say they think, about the law. Japanese scholars are not unaware of the problems of such research. Miyazawa perceptively criticizes survey research on legal culture, and calls for "more thorough questionnaires" to test Kawashima's thesis.[63] Rokumoto also identifies the methodological difficulties of measuring legal culture.[64] These criticisms, while important reminders of the shortcomings of such research, have not led to an overhaul of research methods used to study Japanese legal culture. Moreover, many studies of legal culture in Japan equate law with litigation, so that advanced legal culture (or a high level of legal consciousness, as it is often put) is equated with an eagerness to litigate, and traditional legal culture (or a low level of legal consciousness) means dislike of litigation. With such a limited perspective on what constitutes law and law-related behavior, there is little chance that research on legal culture will explain the place and importance of law in Japanese society.

One Japanese scholar of legal culture who has undertaken a powerful critique of Kawashima is Ōki Masao. In *Nihonjin no Hō Gainen*, Ōki rejects what he sees as Kawashima's strong emphasis on Confucianism as the connection between pre-modern and contemporary legal culture, and questions Kawashima's most basic conclusions.[65] He confesses that he is tempted to accept Kawashima's image of Japanese legal character and culture, because it portrays an appealing, peace-loving, harmonious nation. Nonetheless, by eschewing survey research and turning to events in Japanese history that he believes Kawashima underemphasizes or ignores, Ōki concludes that Japan is a society rife with conflict and violence, imbued with law, and containing a concept of rights limited primarily by authority, not harmony.[66] Like the influential law professor Noda Yoshiyuki, Ōki stresses the enduring importance of geography, history, and the national character of the Japanese in creating this legal culture.[67]

Ōki accepts Kawashima's emphasis on the importance of Japanese legal culture and the need to analyze Japanese legal behavior. In addition, he embraces the assumption that there is a Western meaning of "rights" that can be used as a yardstick of legal culture. He departs significantly from Kawashima's focus on duty and harmony, however, and instead accents the importance of rights and conflict in the past and present of Japanese legal culture. By looking at particular historical events and analyzing their importance, rather than engaging in quantitative research, Ōki observes a radically different reality than does Kawashima. Although his explanation of that reality remains limited to generalizations about national character and geography, it is his description of a nation bursting with rights and conflict that marks a major departure from the paradigm established by Kawashima.

A number of positive lessons for the study of Japanese legal culture can be found in Ōki's approach. Perhaps the most important is his use of history to argue that Japanese legal culture is something that includes not only litigation, but a broad range of social interactions. By turning to history, and examining social conflict, he significantly broadens the territory of work on legal culture. Other scholars, like Mizubayashi Takeshi[68] and Kumagai Kaisaku[69] have also taken historical approaches, but have not shared Ōki's interest in studying conflict.

Ōki's historical work points toward what has become both the most illuminating and the most stifling debate about Japanese legal behavior: the divide between those like Kawashima who believe culture is the primary cause of behavior, and others who point to structural explanations of behavior. As in many other areas of social science research, parties to this debate regularly invoke either/or, culture/structure explanations. Not surprisingly, when academic theorizing is excoriated and we consider how culture and structure are used in daily speech, we discover a sharp division that fuels the academic debate. In common parlance, culture refers to the content of a civilization, its arts, literature, and customs. It is the inside, the furnishings that define a group of people. But structure refers to framework, the cold beams and girders of a society. Structure is scaffold and shell, whereas culture is custom and civilization.

John Haley, an expert on Japanese and comparative law, was among the first to invoke structural/institutional explanations of Japanese disputing behavior. According to Haley, Kawashima perpetuated the myth that the Japanese have "an unusual and deeply rooted cultural preference for informal, mediated settlement of private disputes and a corollary aversion to the formal mechanisms of judicial adjudication."[70] In contrast, Haley writes:

> Is there, then, any evidence of an unusual Japanese aversion toward lawsuits that leads a party to accept a settlement less beneficial than one he anticipates he would gain by suing? The answer, I believe, is negative. What little evidence there is suggests the opposite – that most Japanese are willing to go to court in such circumstances.[71]

Japanese do not sue, he claims, because of "the inability of the formal legal system to provide effective sanctions."[72] Were institutions arranged differently, and going to court rewarded more lucratively, litigation rates would rapidly increase.

Like Kawashima, Haley equates law with litigation, and concentrates on when, why, and how effectively disputes are resolved through lawsuits. Moreover, like Kawashima's reliance on the overbroad term "culture," Haley's use of "institutional arrangements" is deeply ambiguous. Miyazawa writes that he, like many Japanese scholars, understands Haley to be saying that institutional barriers "deliberately introduced by the elite" had a more substantial impact on legal behavior than culture.[73] But whether Haley is actually saying that institutions are *deliberately* manipulated, and how such conscious manipulation can occur, is unclear. The most serious problem is that Haley equivocates about what he means by "institutional." On the one hand, he uses institutions to mean organizations like courts, government ministries, and the Diet. On the other, he writes of access to courts, the number of judges and attorneys, and the limited range of remedies as institutions. How these different sorts of institutions are manipulated by the elite, how the elite comes to be separate from and in control of mass political and legal culture, and what the specific mechanisms are of elite manipulation remain obscure in his argument.

In *Authority Without Power*, Haley supplemented his claims about Japanese legal behavior by distinguishing between customary and institutionalized legal orders. Customary legal orders have informal legal rules; institutionalized orders are formal. Haley writes:

> Nearly all contemporary societies have institutionalized legal orders in which legislatures, administrative bodies, and courts are the basic institutions for lawmaking and law enforcing ... The nature of order depends only in part on the institutional arrangements for both law-making and law enforcing – the traditional concern of lawyers and political scientists. Equally relevant are "cultural" factors: the habits that constitute custom and the values that both shape and sustain consensus and legitimacy.[74]

This claim makes no mention of deliberate intervention by state actors; in contrast, it pays homage to the cultural explanations for-warded by Kawashima. As in his earlier work, however, Haley con-tinues to maintain a divide between institutions and culture, as if they are both important but unrelated influences on law. And like Kawashima he takes as his starting point the need to explain the infrequency of litigation in Japan, rather than addressing the import-ant features, like rights, that characterize the invocation of law.

The false dichotomy between culture and structure, coupled with an overidentification of law with litigation, has distorted much of the literature on law in Japan. It has retarded a better understanding of legal phenomena and detracted from more fruitful avenues of research by treating culture and structure as mutually exclusive categories which alone can explain why Japanese individuals think and act in particular ways about law. With little reflection on the cultural roots of social structures, on institutional cultures, or on the many ways in which culture and structure are intertwined, too many observers of Japanese law have followed in the wake of social scientists in espous-ing one view to the exclusion of the other. Thompson, Ellis, and Wildavsky, in creating a typology for understanding political culture, state:

> A recurring debate among social scientists is whether institutional structures cause culture (defined as values and beliefs, i.e., mental products) or culture causes structure ... we see no reason to choose between social institutions and cultural biases. Values and social rela-tions are mutually interdependent and reinforcing ... Asking which comes first or which should be given causal priority is a nonstarter.[75]

Similarly, Robert Putnam, discussing institutional performance in Italy, has written:

> Social scientists have long debated what causes what – culture or structure . . . Quite apart from the ambiguity of "culture" and "structure," however, this debate is somewhat misplaced. Most dispassionate commentators recognize that attitudes and practices constitute a mutually reinforcing equilibrium . . . Linear causal questions must not crowd out equilibrium analysis. In this context, the culture-vs.-structure, chicken-and-egg debate is ultimately fruitless.[76]

While scholarship on Japanese law and legal behavior has generally been pursued by "dispassionate commentators," many continue to engage in dichotomous thinking. Instead, they must start to conceive of Japanese legal practices as neither solely the product of culture nor structure, but as part of a complex web of cultural and structural influences.

"All of us in social science are looking for bedrock," Aaron Wildavsky writes.[77] Several scholars of Japanese law have sought "bedrock" by moving beyond dichotomous thinking about culture and structure. Frank Upham, for example, focuses on litigation in four contentious cases – environmental pollution, women's employment, social discrimination, and industrial policy. As he puts it, the theme of his work is

> the struggle for control of the process of social change, which entails control over the nature and course of social conflict, which in turn demands legal rules and institutions that allow informality in the process of conflict resolution and that encourage dependence on the government as a central player in that process.[78]

Upham seeks to explain the relationship between litigation and the broader issues of social change by charting the process and substance of the resolution of particular disputes. In so doing, he makes clear the centrality of law in the Japanese political system, highlights the importance of the state as a political and legal actor, and argues that courts and other legal institutions are powerful agents of social change. At the same time, he examines practices and procedures that have both institutional and cultural resonance. He is not bogged down by the argument about whether Japanese legal behavior is best understood from a cultural or institutional perspective. He assumes that both are important, and marshals evidence from each.

Mark Ramseyer takes a different approach. Whereas Upham concludes that law, society, and their interaction in Japan are fundament-

ally different than in the West (his discussion of law using the sub-
headings, "two Western models" and "a Japanese model," makes that
evident), Ramseyer sees deep similarities in the underlying systems,
and believes that "in crucial ways Japanese and American follow the
same internal logic."[79] His work takes a law and economics/rational
choice approach, arguing that legal and political behavior are to some
extent explicable as the actions of rational actors whose basic norm
is to maximize their interests.

With regard to dispute resolution, for example, Ramseyer takes up
one of Haley's points, that the Japanese don't sue because suing
doesn't pay. He argues that "*if* there be any widely accepted nonlitigi-
ous ethic in Japan, its dictates coincide with wealth-maximizing
ploys."[80] Ramseyer emphasizes the predictability of litigation in Japan
as a chief reason that litigants have the ability to determine the likely
outcome of a dispute and decide whether or not to go to court. Elsewhere in his work, particularly in *Odd Markets in Japanese History*,
Ramseyer makes a compelling case for the power and importance of
law and rights in Japan. He carefully examines historical data concerning property rights to land and water, and labor markets for children, cotton spinners, sex workers. He then uses the data to argue
that in each situation people were able to exert a high degree of
control over their working conditions, and courts clearly and forcefully defined and enforced rights. Ramseyer does not dwell on whether
or not there are such things as "rights" in Japan; he does not dismiss
the importance of culture. Instead, he makes use of a vast assortment
of historical sources to make a case for the relationship between
Japanese economic development and the legal system.[81]

The fruitful study of rights in Japan requires a rejection of dichotomous culture/structure approaches. Rights cannot be dismissed as
either inconsistent with the cultural norms of Japan, or outside the
realm of Japanese thought and experience. Rights are not merely what
courts say they are; nor are they reducible to discrete interests that
are asserted by parties and balanced by judges in order to resolve
disputes. Rights are part of a complex legal, political, and social equa-
tion in which they are asserted as a way to unify and mobilize groups.
They are means as well as ends, powerful rhetorical tools as well as
pristine constitutional foundations. They have a long and complicated
history in Japan. It is time to reconsider the importance of rights in
the study of Japanese law and society.

CONCLUSION

The two anecdotes described at the beginning of this book – the apartment rental and automobile accident – both concern conflicts between individuals. The narratives that make up the body of this text, however, discuss conflicts between groups of individuals, and in both cases the conflicts implicate large actors like the Ministry of Health and Welfare, medical associations, pharmaceutical companies, and hospitals. That fact is likely to have a number of consequences; people everywhere speak and feel differently about "the state" or "the company" than they do about their neighbors, and their decisions about which grievances are worth pursuing, and how to frame them, will reflect those differences. In examining the assertion of rights, therefore, it is important to keep in mind who is doing the asserting, about what, and against whom.

The distinction between private, one-on-one conflict, and more public, policy-oriented disputes suggests one important difference between the way in which rights talk is deployed in Japan. Rights talk in Japan appears most likely to be used in conflicts where there is more than one individual who believes s/he is aggrieved. Because the cultural myths about rights powerfully suggests that asserting rights is a sign of selfishness and conceit, people are understandably reluctant to individually and in isolation assert their rights. Asserting the primacy of individual over collective interests must therefore be done with caution. Most often, rights are asserted on behalf of groups, once people with similar concerns are united. Rights assertion itself is one way to create a group of litigants; until there is a critical mass, however, the public, insistent assertion of rights is unlikely. That, at least, is one hypothesis. It would require the examination of a wide range of cases to generate sufficient empirical support for such a claim.

My examination of conflicts over AIDS policy and the definition of death suggests a number of other conclusions about the study of rights in Japan. While the cases I have presented are both in the realm of heath care, there is no reason to think that the assertion of rights is limited to cases in which some aspect of the medical system is in dispute. It would not be difficult to examine a number of other prominent areas of conflict – environmental pollution, the Burakumin (Japan's "outcaste" group), and women, for example – as examples of how different groups have used rights as political resources in their quest for social change.[82] When the study of rights in Japan is taken from its jurisprudential pedestal and made into the focus of political and sociological inquiry, the problem will quickly become how to limit hyperbole about the power of rights in Japan. The question of whether or not they exist will rapidly cease to be interesting.

Why is it that some specialists and virtually all non-specialists of Japanese law have so far failed to embrace an approach to Japanese conflict that takes rights assertion as central? I can only speculate that it is for the same reason that the number of English-language books about Japanese flower arranging, or gardens, or even tattoos, may exceed the number of books about Japanese law. An interest in Japan as a "foreign" culture, the other, what Edward Said describes as Orientalism, has long dominated thinking about Japan. Even at the end of the twentieth century, there are only a handful of experts on Japanese law in the United States who are oriented toward sociolegal study.[83]

Still, only a severe case of hubris could allow me to believe that after decades of legal scholarship by Japanese and Americans, I am the first to discover the importance of rights in Japan. In fact, the truth is much the opposite. Throughout this book, I have noted the work of others that has pointed me in the direction of highlighting the rituals of rights in Japan. Some such work takes for granted what I have labored to explain – that rights assertion in Japan has a long history and a vivid present. Yet even that work almost always limits its scope by equating law with litigation, and none of it has used contemporary policy studies to illustrate the role of rights talk in conflict, nor has it integrated a sociolegal inquiry with both historical analysis and contemporary material. Nonetheless, it is only fair to acknowledge that my claims about the importance of rights assertion in Japan may be more of a surprise to social scientists and non-Japan experts than to the few legal scholars who specialize in Japan.

Studying rights in Japan may also be a refreshing way to think anew about rights in the United States. One of the most compelling reasons to research other legal and social systems is that it opens up a new window onto one's own system. While many Americans are accustomed to thinking about rights and duties as closely linked, for example, various historical conflicts in Japan are thought to have implicated duties but not rights.[84] Western scholars raised on Hohfeld's conception of rights may be able to use such observations

164

about Japan to rethink their beliefs and assumptions about the relationship between rights and duties.

To sum up the message of this book, imagine what would happen if the great great grandson of Alexis de Tocqueville were to turn his gaze on Japan and write a follow-up to the masterwork *Democracy in America*. Clearly, his book would describe the extraordinary power of the Liberal Democratic Party, the powerful links between government and industry, the strength of the agricultural cooperatives, and the proliferation of traditional family businesses in even the most developed and glittering cities. He would note that almost all public servants in Japan are legally trained, as are a great many corporate managers. If he visited the Ministry of Finance, he would discover that it is filled with graduates of Japan's most competitive educational institution, the University of Tokyo's Faculty of Law,[85] as are other elite ministries. He would describe how Japanese legal education looks much like legal education in Germany and other civil law countries; while law graduates are not trained as practitioners, they are taught to read codes, study cases, and become comfortable with the specialized language of the legal profession. And he would learn that while people kept telling him that harmony and consensus were primary social values, they would also inform him about a broad array of conflict. Finally, he would note that when issues really mattered to people, they would band together, say that they had a "right" to something, and engage in a vocal and protracted battle. In Japan, he might say, rights really do matter. After all, the Japanese vigorously assert them in complex and myriad ways.

ENDNOTES

1 Reconsidering rights in Japanese law and society

1. See, for example, Kawashima Takeyoshi, *Nihonjin no Hō Ishiki*, Tokyo: Iwanami, 1967. The historical and contemporary debate over rights in Korea is similar to that in Japan. In *Human Rights in Korea: Historical and Policy Perspectives* (Cambridge, MA: Harvard University Press, 1991), William Shaw writes that "it is difficult to understand why residual Confucianism is a barrier to human rights, but has not constrained rapid industrial growth, world-class corporate conglomerates complete with 12-hour working days for executives, modern urbanization, government by military elites, or other decidedly un-Confucian practices." Other contributors to that volume describe the influence of German and Anglo-American legal thought on the Korean debate over rights, and several emphasize the impact of Japanese legal ideas, as well as Japanese colonial rule, upon the development of rights in Korea. The active role of the Korean state in suppressing the development of rights in the late nineteenth century is also discussed.

2. Karel van Wolferen, *The Enigma of Japanese Power*, New York: Alfred A. Knopf, Inc., 1989, 211.

3. Susan Pharr, *Losing Face: Status Politics in Japan*, Berkeley, CA: University of California Press, 1990, 27.

4. Kawashima, *Nihonjin no Hō Ishiki*.

5. Koga Masayoshi, "Kenri Ishiki ni Tsuite," *Hanrei Taimuzu (Bessatsu)* 3, 1977, 4–21.

6. Arthur Taylor von Mehren, ed., *Law in Japan: The Legal Order in a Changing Society*, Cambridge, MA: Harvard University Press, 1963, 423.

7. Takayanagi Kenzō, "A Century of Innovation: The Development of Japanese Law, 1868–1961," in von Mehren, *Law in Japan*, 39.

8. Leon Kass, "Is There a Right to Die," *Hastings Center Report*, January/February 1993, 34–43, 34.

9. Mary Ann Glendon, *Rights Talk: The Impoverishment of Political Discourse*, New York: The Free Press, 1991, 9, 107.
10. Michael W. McCann, *Rights at Work: Pay Equity Reform and the Politics of Legal Mobilization*, Chicago: University of Chicago Press, 1994; Stewart Scheingold, *The Politics of Rights: Lawyers, Public Policy, and Political Change*, New Haven, CT: Yale University Press, 1974.
11. R. Shep Melnick, "Separation of Powers and the Strategy of Rights: The Expansion of Special Education," 23–46, in Marc K. Landy and Martin A. Levin, eds., *The New Politics of Public Policy*, Baltimore, Johns Hopkins University Press, 1995, 25.
12. Inoue Tatsuo, "The Poverty of Rights-Blind Communality: Looking Through the Window of Japan," *Brigham Young University Law Review*, 1993, 518.
13. *Ibid.*
14. See, for example, Robert C. Ellickson, *Order Without Law: How Neighbors Settle Disputes*, Cambridge, MA: Harvard University Press, 1991 (where his subjects "apply informal norms, rather than formal legal rules, to resolve most of the issues that arise among them" (p. 1)); M. P. Baumgartner, "On the Overlegalized Conception of Modern Society," *Contemporary Sociology* 22 (3), 1993 ("research (contesting the unique importance of law") consistently has found that people in such places as the contemporary United States invoke law only infrequently and instead rely much more upon non-legal strategies of conflict management" (336–337)); Carol J. Greenhouse, *Praying for Justice: Faith, Order, and Community in an American Town*, Ithaca, NY: Cornell University Press, 1986, passim; Laura Nader, "A Litigious People?" *Law and Society Review* 22 (5), 1017–1022, 1988 (writing in her review of Greenhouse that she offers a picture of "Americans who not only avoid legal action but who have even developed a set of injunctions against conflict and the voicing of interpersonal disputes"); Carol J. Greenhouse, Barbara Yngvesson, and David M. Engel, *Law and Community in Three American Towns*, Ithaca, NY: Cornell University Press, 1994, passim; Robert L. Nelson, "Ideology, Scholarship, and Sociolegal Change: Lessons from Galanter and the 'Litigation Crisis,' " *Law and Society Review* 21 (5), 1998, 677–693, passim; Marc Galanter, "Reading the Landscape of Disputes: What We Know and Don't Know (and Think We Know) about Our Allegedly Contentious and Litigious Society," *UCLA Law Review*, 31, 1983, passim; David Engel, "The Oven Bird's Song: Insiders, Outsiders, and Personal Injuries in an American Community," *Law and Society Review* 18, 1984, passim.
15. Scheingold, in *The Politics of Rights*, provides an interesting account of the myth of rights in the United States.
16. Carol J. Greenhouse, "Interpreting American Litigiousness," in June Starr and Jane F. Collier, eds., *History and Power in the Study of Law*, Ithaca, NY: Cornell University Press, 1989, 252–273, 252.
17. John Owen Haley, "The Myth of the Reluctant Litigant," *Journal of Japanese Studies* 4, 1978, 359.

18. The small group of American academics who are experts on Japanese law, numbering fewer than twenty, have mounted an attack on this view over the past decade. Their work has promoted the idea that law in Japan, long seen as irrelevant by political scientists, sociologists, and non-Japan specialist legal academics, is indeed important. See, for example, Frank Upham, *Law and Social Change in Postwar Japan*, Cambridge, MA: Harvard University Press, 1987, which argues that an understanding of law is essential to the understanding of postwar Japanese social conflict, and J. Mark Ramseyer and Minoru Nakazato, "The Rational Litigant: Settlement Amounts and Verdict Rates in Japan," *Journal of Legal Studies* 18, 1989, 263, which argues that in cases of fatal traffic accidents, "families of the victims assert their legal rights" (289). Such reappraisals of law in Japan, while intellectually powerful, have had a limited impact upon legal comparativists, social scientists, and others, who continue to view Japan as devoid of law and rights.
19. "Subway Stations Provide Little Relief," *Asahi Evening News*, April 20, 1991, 5.
20. "Korean urges 'Furigana' on Registry," *The Japan Times*, September 25, 1992, 2.
21. Nagoya Satoru, "Left Wing Rips Bid to Curb Loudspeakers," *The Japan Times*, May 26, 1992, 3.
22. Scheingold, *The Politics of Rights*, passim.
23. David J. Rothman, "Three Views of History: View the First," *Hastings Center Report*, Special Supplement, November–December 1993, S11–S12.
24. Ibid., S12.
25. McCann, *Rights at Work*.
26. Miyoshi Masao, *Off Center: Power and Culture Relations between Japan and the United States*, Cambridge, MA: Harvard University Press, 1991, 17.
27. Stephen R. Reed, *Making Common Sense of Japan*, Pittsburgh, PA: University of Pittsburgh Press, 1993, 6, 24.
28. See, for example, Chalmers Johnson, *Japan: Who Governs*, New York: W.W. Norton & Company, 1995.
29. Peter Dale, *The Myth of Japanese Uniqueness*, New York: St. Martin's Press, 1986.
30. There are particular hazards for an American studying rights in Japan, since the differences between Japanese and American practices are far more acute than those between Japan and most European jurisdictions. From a German legal scholar's perspective, for example, it must seem obvious that many basic aspects of the Japanese legal system are perfectly in line with "normal" practices.
31. Paul Bohannan, *Justice and Judgment Among the Tiv*, London: Oxford University Press for the African Institute, 1957.
32. Ibid., 104.
33. Max Gluckman, *The Ideas in Barotse Jurisprudence*, quoted in J. C. Smith, "The Unique Nature of the Concepts of Western Law," *The Canadian Bar Review* 46 (2), May 1968, 9.

34. Max Gluckman, "Natural Justice in Africa," in Csaba Varga, ed., *Comparative Legal Cultures*, New York: New York University Press, 1992, 191.
35. Ibid., 192.
36. Mary Ann Glendon, *Abortion and Divorce in Western Law*, Cambridge, MA: Harvard University Press, 1987, 3.
37. Ibid., 4.
38. Reinhard Bendix, *Nation-Building and Citizenship: Studies in Our Changing Social Order*, Berkeley, CA: University of California Press, 1964, 2.
39. Chalmers Johnson, "Trade, Revisionism, and the Future of Japanese-American Relations," 105–136, in Yamamura Kozo, ed., *Japan's Economic Structure: Should it Change?*, Society for Japanese Studies, 1990, 119.

2 Rights in Japanese history

1. The complex relationship between peasants and proprietors with regard to land use, occupancy, and profit in the eleventh and twelfth centuries, for example, was based on an interlocking group of privileges and obligations that would be called rights in a Western context. The same is true, during the same period, of interests in land that entitled the bearers (non-peasants of various social positions) to income. These were negotiated, disputed, and litigated through the highly developed Kamakura legal system. Even peasants had definable, legitimate expectations, which proprietors had an obligation to grant. See, for example, Carl Steenstrup, *A History of Law in Japan Until 1868*, New York: E. J. Brill, 1991, 66–70.
2. Maeda Masaharu, "Kenri to Kenri Kakusho," *Hō to Seiji* 25 (3–4), 1975, 347–86; Yanabu Akira, *Honyakugo Seiritsu Jijyō*, Tokyo: Iwanami Shoten, 1982.
3. John O. Haley, in *Authority Without Power: Law and the Japanese Paradox*, New York: Oxford University Press, 1991, discusses this (69). Two other books about the translation of Western words into Japanese during the Meiji era are Saitō Tsuyoshi, *Meiji no Kotoba*, Tokyo: Kōdansha, 1977, and Yanabu Akira, *Honyaku no Shisō: Shizen to Nature*, Tokyo: Heibunsha, 1977.
4. Carmine Blacker, *The Japanese Enlightenment: A Study of the Writings of Fukuzawa Yūkichi*, Cambridge: Cambridge University Press, 1964, 104–105.
5. Donald Calman, *The Nature and Origins of Japanese Imperialism*, New York: Routledge, 1992, 272–273.
6. Frans B. Verwayen, "Early Transplantations of Dutch Law Texts," Paper presented at the Japan–Netherlands Institute, November 16, 1992, 1–3.
7. Ibid., 11–12.
8. Yanabu, *Honyakugo Seiritsu Jijyō*, 152–153.
9. Calman, *Japanese Enlightenment*, 272–274.
10. For a more detailed discussion of the etymology discussed in the following paragraphs, see Noda Yoshiyuki, "Kenri to yū Kotoba no Imi ni

Tsuite," *Gakushūin Daigaku Hōgakubu Kenkyūbu Kenkyū Nempō* 14, 1979, 23–24.

11. Maeda, "Kenri to Kenri Kakusho," 347–386.

12. Suzuki Shōji, *Nihon Kango to Chūgoku*, Tokyo: Chūkoshinshō 626, 1981, Ch. 1, "'Sanken Bunritsu' ni Matsuwaru Yogo: 'Kenri' to 'Gimu'," 45, compares the unfortunate identification of rights, power, and interest in traditional China with the Japanese understanding of these concepts.

13. Some scholars seem to assume the lack of understanding of rights in Japan, and focus their work exclusively on exploring rights in Western texts. For example, Ōta Tomoyuki, "Kenri to yū Kotoba no Imi ni Tsuite," *Shisō* 5, (479), 1964, 25–35, seeks to better understand the meaning of rights but makes no reference to the Japanese experience.

14. Mary Ann Glendon, *Rights Talk: The Impoverishment of Political Discourse*, New York: The Free Press, 1991, xii.

15. Mark Ramseyer, *Odd Markets in Japanese History: Law and Economic Growth*, New York: Cambridge University Press, 1996, 163.

16. Thomas Kierstead, *The Geography of Power in Medieval Japan*, Princeton, NJ: Princeton University Press, 1992, 94–95.

17. Ibid.

18. Ibid., 95; John W. Hall, *Japan from Prehistory to Modern Times*, New York: Dell Publishing Co., 1970, 71, cited in Kierstead, 150, n.76.

19. Gregory Vlastos, "Justice and Equality," 41–76, in Jeremy Waldron, *Theories of Rights*, New York: Oxford University Press, 1984, 47. Also see John Dunn, "Rights and Political Conflict," in Larry Gostin, ed., *Civil Liberties in Conflict*, New York: Routledge, 1988, 21–38.

20. Kierstead, *Geography of Power*, at 126–7. See also Ishii Ryōsuke, *Nihon Hōseishi Gaisetsu*, Tokyo: Kōfundō, 2d ed. 1949, 302–305; Jeffery P. Mass, *The Development of Kamakura Rule*, Stanford, CA: Stanford University Press, 1979, at xv, 131–142; John Carey Hall, *Japanese Feudal Law*, Washington, DC, University Publications of America, 1979, 71.

21. Takayanagi Kenzo, "A Century of Innovation: The Development of Japanese Law, 1868–1961," 5–40, in Arthur Taylor von Mehren, ed., *Law in Japan: The Legal Order in a Changing Society*, Cambridge, MA: Harvard University Press, 1963, 24.

22. Ōki Masao, *Nihonjin no Hō Kannen*, Tokyo: Tokyo University Press, 1983, 159, says the Bukeiho of the Kamakura period was the source of the rule of law in Japan, and significantly more accessible than earlier legal codes. See also Kierstead, *Geography of Power*, who cites Satō Shin'-ichi and Ikeuchi Yoshisuke, comps., *Chūsei Hōsei Shiryōshū*, vol. I, *Kamakura Bakufu Hō*, vol. II, *Muromachi Bakufu Hō*, Tokyo: Iwanami Shoten, 1955–1957. Translation of Muromachi laws are available in Kenneth Grossberg, ed. and trans., *The Laws of the Muromachi Bakufu*, Tokyo: Monumenta Nipponica, 1981.

23. Haley, *Authority*, 42.

24. Ibid., 44–5, quoting John Carey Hall.

25. Kawashima Takeyoshi, "The Status of the Individual in the Notion of Law, Right, and Social Order in Japan," in Charles A. Moore, ed., *The*

Japanese Mind: Essentials of Japanese Philosophy, Honolulu: East-West Center Press, University of Hawaii Press, 1967, 265.

26. Carl Steenstrup, "The Legal System of Japan at the End of the Kamakura Period from the Litigants' Point of View," 73–109, in Brian E. McKnight, ed., *Law and the State in Traditional East Asia*, Honolulu: University of Hawaii Press, 1987, 98.

27. One interesting discussion of peasant revolts is Namba Nobuo, "Hyakushō Ikki no Hō Ishiki," in Aoki Michio, ed., *Ikki*, vol. IV, of *Seikatsu, Bunka, Shisō*, Tokyo: University of Tokyo Press, 1981, 43–88.

28. Quoted in E. H. Norman, *Origins of the Modern Japanese State*, John W. Dower ed., New York: Pantheon, 1975, 326.

29. Herbert Bix, *Peasant Protest in Japan, 1590–1884*, New Haven, CT: Yale University Press, 1986, citing Yokoyama Toshio, *Hyakushō Ikki to Gimin Denshō*, Tokyo, 1977.

30. Roger W. Bowen, *Rebellion and Democracy in Meiji Japan: A Study of Commoners in the Popular Rights Movement*, Berkeley, CA: University of California Press, 1980, 72, citing Aoki Kōji, *Hyakushō Ikki no Sōgō Nempyō*, Tokyo, Sanichi Shobo, 1971.

31. Anne Walthall, *Social Protest and Popular Culture in Eighteenth-Century Japan*, Tucson, AZ: University of Arizona Press, 1986, provides an account of some of them.

32. See, for example, Stephen Vlastos, "*Yonaoshi* in Aizu," in Najita Tetsuo and J. Victor Koschmann, eds., *Conflict in Modern Japanese History: The Neglected Tradition*, Princeton, NJ: Princeton University Press, 1982.

33. Hashimoto Mitsuru, "The Social Background of Peasant Uprisings in Tokugawa Japan," 163, in Najita and Koschmann, *Conflict*.

34. Vlastos at 175–6, in Najita and Koschmann, *Conflict*.

35. Bowen, *Rebellion*, 180–1. On Ogyū Sorai, see Harry Harootunian, "Ideology as Conflict," 31–36, in Najita and Koschmann, eds., *Conflict*. Ōki, *Nihonjin no Hō Kannen*, 13–16 argues that comparative law scholars consistently err by lumping Japan with China under the rubric of Asian law, and finding in both of them a strong element of Confucianism that results in a reluctance to litigate or use the courts, an emphasis on harmony, etc. He believes that the influence of Confucianism in Japan was always mixed with other elements (for example, the many non-Confucian rules in the *Ritsuryō*), and that also in China the importance of Confucianism has waned.

36. Irwin Scheiner, "Benevolent Lords and Honorable Peasants: Rebellion and Peasant Consciousness in Tokugawa Japan," in Najita Tetsuo and Irwin Scheiner, *Japanese Thought in the Tokugawa Period*, Chicago: University of Chicago Press, 1978, 52.

37. Takayanagi, "A Century of Innovation," 24.

38. Thomas C. Smith, *The Agrarian Origins of Modern Japan*, Stanford, CA: Stanford University Press, 1959, 183.

39. Mark Ramseyer, "Water Law in Imperial Japan: Public Goods, Private Claims, and Legal Convergence," *The Journal of Legal Studies*, January 1989, 51–77.

40. Bowen, *Rebellion*, 119.
41. Ibid., 177.
42. Ibid., 117–118.
43. Ibid.
44. Traditions of protest and civil unrest inherited from the Tokugawa and Meiji continued as a significant feature of Taishō Japan (Among the many books on this period are Robert Scalapino, *Democracy and the Party Movement in Prewar Japan*, Berkeley, CA: University of California Press, 1967; Ike Nobutaka, *The Beginnings of Political Democracy in Japan*, New York: Greenwood Press, 1969; Bernard S. Silberman and H. D. Harootunian, eds., *Japan In Crisis: Essays on Taishō Democracy*, Princeton, NJ: Princeton University Press, 1974; and J. Thomas Rimer, ed., *Culture and Identity: Japanese Intellectuals During the Interwar Years*, Princeton, NJ: Princeton University Press, 1990). The immediate cause was the price of rice, which farmers claimed was unconscionably low. Workers also carried forward the legacy of the PRM. Many had previously worked as farmers, and left to work in urban companies. Laws protecting workers' rights were in existence; the perception that such laws did not reduce the exploitation of workers made them a focus of protest (see Koga, "Kenri," 18).

As with peasant revolts and Tokugawa movements, Taishō period protests can be interpreted as a general demand for broader democratic rights. An editorial from the *1918 Tōyō Keizai Shinpō* newspaper refuted the government's claim that the people's hearts needed to be quieted by discipline: "How about universal suffrage? This, too, is something the people's hearts desire . . . How about legally recognizing the right of labor organization? Something else desired by public sentiment" (Michael Lewis, *Rioters and Citizens: Mass Protest in Imperial Japan*, Berkeley, CA: University of California Press, 1990, 133). Not content to rely on the benevolence of their leaders, rioters demanded the rights of factory workers, women, burakumin, and farmers. "All of these movements had existed in some form before," writes historian Michael Lewis, "but they had become largely inactive under the weight of bureaucratic politics and restrictive police laws . . . " (Lewis, 248–250). Social movements were ultimately unsuccessful by most concrete measures, not because they used non-Japanese concepts like rights, but because advocating for rights and freedom posed a threat to the ideology and stability of the state.
45. See Bix, *Peasant Protest*, passim.
46. Bowen, *Rebellion*, 109, citing Ike, *Political Democracy*, 67.
47. W. G. Beasley, *The Rise of Modern Japan*, London: Weidenfeld and Nicolson, 1990, 76.
48. P. Duus, *The Rise of Modern Japan*, Boston: Houghton Mifflin Co., 1976.
49. Calman, *Japanese Imperialism*, 98, 102, 254, citing Matano Hansuke, *Etō Nampaku*, Hara Shobō, 1914, 2nd ed. 1968, 106ff.
50. Calman, *Japanese Imperialism*, 254.
51. Fukuzawa Yūkichi, *An Outline of a Theory of Civilization*, trans. David A.

Dilworth and G. Cameron Hurst, Tokyo: Sophia University, 1973, 184.

52. Hane Mikiso, "The Movement for Liberty and Popular Rights," 95, in Harry Wray and Hilary Conroy, eds., *Japan Examined: Perspectives on Modern Japanese History*, Honolulu: University of Hawaii Press, 1983.
53. Blacker, *Japanese Enlightenment*, 114.
54. Calman, *Japanese Imperialism*, 269–70.
55. An interesting series of articles that examines the PRM and its relationship to contemporary social movements is Tanaka Shigeaki, "Shimin Undō ni Okeru Kenri to Saiban: Sono Hōteki Senryaku no Haikei to Igi o Megutte," *Minshō Hō Zasshi* 76, 1977, 633 (part 1); 76, 1977, 779 (part 2); 77, 1977, 161 (part 3); 77, 1977, 321 (part 4).
56. Fukuzawa, *An Outline*, 184.
57. Hane, "The Movement," 90.
58. Duus, *Modern Japan*, 96. See also James L. Huffman, "The Popular Rights Debate: Political or Ideological?," 98–103, in Harry Wray and Hilary Conroy, eds., *Japan Examined: Perspectives on Modern Japanese History*, Honolulu: University of Hawaii Press, 1983.
59. Irokawa Daikichi, in Bowen, *Rebellion*, 201. Maeda points out that even though the PRM advocated democratic rights, many of its leaders were disdainful of Western culture.
60. Beasley, *Modern Japan*, 76.
61. Bowen, *Rebellion*, 116.
62. Duus, *Modern Japan*, 102.
63. Koga, "Kenri Ishiki ni Tsuite," 8–9.
64. Bowen, *Rebellion*, 206.
65. Ibid., 20.
66. Blacker, *Japanese Enlightenment*, 105, translating *Gakumon no Susume*, in *Fukuzawa Zenshū*, vol. III, 10–11. Another translation reads: "When heaven gives birth to man, it gives him faculties of body and mind and the powers to realize his rights in practice. Therefore under no circumstances should a man be deprived of his rights. The lives of the feudal daimyō and their porters were equal in essential value. A rich merchant protects his million ryō no more than the candy vendor protects his four mon, each as their own personal property ... What was distressing for the peasants was also distressing for the lord of the manor; what was sweet for the lord was also sweet for the peasants," in Fukuzawa Yūkichi, *An Encouragement of Learning*, trans. David A. Dilworth and Hirano Umeyo, Tokyo: Sophia University Press, 1969, 11.
67. Blacker, *Japanese Enlightenment*, 106.
68. Benjamin Jowett, trans., *The Dialogues of Plato*, in *Great Books of the Western World*, ed. Robert Maynard Hutchins, Chicago: Encyclopaedia Britannica, 1952, 191.
69. Gregory Vlastos taught a brilliant class on this dialogue in his graduate philosophy seminar at U.C. Berkeley in 1988. I am indebted to him for his explanation of Socrates' view of courage.
70. See Ann Waswo, *Modern Japanese Society, 1968–1984*, New York:

Oxford University Press, 1996, 54–75, for an interesting discussion of how the state handled what she calls "protest from below."

71. Carol Gluck, *Japan's Modern Myths: Ideology in the Late Meiji Period*, Princeton, NJ: Princeton University Press, 1985, 275.

72. Peter Dale, *The Myth of Japanese Uniqueness*, New York: St Martin's Press, 1986, 106.

73. Maruyama Masao, *Thought and Behavior in Modern Japanese Politics*, ed. Ivan Morris, New York: Oxford University Press, 1969, 3–5.

74. Andrew Barshay, *State and Intellectual in Imperial Japan: The Public Man in Crisis*, Berkeley, CA: University of California Press, 1988, xiii.

75. Chalmers Johnson, "The Foundation of Japan's Wealth and Power and Why They Baffle the United States," presented to the workshop on "Japan as Techno-Economic Superpower: Implications for the United States," Los Alamos National Laboratory, Santa Fe, New Mexico, November 18–19, 1993, 19–22.

76. Dale, *The Myth*, 65.

77. Patricia Boling, "Private Interest and the Public Good in Japan," *The Pacific Review* 3 (2), 1990, 190, 147.

78. Many have used the prevalence of conciliation as evidence that Japanese prefer to informally resolve disputes in order to maintain harmony. See, for example, Richard Minear, *Japanese Tradition and Western Law: Emperor, State, and Law in the Thought of Hozumi Yatsuka*, Cambridge, MA: Harvard University Press, 1970.

79. Ōki, *Nihonjin no Hō Kannen*, 165–167.

80. Dan Fenno Henderson, *Conciliation and Japanese Law: Tokugawa and Modern*, Seattle, WA: University of Washington Press, 1965, 2 volumes.

81. Ibid., vol. I, 7.

82. Ibid., 8–9.

83. Ishii Ryōsuke, Review, trans. K. Duff, of Dan Fenno Henderson's *Conciliation and Japanese Law – Tokugawa and Modern Law in Japan: An Annual* 2, 1968, 202.

84. Koga, "Kenri Ishiki ni Tsuite," 6–7.

85. Kawashima Takeyoshi, *Nihonjin no Hō Ishiki*, Tokyo: Iwanami, 1967, 50–57.

86. Frank Upham, *Law and Social Change in Postwar Japan*, Cambridge, MA: Harvard University Press, 1987, passim.

87. Martin Shapiro, *Courts: A Comparative and Political Analysis*, Chicago: University of Chicago Press, 1981, 8–17.

87. Duus, *Modern Japan*, 99.

89. Ōki, *Nihonjin no Hō Kannen*, 178.

90. Beasley, *Modern Japan*, 76.

91. Winston Davis, *Japanese Religion and Society: Paradigms of Structure and Change*, Albany, NY: State University of New York Press, 1992, 60.

92. Lewis, *Rioters and Citizens*, 250.

93. Ōki, *Nihonjin no Hō Kannen*, 201.

94. Kawashima Takeyoshi, "The Status of the Individual in The Notion of Law, Right, and Social Order in Japan," in Moore, ed., *The Japanese Mind*, 276.

3 Patients, rights and protest in contemporary Japan

1. John Owen Haley, "The Myth of the Reluctant Litigant," *Journal of Japanese Studies* 4 (2), 1978.
2. Proceeding from a Symposium of the National Study Group on the Constitution, in which a number of these rights were discussed in depth, can be found in "Atarashii Jinken," *Jurisuto* 606, February 15, 1976, 49–69; citizens' movements, and the judicial development of the new rights of sunshine and the environment, are discussed in Julian Gresser, Fujikura Kōichiro, and Morishima Akio, *Environmental Law in Japan*, Cambridge, MA: MIT Press, 1981.
3. Tanaka Shigeaki, *Gendai Nihon Hō no Kōzu*, Tokyo: Kōtokusha Chikuma Shobō, 1987, 14–15.
4. Yamada Takao, "Kenri no Katarogu Zukuri ni Mukete," *Hō Shakaigaku* 39, 1987, 2–10.
5. Inamoto Yonosuke, "'Atarashii Kenri' no Kategorii to Sōgō Sakuyō," *Hō Shakaigaku* 40, 1988, 2–8.
6. Konishi Minoru, "Kenri Gainen o Meguru Ichi Kōsatsu," 266–284, in Inoue Shigeru, *Gendai no Hō Tetsugaku*, Tokyo: Yūhikaku, 1981, 269–270.
7. Awaji Takehisa, "Minji Hō no Ryōiki," *Hō Shakaigaku* 38, 1986, 14; Kobayashi Naoki, "Atarashii Kihonken no Tenkai," *Jurisuto* 606, February 15, 1976, 15–27.
8. Tanaka Shigeaki, *Saiban o Meguru Ho to Seiji*, Tokyo: Yūhikaku, 1979, 213–309.
9. Tanaka Shigeaki, "Nihonjin no Hō Ishiki to sono Kenkyū no Genjyō ni tsuite," *Hō Shakaigaku*, 37, 1985.
10. Ibid.
11. See, for example, Tanaka Shigeaki, "Kenri, Gimu no Gainen," in Inoue Shigeru, ed., *Gendai no Hō Tetsugaku*, Tokyo: Yūhikaku, 1981, 285–310; Tanaka Shigeaki, "Hō, Kenri, Saiban ni tsuite no Ichi Kōsatsu," in Katō Shinpei, ed., *Hō Rigaku no Shō Mondai*, Tokyo: Yūhikaku, 1976, 101–129.
12. Awaji, "Minji Hō no Ryoiki," 8.
13. Margaret A. McKean, *Environmental Protest and Citizen Politics in Japan*, Berkeley, CA: University of California Press, 1981, 78; Patricia Boling makes a similar point in "Private Interest and the Public Good in Japan," *The Pacific Review* 3(2), 1990, 143.
14. McKean, *Environmental Protest*, 267.
15. Hasegawa Kōichi, "Gendaigata Soshō no Shakai Undōronteki Kōsatsu," *Hōritsu Jihō* 61 (12), October 1989, 67–8.
16. Gerald Rosenberg, *The Hollow Hope: Can Courts Bring About Social Change?*, Chicago: University of Chicago Press, 1991.
17. Frank Upham, *Law and Social Change in Postwar Japan*, Cambridge, MA: Harvard University Press, 1987.
18. Susan Pharr, *Losing Face: Status Politics in Japan*, Berkeley, CA: University of California Press, 1990.
19. There is in the United States as well a debate about the extent to which

litigation and courts bring about social change. See Rosenberg, *The Hollow Hope*. For a lively exchange on the central themes of this book, see Michael W. McCann, "Reform Litigation on Trial," Malcolm M. Feeley, "Hollow Hopes, Flypaper, and Metaphors," and Gerald N. Rosenberg, "Hollow Hopes and Other Aspirations: A Reply to Feeley and McCann," all in *Law and Social Inquiry* 17(4), 1992.

20. Miyazawa Setsuo, "Kenri Keisei/Tenkai no Shakai Undō Moderu o Mezashite," *Hō Shakaigaku* 40, 1988, 43–44; a similar argument is presented in Miyazawa Setsuo, "Social Movements and Contemporary Rights in Japan: Relative Success Factors in the Field of Environmental Law," *Kobe University Law Review* 22, 1988, 63.

21. Abe Yasutaka, "Kenri no Keisei to Hatten," *Hō Shakaigaku* 39, 1987, 24.

22. Inoue Kyoko, in her linguistic approach to postwar legal reform, argues that the American and Japanese versions of the constitution are quite different in tone and meaning. She believes that the Japanese version does not capture the American idea that individuals have rights that the government cannot infringe and must protect, but instead allocates more power and responsibility to the government. By arguing that the "illocutionary force" of the two documents is different, she implies that the Japanese version of the postwar constitution may not be as strongly symbolic as many legal scholars claim. Inoue Kyoko, *MacArthur's Japanese Constitution: A Linguistic and Cultural Study of Its Making*, Chicago: University of Chicago Press, 1991, 102–103.

23. Tanase Takao, "Kenri Seisei no Shisutemu Teki Kōsatsu," *Hō Shakaigaku* 39, 1987, 16.

24. Imai Shōzō, "Nihon ni Okeru Jinken no Kenkyū Dōkō," in Hasegawa Masayasu, ed., *Gendai Jinken Ron (Kōhō Jinken Ron I)*, Tokyo: Hōritsu Bunkasha, 1982, 289–291.

25. Awaji, "Minji," 12.

26. An earlier version of some of the following material can be found in Eric A. Feldman, "Patients' Rights, Citizens' Movements, and Japanese Legal Culture," in David Nelken, ed., *Comparing Legal Cultures*, Aldershot: Dartmouth Publishing Company, 1997.

27. Ikegami Naoki and John Creighton Campbell, eds., *Containing Health Care Costs in Japan*, Ann Arbor, MI: University of Michigan Press, 1996.

28. For two interesting discussions of informed consent, see Marjorie Maguire Schultz, "From Informed Consent to Patient Choice: A New Protected Interest," 95 *Yale Law Journal* 219, 1985; Peter H. Schuck, "Rethinking Informed Consent," *Yale Law Journal* 103, 1993, 899.

29. For a comprehensive and authoritative analysis of informed consent in Japan, see Robert B. Leflar, "Informed Consent and Patients' Rights in Japan," *Houston Law Review* 3 (1), 1996, 1–112. Maruyama Eiji, in "Informed Consent: Ishi no Setsumei to Kanja no Shōdaku," *Hōgaku Kyōiku* 120, September 1990, and "Japanese Law of Informed Consent," *Kobe University Law Review* 25, 1991, 39–43, provides an excellent discussion of the development of informed consent law in Japan.

30. Kimura Rihito, "Bioethics as Prescription for Civic Action: The

Japanese Interpretation," *The Journal of Medicine and Philosophy*, 12, 1987, 271.

31. Quoted in Shibazaki Tomoko, "Medical Secretiveness is Under Attack," *The Japan Times*, July 4, 1991, 4.

32. One of Bai Kōichi's efforts in this regard is *Iryō to Jinken*, Tokyo: Chūō Hōki Shuppan, 1985.

33. For example, Bai Kōichi, *Iji Hōgaku e no Ayumi*, Tokyo: Iwanami, 1970 (originally published 1965).

34. Hirasawa Masao, "Iryō Henkaku to Shimin Undō," *Jurisuto*, Tokushū, *Iryō to Jinken* 548, November 25, 1973, 273–277.

35. Ibid., 273.

36. Makino *v.* Red Cross, Nagoya District Court Judgment, May 29, 1989, *Hanji* 1325, 103, 107, translated by Higuchi Norio. A review of this and other cases can be found in Higuchi Norio, "The Patient's Right to Know of a Cancer Diagnosis: A Comparison of Japanese Paternalism and American Self-Determination," *Washburn Law Journal* 31 (3), 1992, 455–473.

37. Norman Field airs a slightly different interpretation of this case when interviewing Mayor Motoshima of Hiroshima: "I've been thinking about the still-common Japanese practice of not telling cancer patients the nature of their illness. Do you remember the court case in Nagoya earlier this year, where the bereaved daughter and husband of a woman who had not pursued any treatment because she hadn't been told of her cancer brought suit against the physicians and the hospital, and the court held that it was the physician's prerogative to withhold such information? Not to mention Emperor Shōwa's cancer. I've begun to think that this practice is another form of the Emperor system, so to speak. The reason everybody gives is that Japanese are too fainthearted to be told such distressing news, that patients would die needlessly of shock. I don't believe that anymore. I think it makes it easier for doctors to manage cancer patients if they don't have to tell them. They don't have to address their fears and anxieties. Cancer patients tend to suspect their condition anyway, and it's common enough for people who don't have cancer to worry that they do. Current Japanese practice precludes, forbids, the airing of these feelings even between the dying and their families." Norma Field, *In the Realm of a Dying Emperor: A Portrait of Japan at Century's End*, New York: Pantheon, 1991, 243.

38. Maruyama, "Japanese Law," 43.

39. Suzuki Toshihiro, "Atarashii Shimin Undō o Minna no Chikara de," in Kanja no Kenri Hō o Tsukuru Kai, *Kanja no Kenri o Tsukuru*, Tokyo: Meiseki Shoten, 1992, 19–22.

40. The Declaration, its background, and other attempts to catalyze patients' rights legislation are discussed in Ikenaga Mitsuru, " 'Kanja no Kenri Hō' Seitei Undō no Igi to Gen Dankai," *Iji Hōgaku*, June 1992, 72–78.

41. Suzuki Toshihiro, "Kanja no Kenri Sengen," *Jurisuto* 826, December 1, 1984, 48–51.

42. Nihon Ishikai Seimei Rinri Kondan Kai, " 'Setsumei to Dōi' ni tsuite no

Hōkoku," *Jurisuto* 950, February 15, 1990, 149–157; A discussion of the report can be found in "'Setsumei to Dōi' ni tsuite no Hōkoku," *Iji Hōgaku*, June 6, 1991, 164–168.

43. "Malpractice Plaintiffs Form Group," *The Japan Times*, October 21, 1991, 2.
44. Kanja no Kenri Hō o Tsukuru Kai, *Kanja no Kenri Hō o Tsukuru*, 237–257.
45. "Group Lodges Demands for Patients' Rights," *The Japan Times*, March 2, 1993, 2.
46. "Kanja ni 'Kenri Shōten' – 'Setsume to Dōi' nado Meiki," *Asahi Shimbun*, July 6, 1993, 10.

4 AIDS policy and the politics of rights

1. David L. Kirp and Ronald Bayer, eds., *AIDS in the Industrialized Democracies: Passions, Politics, and Policies*, New Brunswick, NJ: Rutgers University Press, 1992, 371–372.
2. Ronald Bayer, *Private Acts, Social Consequences: AIDS and the Politics of Public Health*, New York: The Free Press, 1989, 15.
3. Ebashi Takashi, "Kansenbyō Taisaku to Jinken," in Yamada Takuo, Ōi Gen, Negishi Masayoshi, *et al.*, *AIDS ni Manabu*, Tokyo: Nihon Hyōronsha, 1991, 151.
4. Hatakeyama Takemichi, "AIDS Hōan o Meguru Sho Mondai," *Jurisuto* 888, June 15, 1987, 83–87, 84.
5. Tamashiro Hidehiko, "21 Seiki ni wa, Asia no Hasseisha Kazu wa Afurika yori Ōkunatte Iru Darō," *Rengō*, November 1992, 4–7, 6.
6. Steven Epstein, *Impure Science: AIDS, Activism, and the Politics of Knowledge*, Berkeley, CA: University of California Press, 1996.
7. For a less rights-focused and earlier version of this analysis of Japanese AIDS policy, see Eric A. Feldman and Yonemoto Shohei, "Japan: AIDS as a Non-issue," in Kirp and Bayer, eds., *AIDS in the Industrial Democracies: Passion, Politics, and Policies*.
8. For a more detailed discussion of the epidemiology of AIDS in Japan, see Kihara Masahiro and Kihara Masako, "Wagakuni no HIV Kansen Hayari no Ekigaku," *Kikan Rōdōhō* 168, 1993, 34–42; Kihara Masahiro, "Saikin Nihon Gaikokujin HIV Kansenshasū no Zōka o Dō Miruka," *Nihon Kōshū Eisei Zasshi* 40 (11), November 15, 1993, 1001–1005.
9. Ministry of Health and Welfare, *AIDS Report*, August 1997.
10. Ibid.
11. The use of controlled substances in Japan is severely limited by various factors, among them two strict laws, the Narcotics Control Law (*Mayaku Torishimari Hō*) and the Awakening Drug (stimulant) Law (*Kakuseizai Torishimari Hō*). The former imposes a jail sentence of three years to life and a fine of up to 5 million yen ($43,500) for anyone caught buying or selling a controlled narcotic. For carrying, using, giving away, making, or importing a controlled substance, the penalty is up to ten years in prison and up to 3 million yen ($26,100) in fines. In 1988, 20,716 people were arrested for violating the Awakening Drug Law, but only a small

percentage of them were likely to have been administering the drugs intravenously (Ministry of Justice, *White Paper on Crime* 1989, 24). In addition to these laws, other socioeconomic factors such as a low unemployment rate and a high overall standard of living contribute to the infrequency of illicit drug abuse.

Further, among those who do use intravenous drugs, the culture of use in Japan is quite different from that in the United States. Drug users tend to be more private about their habits, shooting up alone rather than in urban "shooting galleries." This helps to account for the limited sharing of needles. Data collected in the late 1980s indicate that out of 2753 drug users given an HIV test, only one tested positive. (Soda Kenji, "Present Situation of AIDS and HIV Infection in Japan," *HIV Ekigaku Kenkyūhan Kenkyū Hōkokusho* (March 1989), 19.) Thus, drug abuse is currently an insignificant factor in the spread of AIDS in Japan.

12. "Number of AIDS Sufferers Reaches 371," *The Japan Times*, April 24, 1991, 2.
13. "Doctors Keep Hemophiliacs in the Dark," *Mainichi Daily News*, March 24, 1987, 12.
14. Ishida Yoshiaki, "AIDS Taisaku no Hō Seika ni Hantai," *Asahi Shimbun* February 9, 1987.
15. Soda, "Present Situation," 287.
16. Institute of Medicine, National Academy of Sciences, *Mobilizing Against AIDS*, Cambridge, MA: Harvard University Press, 1986, 26.
17. Kyoto Chapter of Japanese Society of Friends of Hemophiliacs, "Yunyū Ketsueki Seizai Higai Jitai Chōsa Ankēto," February 1989.
18. "Hemophiliacs Targets of Abuse, Poll Shows," *The Daily Yomiuri* April 12, 1988, 2.
19. Ibid.
20. Kyoto Chapter of Japanese Society of Friends of Hemophiliacs.
21. Ihara Saikaku, *The Great Mirror of Male Love*, trans. Paul Gordon Shalow, Stanford, CA: Stanford University Press, 1990.
22. See, for example, Sawazaki Yasushi, "Gay Men and HIV in Japan," 47–50, in Mitchell Feldman, Eric Feldman, and Thomas Coates, eds., "Partners in AIDS Prevention: A US/Japan Collaboration," special supplement to *Journal of Acquired Immune Deficiency Syndromes and Human Retrovirology* 14 (Supplement 2), 1997.
23. Personal communication with Yamaguchi Katsuhisa, HIV–Human Rights Information Center, September 27, 1990.
24. Sawazaki Yasushi, "AIDS-Related Health Behavior Among Gay Men in Japan," Presented at the Fifth International Conference on AIDS, San Francisco, CA, June 21, 1990.
25. Ibid. Personal communication with Jim Fredrick, International Friends, October 6, 1990.
26. *The Japan Times*, January 23, 1987.
27. William Weatherall, "Japan Curses Gaijin and AIDS Still Spreads," *Far Eastern Economic Review*, April 9, 1987, 111.
28. "Health Ministry Mulls AIDS Prevention Law," *Mainichi Daily News*,

January 20, 1987, 1; "Law Considered to Bar Entry of AIDS Carriers," *The Japan Times*, February 4, 1987, 12.

29. "News of Pregnant AIDS Carrier Fires Talk of Legislation," *The Japan Times*, February 18, 1987, 1.
30. Ishida, "AIDS Taisaku no Hō Seika ni Hantai."
31. "AIDS Reporting Plan Proposed in Drafts of Prevention Bill," *The The The Japan Times*, February 19, 1987, 2; "LDP Has Draft AIDS Bill," *Mainichi Daily News*, February 21, 1987, 12.
32. The draft did not explicitly limit penalties to those who engaged in *unsafe* sexual acts, but this limitation can be implied from the language of the bill.
33. While the draft did not clearly say that names had to be reported, this requirement can be implied from the language of the bill.
34. "AIDS Bill Draft Watered Down," *Daily Yomiuri*, March 7, 1987, 1.
35. Ishida Yoshiaki, "Objection to the Legalization of AIDS Countermeasures," unpublished document, Kyoto Branch, Japanese Society of Friends of Hemophiliacs, 1987.
36. Jocelyn Ford, "Innocent Victims of AIDS Worry that Government Ignores their Rights," *Daily Yomiuri*, March 1, 1987, 5.
37. Osaka Tomo no Kai, "Osaka Tomo no Kai Nyūsu," 65, May 1987.
38. Yasuda Yukuo, "AIDS Higai to Kuni no Sekinin," *Hōgaku Seminā* 406, October 1988, 14–17, 17.
39. See, for example, Ford, "Innocent Victims," 2.
40. Kirp and Bayer, *AIDS*, 364.
41. "Kōsei Kei Kyōkai," *Kōsei no Shihyō*, Tokyo: 1989.
42. Personal communication with Dr. Negishi Masayoshi, Department of Infectious Diseases, Tokyo Metropolitan Komagome Hospital.
43. Negishi Masayoshi, "AIDS Kansensha no Jinken Mamori," *Asahi Shimbun*, March 11, 1987, 5.
44. "LDP Panel Approves Ministry's AIDS Bill," *The Japan Times*, March 7, 1987, 2.
45. *Law Concerning the Prevention of Acquired Immunodeficiency Syndrome*, Ministry of Health and Welfare, March 6, 1987.
46. Ibid.
47. Niwayama Shōichiro, "Kokkai Tsūka o Isoida AIDS Yobō Hōan no Kikensei," *Shin Iryō*, December 1988, 34–36, 35.
48. Ishida, "AIDS Taisaku no Hoseika ni Hantai."
49. Uchiyama Yayoi, "Draconian AIDS Legislation," *Mainichi Daily News*, May 15, 1987, 6.
50. Ibid.
51. Ibid.
52. Jiyū Jinken Kyōkai, " 'AIDS Taisaku' wa Dō Aru Bekika," Tokyo, March 10, 1988.
53. "Relief for Transfusion AIDS Patients Mulled," *Mainichi Daily News*, May 15, 1987, 16.
54. Margaret Powell and Anesaki Masahira, eds., *Health Care in Japan*, New York, Routledge, 1990, 179–186.

55. "Ministry Will Help Tainted Blood Victims," *The Japan Times*, October 17, 1993, 2.
56. Interview with Dr. Sakurai Yoshiki, October 9, 1990.
57. Marcia Stepanek, "Japan's New Gay Activists Battle Bias, Indifference," *San Francisco Examiner*, May 26, 1991, 1.
58. HIV to Jinken Yobō Sentā, "AIDS kara HIV e," Tokyo, 1990.
59. HIV to Jinken Yobō Sentā, "HIV Mondai ni Kansuru Yobōsho," Petition to the minister of health and welfare, March 5, 1991.
60. Ministry of Health and Welfare, "AIDS Control in Japan," May 1993, 10.
61. "AIDS Mondai Sōgō Taisaku Taikō," Ministry of Health and Welfare, Internal Document, March 19, 1992.
62. "Cabinet Presses War on AIDS," *The Japan Times*, March 20, 1992, 1.
63. "AIDS Becomes a Notifiable Disease in Japan Despite Protests," *Nature* 326, March 19, 1987, 232.
64. "Kokusai AIDS Kaigi Nekku wa Nyūkoku Mondai," *Yomiuri Shimbun*, July 25, 1993, 26;
65. "Entry OK for AIDS Meeting," *Asahi Evening News*, December 24, 1993, 4.
66. Takeda Bin, "AIDS Kyōiku ni Motomerareru Mono," *Sekai*, October 1992, 68–71, 71.
67. For a description of the gay community in Japan, and its recent emergence from social invisibility, see Ōiwa Yūri, "Nihon no Gei," *Aera*, August 27, 1991, 18–22.
68. Personal communication with Sawazaki Yasushi, September 24, 1990.
69. Interviews with staff of AIDS, Tuberculosis, and Other Infectious Diseases Control Bureau, Ministry of Health and Welfare, July 23, 1993.
70. Kawaguchi Takao, "The Conversation: Minami Teishiro," *Tokyo Journal*, August 1992, 23–25, 23.
71. Japan Institute for People with HIV, Appeal to Tsuchiya Yoshihiko, President of the House of Councilors, and Sakurauchi Yoshio, Speaker of the House of Representatives, May 15, 1990.
72. "AIDS Patients Receive Little Aid or Comfort," *Asahi Shimbun Japan Access*, September 9, 1991, 3.
73. "Surgery Refused Due to AIDS Fear," *The Japan Times*, March 12, 1993, 3.
74. "Hemophiliacs Targets of Abuse, Poll Shows," *Daily Yomiuri*, April 12, 1988, 2.
75. "Doctors Keep Hemophiliacs in the Dark," *Mainichi Daily News*, March 24, 1987, 12.
76. Ibid.
77. "HIV Carrier Lashes Out in Court," *Daily Yomiuri*, October 19, 1993.
78. "Doctors Keep Hemophiliacs in the Dark," *Mainichi Daily News*, March 24, 1987, 12.
79. "Data About AIDS Patients Printed Without Permission," *Daily Yomiuri*, March 31, 1993, 2.
80. Ibid.

81. Obata Yōichi, "Fear of AIDS Extends to Medical Community," *Daily Yomiuri*, January 12, 1993, 9.
82. Ibid.
83. "AIDS, HIV Cases Show Record Rise," *The Japan Times*, July 24, 1991, 2.
84. Kōseishō Hoken Iryō Kyōku, AIDS Kekkaku Kansenbyō Kachō, "HIV Kensa no Jisshi ni Tsuite," Ministry of Health and Welfare directive on HIV testing, sent by the chief of the AIDS, Tuberculosis, and Infectious Diseases Department to city and prefectural governments, July 13, 1993.
85. Interview with Niwayama Shōichiro, August 12, 1991, Tokyo, Japan.

5 Asserting rights, legislating death

1. Two laws concerning the transplantation of organs have been enacted. The first, "An Act Relating to Cornea Transplantation," was passed in 1957. It stipulated that the removal of corneas be authorized by the written consent of a donor's family, and only when a specific recipient was available. This law was superseded in 1979, when "An Act Concerning the Transplantation of Cornea and Kidneys" was passed.

   Drafted by a Diet member rather than a ministry bureaucrat, the enactment of "An Act Concerning the Transplantation of Cornea and Kidneys" closely followed a campaign by the Kidney Transplantation Promoting Association and the Japan Society of Transplantation. The campaign urged an increase in kidney donation, coverage of kidney transplants by the health insurance system, and the inauguration of a National Center of Kidney Transplantation. The Act governs only kidneys and corneas, both of which can be removed from bodies declared dead by conventional criteria. Unlike the older cornea law it does not require the existence of a specified recipient. Surgeons removing kidneys are exempt from prosecution for damaging a corpse under Article 190 of the Penal Code.

   Despite this law, most kidneys for transplantation are donated by living relatives. The scarcity of organs taken from corpses may in part be due to the necessity of obtaining family consent for their removal. If a donor has left a written consent, relatives must be notified, and can prohibit organ removal if they choose. Irrespective of a donor's desires, relatives may consent to organ removal if they are so inclined. The power vested in relatives, justified by what Bai Kōichi calls "the right of self-determination of a surviving relative," is difficult to exercise and limits the supply of donated kidneys.

   Differences in the meaning and style of charity may also mitigate against kidney donation in Japan. Some Western sociological literature has approached organ transplantation from the perspective of gift-giving, and identified the donation of one's body parts as firmly within the Christian tradition of providing charity to strangers. With more emphasis in Japan on one's immediate group than on anonymous giving, some sociologists and anthropologists have emphasized the difficulties involved in institutionalizing organ donation. But this ignores the fact that there is an acute shortage of donated organs in the West, as well as the rampant ritualized gift-giving in Japan that sees an exchange of commodities between near-strangers that is unknown in other lands.

The limited number of voluntary organ donors is in part a side effect of the debate over brain death and transplantation, which has poisoned the general atmosphere for the donation of organs. The general public is not sophisticated about the nuances of medical practice, and many are certainly unaware of which organs can be transplanted from those declared dead by conventional means and which require brain dead donors. Moreover, between 1980 and 1985, despite the proscription on legally recognizing brain death, the head of the Japan Society for Transplantation has estimated that over 100 kidneys were transplanted from brain dead donors. Several of the transplant surgeons have been indicted for murder, but those who have taken only one kidney are beyond the reach of the law, since humans can live with just one kidney. The confusion and publicity surrounding these transplants is a powerful disincentive for those ambivalent about kidney donation.

A recent campaign by the National Policy Agency (NPA) may help to address the scarcity of kidneys and corneas. As the result of a "request" by Parliamentary Vice Health Minister, Noro Akihiko, to NPA chief, Kanazawa Akio, donor forms will become available at police stations and drivers' license testing centers and can be submitted along with license renewal applications. With over 60 million registered drivers, the number of prospective donors registered at kidney banks, now 250,000, could substantially increase. But until there is a more settled national policy on brain death and organ transplantation, the number of people willing to voluntarily donate their organs will remain low.

2. Japan has no statutory definition of death, and no law that requires death to be determined with regard to any particular criteria. The medical profession relies on accepted norms of medical practice and judgment to decide when an individual is to be declared dead. These accord with what is thought of as death by the layperson – termination of heartbeat and respiration, lack of reflexes – and were not questioned until the possibility of determining death based on brain criteria emerged in the 1960s.

3. A heart, liver, or pancreas taken from a body declared dead in the traditional sense – termination of pulse, breath, and reflexes – quickly becomes "stale" and untransplantable. The same organs from a donor declared brain dead but maintained by a respirator are "fresh" and reusable. Without brain dead donors, therefore, transplantable organs are unavailable.

4. Honda Katsunori and Andō Hiroyuki, "Brain Death and Patients' Rights," paper presented at the International Conference on Health Law and Medicine, Sydney, Australia, August 20, 1986, 25.

5. Nudeshima Jirō, *Nōshi/Zōki Ishoku to Nihon Shakai*, Tokyo: Kōbundo, 1991, passim.

6. For related discussions of the definition of death in Japan, see Eric A. Feldman, "Culture, Conflict, and Cost: Perspectives on Brain Death in Japan," *International Journal of Technology Assessment in Health Care* 10, 1994, 447–463, and "Over My Dead Body: The Enigma and Economics of Brain Death in Japan," in Ikegami Naoki and John C. Campbell, eds., *Containing Health Care Costs in Japan*, Ann Arbor, MI: University of Michigan Press, 1996).

7. Umehara Takeshi, "Gendaijin no Sei to Shi," *This Is* 6(10), 1989, 20.

8. Nudeshima, *Nōshi/Zōki.*

9. Margaret Lock and Christina Honde, "Reaching Consensus about Death: Heart Transplants and Cultural Identity in Japan," in G. Weisz, ed., *Social Science Perspectives on Medical Ethics*, Dordrecht: 1990, 100; Emiko Ohnuki-Tierney, "Socio-cultural Dimensions of Renal Transplants in Japan," *Health Policy* 6, 1986, 279; Akatsu Haruko, "The Heart, the Gut, and Brain Death in Japan," *Hastings Center Report*, March/April 1990, 2.

10. Lock and Honde, "Reaching Consensus," 109; Ohnuki-Tierney, "Renal Transplants," 281; Akatsu, "The Heart," 2.

11. Takie S. Lebra, *Japanese Patterns of Behavior*, Honolulu: University of Hawaii Press, 1976, 190.

12. Lafcadio Hearn, *Japan: An Attempt at Interpretation*, Rutland, VT: Charles C. Tuttle Co., 1955 (originally published 1904), 32.

13. Stuart D. B. Picken, "The Understanding of Death in Japanese Religion," *Japanese Religions* 9 (4), July 1977, 48.

14. See Basil Hall Chamberlain, trans., *Ko-Ji-Ki*, Kobe: J. L. Thomson and Co., 1932.

15. Ibid.

16. Anesaki Masaharu, *History of Japanese Religion with Special Reference to the Social and Moral Life of the Nation*, London: K. Paul, Trench, Trubber & Co., 1930.

17. Hearn, *Japan*, 25–31.

18. David W. Plath, "Where the Family of God is the Family: The Role of the Dead in Japanese Households," *American Anthropologist* 66(2), April 1964, 310.

19. Emiko Ohnuki-Tierney, *Illness and Culture in Contemporary Japan*, New York: Cambridge University Press, 1984, 70.

20. Hozumi Nobushige, *Ancestor Worship and Japanese Law*, New York: Books for Libraries Press, 1912 (reprinted 1973), 77–83.

21. Jean Herbert, *Shintō*, New York: Stein and Day, 1967, 54.

22. Hozumi, *Ancester Worship*, 29.

23. Picken, "Understanding of Death," 47.

24. Ibid., 52.

25. Hearn, *Japan*, 201–202.

26. Herbert, *Shintō*, 64.

27. William R. LaFleur, "Japan," in Frederick H. Holck, ed., *Death and Eastern Thought: Understanding Death in Eastern Religions and Philosophies*, Nashville, TN: Abingdon Press, 1974, 229.

28. Anesaki, 81.
29. Hearn, *Japan*, 179.
30. Bai Kōichi, *Iji Hōgaku e no Ayumi*, Tokyo: Iwanami, 1970 (originally published 1965).
31. Bai Kōichi and Hirabayashi Katsumasa, "The Legal Situation in Japan" and "Whose Consent Shall Make Organ Removal Lawful," in "Symposium: A Comparative Legal Study of Organ Transplantation: Requirements for Organ Removal from Cadavers," *Comparative Law Journal* 46, 1984, 298.
32. A summary of an anticipated draft transplant law was printed in "Zōki Ishoku Hōan Yōkōan no Yōshi," *Asahi Shimbun*, December 3, 1993.
33. "'Honnin no Ishi' Doko Made," *Asahi Shimbun*, December 3, 1993; "Zōki Teikyō no Ishi Seimei no Gendo Suisatsu," *Asahi Shimbun*, January 12, 1994, 1; "Bill Would Let Relatives 'Surmise' Donor's Intent," *Daily Yomiuri*, January 12, 1994.
34. Aita Kaoruko, "Brain Death Talks Set to Come Alive," *The Japan Times*, March 16, 1994, 3.
35. "Definition of 'Death' Still a Matter of Dispute," *Daily Yomiuri*, February 11, 1994.
36. Lock and Honde, "Reaching Consensus," 104–105.
37. Tsukamoto Yasushi, "Arguments about the Criteria of Brain Death in Japan," *Journal of Behavioral and Social Sciences (Kōdō Kagaku Kenkyū)* 41, 1992, 25.
38. *The Japan Times*, July 10, 1985, 13.
39. *The Japan Times*, May 14, 1985, 2.
40. See, for example, "Health Ministry Seeks Clearer Definition of Brain Death," *Asahi Evening News*, May 14, 1985, 1, and "Panel Releases Results of Study on Standards for Brain Death," *The Japan Times*, May 14, 1985, 2.
41. "Brain Death Criteria Vary Case to Case," *Mainichi Daily News*, May 15, 1985, 12.
42. *Asahi Evening News*, May 14, 1985, 1.
43. "Kōseishō Kenkyūhan ni yoru Nōshi no Hantei Kijyun" [Brain Death Determination Criteria of the Ministry of Health and Welfare's Research Group], December 6, 1985.
44. Clyde Haberman, *New York Times*, February 10, 1987, 4.
45. "National Standard on Brain Death Drawn Up," *Mainichi Daily News*, December 7, 1985, 1.
46. Editorial, "Brain Death," *Mainichi Daily News*, December 11, 1985, 2(B).
47. "Sidelight: Control over Death," *Mainichi Daily News*, December 11, 1985, 2(B).
48. Editorial, "In the Shadow of Death," *The Japan Times*, December 15, 1985, 12.
49. For discussion of the Science Council of Japan's deliberations, see "Brain Death = Human Death, Science Committee Decides," *The Japan Times*, February 26, 1987, 2; Ikeda Daisaku, "Nōshi Mondai ni Kansuru Ichi Kosatsu," *Tōyōgaku Kenkyū* 26 (2), 1987, 135; Nihon Gakujyutsu Kaigi,

Iryō Gakujyutsu to Ningen no Seimei Tokubetsu Iinkai Hōkoku, "Nōshi ni Kansuru Kenkai," October 23, 1987; "Nōshi Kenkai de Fukyū Tsuzukeru Gakujyutsu Kaigi," *Asahi Shimbun*, 1987; "Science Council Rejects Brain Death Report," *The Japan Times*, April 24, 1987, 2.

50. Nihon Ishikai Seimei Rinri Kondankai, "Nōshi Oyobi Zōki Ishoku ni Tsuite," (Japan Medical Association Life Ethics Deliberative Council, "Concerning Brain Death and Organ Transplantation"), Chukan Hōkoku, March 25, 1987; Saishū Hōkoku, January 12, 1988.

51. Katō Ichirō, *Nōshi Zōki Ishoku to Jinken*, Tokyo: Yūhikaku, 1986.

52. Katō Ichirō, "Nōshi Mondai: Shakai teki Gōi wa Shinkirō," *Bungei Shunjyū* 4, 1988, 106–115.

53. In their article "Reaching Consensus about Death," Lock and Honde appear to take the report of the JMA's Life Ethics Deliberation Council as legally enforceable. The question they seek to answer is why, given its legality, transplantation is not widespread. This leads them to overlook the more fundamental question about brain death in Japan – whether it ought to be a legal definition of death.

54. Bai Kōichi, "Nōshi Riron no Ronri: 'Saigo Hōkokusho' Hihan," *Sekai*, October 1988, 32–46; See also Maruyama Eiji, "History and Theories of Brain Death in Japan Since 1985," *Journal of Behavioral and Social Sciences (Kōdō Kagaku Kenkyū)* 41, 1992, 45–57.

55. Yamauchi Masaya, "Transplantation in Japan," *British Medical Journal* 301, 507, 1988.

56. Clyde Haberman, "Ruling on Death Opens Way for Transplants," *New York Times*, January 14, 1988, B7.

57. Nihon Bengoshi Rengōkai, "Nihon Ishikai Seimei Rinri Kondankai 'Nōshi Oyobi Zōki Ishoku ni Tsuite no Saishū Hōkoku' ni Taisuru Ikenshō," 1988, written opinion No.5, "Determination of Brain Death and the Wishes of Patient and Family," and No.7, "Social Consensus."

58. Tachibana Takashi, *Nōshi*, Chūō Kōron Shupansha, 1986.

59. Ibid., and *NHK Supesharu: Nōshi*, 1991, partially aired as a television special titled, Nōshi, December 15, 1990.

60. In February 1990, the Ethics Review Committee of Tokyo University's Institute of Medical Science approved the use of brain death donors for liver transplants. Osaka University's Ethics Committee, in the summer of 1990, approved the transplantation of hearts, livers, and kidneys from brain dead donors.

61. "Indecision Plagues Organ Donor Issue," *Daily Yomiuri*, July 11, 1990, 3.

62. Rinji Nōshi Oyobi Zōki Ishoku Chōsa Kai Secchi Hō, Law Number 70, December 8, 1989.

63. Groups wanting *osumitsuki*, or an official "go ahead," will sometimes pressure a particular section of the government to create a study group to approve a new policy. For an excellent discussion of Japanese consultative councils, see Frank J. Schwartz, *Advice and Consent: The Politics of Consultation in Japan*, New York: Cambridge University Press, 1998.

64. Rinji Nōshi Oyobi Zōki Ishoku Chōsa Kai, "Nōshi Oyobi Zōki Ishoku Ni Kansuru Jyūyō Jikō ni Tsuite (Chūkan Iken)," Kōseishō, June 14, 1991.

65. Ibid., 9.
66. Ibid., 15–16.
67. Translation from "Brain-Death Debate Moves to Public Arena," *Asahi Shimbun Japan Access*, 24, June 1991, 3.
68. Maruyama, "History," also emphasizes these points.
69. "Anxieties over Report on Brain Death," *The Japan Times*, July 7, 1991, 22; this is a translation of Shimen Tenbō (survey of editorials) from Shimbun Kyōkai-hō; quote comes from *Nishi-Nippon Shimbun*.
70. "Brain Death Report Divides Experts," *The Japan Times*, June 15, 1991, 2.
71. Translation from "Brain-Death Debate Moves to Public Arena," *Asahi Shimbun Japan Access* 24, June 1991, 3.
72. "Prosecutor Raps Brain Death Criteria," *The Japan Times*, June 19, 1991, 2.
73. "Brain Death is not Legal, Lawyers Say," *The Japan Times*, June 30, 1991, 2.
74. "Police Warning on Brain Death Leads Hospital to Cancel Liver Transplant," *The Japan Times*, July 4, 1991, 2.
75. Seimei Rinri Kenkyūkai, "Zōki no Tekishutsu ni Kansuru Hōritsu," *Jurisuto* 1001, 52–64.
76. Rinji Nōshi Oyobi Zōki Ishoku Chōsa Kai, "Nōshi Oyobi Zōki Ishoku ni Kansuru Jyūyō Jikō," Ministry of Health and Welfare, January 22, 1992.
77. "Nōshi Ishoku," *Yomiuri Shimbun*, January 23, 1992, 1.
78. "Nōshi wa Hito no Shi . . ." *Asahi Shimbun*, January 23, 1992, 1.
79. Umehara Takeshi, "Watakushi wa Naze, 'Nōshi = Ningen no Shi' ni Shitsuyō ni Hantaishi Tsuzukeru no ka?" *Sapio*, January 9, 1992, 76–80.
80. Tachibana Takashi, "Nōshi to Hito no Shi," *Gekkan Asahi*, March 1992, 21–25.
81. "'Nōshi' Rippōka ni Nao Kadai," *Asahi Shimbun*, January 23, 1992, 3.
82. "Tōmen wa Shisei Kaezu," *Asahi Shimbun*, January 23, 1992, 3. In addition, the Ministry of Justice indicated that because of this continuing legal ambiguity, the indictments brought by the Patients' Rights Conference were unlikely to be disposed of in the near future.
83. "Brain Death Dispute Delays Organ Removal," *The Japan Times*, February 1, 1992, 3.
84. Rinji Nōshi Oyobi Zōki Ishoku Chōsa Kai (1992), 11.
85. Ibid., 23–4.
86. *Gekkan Asahi*, "Zōki Ishoku ni Gō Sign wa Detaka?" interview with Ōta Kazuo and Nishioka Yoshiki, March 1992.
87. Interestingly, and in contrast to the debate over organ transplantation in the United States, concern over the cost of organ transplants in Japan has rarely been openly discussed. The AHC explicitly avoided the question of whether transplants could be an unwelcome addition to overall health care costs, as well as the question of who should pay. After the AHC's final report was announced and the possibility of a transplant program began to take form, however, articles began to appear in the

newspaper reporting on a disagreement between the MHW and the transplant physicians as to who should pay. The possibility of establishing a special fund apart from national health insurance was discussed, as was providing no governmental assistance at all.

88. *Gekkan Asahi.*
89. Katō Ichirō *et al.*, "Nōshi Rinchō Saishū Tōshin o Megutte," *Jurisuto* 1001, June 1, 1992, 9–34.
90. "Tōmen wa Shisei Kaezu," *Asahi Shimbun*, January 23, 1992, 3.
91. "Nōshi to Zōki Ishoku #4," *Asahi Shimbun*, June 13, 1991.
92. Umehara, "Watakushi wa Naze," 76–80.
93. "Iryō Fuan no Kōzō Shiteki," *Asahi Shimbun*, January 23, 1993, 5.
94. Seimei Rinri Kenkyūkai, "Zōki no Tekishutsu ni Kansuru Hōritsu (Shian)," *Jurisuto* 1001, June 1, 1992, 52–64.
95. Maruyama, "History," 45–57.
96. Aita Kaoruko, "Rights of Donors is the Key Issue,"*The Japan Times*, June 18, 1997, 3.

6 Litigation and the courts: talking about rights

1. Noda Yoshiyuki, *Introduction to Japanese Law*, ed. and trans. Anthony H. Angelo, Tokyo: University of Tokyo Press, 1976, 161.
2. Ibid.
3. John O. Haley, "The Myth of the Reluctant Litigant," *Journal of Japanese Studies* 4 (2), 1978, 389.
4. Important works by Western scholars that have carefully considered courts and cases include Mark Ramseyer's *Odd Markets in Japanese History: Law and Economic Growth*, New York: Cambridge University Press, 1996 and Frank Upham's *Law and Social Change in Postwar Japan*, Cambridge, MA: Harvard University Press, 1987.
5. See, for example, Upham, *Law and Social Change*; Jeffery Broadbent, *Environmental Politics in Japan: Networks of Power and Protest*, New York: Cambridge University Press, 1998; Margaret McKean, *Environmental Protest and Citizen Politics in Japan*, Berkeley, CA: University of California Press, 1981.
6. Earlier versions of some of the following material can be found in Eric A. Feldman, "Legal Transplants, Organ Transplants: The Japanese Experience," *Social and Legal Studies* 3, 1994, 71–91, and Eric A. Feldman, "HIV and Blood in Japan: Transforming Private Conflict into Public Scandal," in Eric A. Feldman and Ronald Bayer, eds., *Blood Feuds: AIDS, Blood, and the Politics of Medical Disaster*, New York: Oxford University Press, 1999.
7. I am indebted to Dr. Mitchell Feldman, University of California, San Francisco, Division of General Internal Medicine, for this scientific background.
8. A more detailed description of the pharmaceutical industry can be found in Margaret Powell and Anesaki Masahira, eds., *Health Care in Japan*, New York: Routledge, 1990, 179–186.
9. This may account for Japan's use of a disproportionate amount of the

world plasma supply, an allegation that I have heard frequently but have been unable to confirm.

10. For an overview of the litigation, see Kamei Masateru, "HIV Soshō no Gaiyō," *Hōgaku Seminā* 481, January 1995, 22–26; Iwao Ikoma, "Tokyo HIV Soshō no Mezasumono," *Nihon no Kagakusha* 28, July 1993, 388– 93.

11. "Ketsuyūbyō Kanja no 4 Wari," *Asahi Shimbun*, September 18, 1987.

12. "Hemophiliac Group to Seek Compensation," *Mainichi Daily News*, February 5, 1988, 3.

13. Tokyo HIV Soshō Genkoku Dan, HIV Soshō o Sasaeru Ketsuyūbyō no Kai, "Ima, Inochi no Omosa wa," pamphlet with selections from the oral arguments in the Tokyo District Court regarding litigation over distribution of HIV-contaminated blood. The argument here was presented in the Tokyo District Court, March 4, 1991.

14. Absent from the list of defendants was the Japanese Red Cross. While the JRC had no active role in importing, distributing, or approving blood products used by hemophiliacs, zealous plaintiffs could have argued that the JRC neglected its duty to ensure a safe blood supply in Japan by failing to collect enough blood to manufacture blood products domestically. But the honorary chair of the JRC has since the Meiji period been a member of the Japanese royal family, which has bestowed a peculiar kind of sanctity on the organization, and made suing the JRC taboo.

15. A detailed chronology of the important dates and events surrounding the importation and distribution of tainted blood can be found in Katahira Kiyohiko and Satō Tsugumichi, "AIDS Hassei no Shoki ni Okeru Nihon no Ketsuyūbyō-Ketsueki Seizai Kankeisha no Ninshiki to Taiō," *Nihon no Kagakusha* 28 (306), July 1993, 17–22.

16. Aita Kaoruko, "HIV-Positive Hemophiliacs Want Government, Drug Firms to Pay," *The Japan Times*, October 30, 1992, 3.

17. Ibid.

18. Ibid.

19. Personal communication with Sugiyama Shinichi, February 5, 1993, Tokyo, Japan.

20. The best description of the legal points at issue in the litigation, albeit from the plaintiffs' perspective, is "HIV Soshō Benkyō Kai," *Ki Shihō Shūshūsei Natsu no Shūkai Hōkokushū* 44, Kyoto, April 27–28, 1991, 96– 117. It provides a framework for the following discussion.

21. Ibid., 98–99.

22. Katahira Kiyohiko and Satō Tsugumichi, "AIDS as Drug-Induced Suffering in Japan," in S. Araki, ed., *Behavioral Medicine: An Integrated Biobehavioral Approach to Health and Illness*, Dordrecht: Elsevier Science Publishers, 1992, 229–234.

23. John Dower, *War Without Mercy: Race and Power in the Pacific War*, New York: Pantheon, 1986, 348, note 40.

24. Ibid.

25. Katahira and Satō, "AIDS," 232, which describes the testimony of Dr. Kaneo Yamada, Marianna University School of Medicine, June 7, 1991, Tokyo District Court.

26. Blood Services Department, Japanese Red Cross Society, *Blood Services*, Tokyo: Japanese Red Cross Society, 1993, 29–30.
27. These views are summarized in Ministry of Health and Welfare, "Saiban no Jyōkyō," unpublished, on file with author, 1995.
28. Institute of Medicine, *HIV and the Blood Supply*, Washington, DC: National Academy Press, 1995.
29. Passim, legal briefs of defendants.
30. Takasugi Shingo, "Abe Takeshi: "Watakushi wa AIDS Kansen no Dōgi-teki Geshunin Da," *Gendai*, October 1987, 250–265, 261.
31. Interview with Sasaki Hiroshi, Pharmaceutical Affairs Bureau, Ministry of Health and Welfare, July 22, 1993.
32. A review of such incidents can be found in Katahira Kiyohiko *et al.*, "Improvement of the Law and Procedures to Relieve Drug-Induced Suffering and to Prevent its Occurrence: Lessons from the Clioquinol Lawsuit and Other Cases in Japan," Proceedings of the Kyoto International Conference Against Drug-Induced Suffering, April 14–18, 1979, International Congress Series 513. A recent case, deaths caused by the antiviral sorivudine, is discussed in Mark Robinson, "Making a Killing," *Tokyo Journal*, December 1994, 32–37.
33. "HIV Soshō Benkyō Kai," 108.
34. Institute of Medicine, *HIV and the Blood Supply*.
35. "Kokumin mō Damatte Inai," *Newsweek* (Japanese edition), March 3, 1996, 12–14.
36. "HIV Hemophiliacs Vow to Fight for Apology," *The Japan Times*, October 8, 1995.
37. Two attorneys for the plaintiffs discuss the proposed settlement in Iizuka Tomoyuki and Itō Toshikatsu, "Wakai Kankoku o Dō Miru Ka," *Hōgaku Seminā* 492, December 1995, 17–20.
38. "Wakai Kankoku ni Atatte no Shoken," *Hō to Minshushugi* 303, November 1995, 6–7.
39. Ibid.
40. "Rallies Slam Ministry for HIV Stance," *The Japan Times*, December 13, 1995, 2.
41. "HIV Group Tries New Tactics," *The Japan Times*, February 17, 1996, 3.
42. "Kaiketsu 'Mō Matte-innai,'" *Yomiuri Shimbun*, February 14, 1996, 26.
43. Ibid.
44. "State Admits HIV Guilt," *The Japan Times*, February 17, 1996, 1.
45. "Blood Product Marketing Thought Willfully Delayed," *Mainichi Daily News*, February 7, 1988, 12.
46. Hemophiliacs were previously responsible for paying 10,000 yen/month ($87.00) for their medical care, but for the past decade there has been no co-payment.
47. HIV Soshō o Sasaeru Kai, petition circulated after the first settlement proposal.
48. "Courts Issue Second Plan in HIV Suits," *The Japan Times*, March 8, 1996, 1.
49. Press Release, Bayer Yakuhin, March 14, 1996.

50. Statement Released to Plaintiffs, Baxter, March 14, 1996.
51. Tokyo Chihō Saibansho, Wakaichōsho Kisai Jikō, Hatasawa Preliminary Translation, Mr. Hatasawa Tamotsu, Hatasawa and Wakai Law Offices, Tokyo, Japan, April 5, 1996.
52. The Japanese criminal law provides that in particular situations individuals not directly injured may notify investigating officials that they would like a particular matter prosecuted. This first stage, the complaint, carries no official weight, and ordinarily gives rise to an investigation of the alleged offense by the police or public prosecutor. After the investigation is conducted and the evidence evaluated, a decision is made as to whether a case will be prosecuted. Dando Shigemitsu, *Japanese Criminal Procedure*, trans. B. J. George, South Hackensack, NJ: Fred B. Rothman & Co., 1965, 95, 323.

   Because the Criminal Code does not specify a time within which investigations must be completed, complaints can be indefinitely prolonged if the investigating officials say that the investigations are ongoing.
53 Ibid.
54 Hemophiliacs, almost all men, suffer from a condition in which their blood does not spontaneously clot. The severity of the disease depends upon the exact element missing from one's blood. For years, hemophiliacs were forced to limit their daily activities to avoid the possibility of excessive blood loss and death. The burden of hemophilia was greatly lightened when medical science isolated clotting factors 8 and 9, coagulant proteins, from blood.
55. John Henry Merryman, *The Civil Law Tradition*, Stanford, CA: Stanford University Press, 1969, 124–132, contains an excellent discussion of the fundamental differences between criminal procedure in common and civil law systems.
56. Ibid., 127.
57. B. J. George, Jr., "Discretionary Authority of Public Prosecutors in Japan," *Law in Japan* 17, 1984, 42–76, 55–56.
58. Shigemitsu, *Japanese Criminal Procedure*, 323.
59. Prosecutorial discretion is an issue discussed by a variety of commentators, including Dando Shigemitsu, "System of Discretionary Prosecution in Japan," *American Journal of Comparative Law* 18, 1970, 518–531; George, "Discretionary Authority," 42–76; Marcia E. Goodman, "The Exercise and Control of Prosecutorial Discretion in Japan," *UCLA Pacific Basin Law Journal* 5, 1986; and Daniel H. Foote, "The Benevolent Paternalism of Japanese Criminal Justice," *California Law Review* 80, 1992, 317–390. John Haley says that the biggest difference between criminal procedure in Japan and Germany is the high degree of discretion allowed to police, prosecutors, and judges. See John Haley, *Authority Without Power: Law and the Japanese Paradox*, New York: Oxford University Press, 1991, 126.
60. This section relies on the excellent analysis provided in Yonemoto Shōhei's *Sentan Kakumei Iryō*, Tokyo: Chūō-Kōron Shupansha, 1988.

61. Ibid., Chapter 2, particularly its treatment of the Wada incident, provides an excellent account of the debate over brain death and organ transplantation in Japan.
62. My discussion of these questions is based on a more detailed description provided in Mizuno Hajime, *Nōshi to Zōki Ishoku*, Tokyo: Kinokuniya, 1991, 13–29.
63. Both Yonemoto and Mizuno take this position.
64. Teruo Fujimoto, "Hōken Shoken Kara Mita Shin Ishoku," *Saishin Igaku*, March 1969.
65. Miyahara Mitsuo, "Shinzō Ishoku Tōki ni Okeru Seishi Hantei," *Naika*, special issue, "Rinshōka no tame no Seishi Hantei," May 1969.
66. Mizuno, *Nōshi*, 21–22.
67. Yonemoto, *Sentan*, 45.
68. Ibid., 45.
69. Honda Katsunori and Andō Hiroyuki, "Brain Death and Patients' Rights," presented at the International Conference on Health Law and Medicine, Sydney, Australia, August 20, 1986, 12.
70. One of them, the so-called 9.5 incident in Osaka, is the subject of a book, Osaka Byōin "Nōshi" to Zōki Ishoku no Mondai o Sasaeru Kai, *Zōki Tekishutsu wa Tadashikatta ka*, Tokyo: Azusa Shoten, 1991.
71. Interview with Mitsuishi Tadahiro, July 25, 1991, Tokyo, Japan.
72. Interview with Hirano Ryōichi, November 27, 1991, Tokyo, Japan.
73. Interview with Hironaka Junichirō, August 6, 1991, Tokyo, Japan.
74. Interview with Ogata Tsuyoshi, July 21, 1993, Tokyo, Japan.
75. Honda and Andō, "Brain Death," 22.

7 A sociolegal perspective on rights in Japan
1. Frank Upham, in a recent review of the field of Japanese legal studies, writes that in the 1980s, "the idea that law was either socially or politically insignificant or culturally determined in a strong sense was pretty well dead within the coterie of Japanese law scholars. It remains alive in the world of mainstream comparative law ...." Frank Upham, "The Development of Japanese Legal Studies in American Law Schools," prepared for the Reischauer Institute 25th Anniversary Symposium on the Postwar Development of Japanese Studies, Fall, 1996.
2. Reinhard Bendix, *Nation-Building and Citizenship: Studies in Our Changing Social Order*, Berkeley, CA: University of California Press, 1964, 361–434.
3. Ibid., 364.
4. Ibid., 410.
5. Harry Eckstein, *Regarding Politics: Essays on Political Theory, Stability, and Change*, Berkeley, CA: University of California Press, 1992, 232.
6. Bendix, *Nation-Building*, 418–419.
7. For three consecutive years the annual journal of the Japanese Association of Sociology of Law was devoted to an examination of legal consciousness in Japan. See Nihon Hō Shakaigaku Kaihen, "Shimpojyūmu: Hō Ishiki o Meguru Shomondai," *Hō Shakaigaku*, 1984–1986, 36–38.

Some of the Japanese literature on legal consciousness is reviewed in Miyazawa Setsuo, "Taking Kawashima Seriously: A Review of Japanese Research on Japanese Legal Consciousness," *Law and Society Review* 21 (2), 1987. A good overview of the field of legal sociology in Japan can be found in Rokumoto Kahei, *Hō Shakaigaku*, Tokyo: Yūhikaku, 1986, 141–161, and Rokumoto Kahei, "'Nihonjin no Hō Ishiki' Kenkyu Gaikan – Hō Kannen o Chūshin Toshite," *Hō Shakaigaku* 35, 1983, 14–33, which contains an eight page supplement of sources on legal consciousness.

Miyazawa, in "Taking Kawashima Seriously," writes that "legal consciousness is another term for [legal culture]" (221). In fact, there may be a slight difference in nuance – legal consciousness refers more explicitly than legal culture to individual thoughts and beliefs, which as will be discussed later in this chapter, is what Japanese legal sociologists have studied. But the terms are broadly overlapping, and I will use them interchangeably except when the terms themselves are being discussed.

8. Winston Davis, *Japanese Religion and Society: Paradigms of Structure and Change*, Albany, NY: State University of New York Press, 1992, 253–270, contains an excellent discussion of what he calls the *Nihonron* literature.

9. Kawashima Takeyoshi, "Nihonjin no Gengo Ishiki to Hōritsu," *Sekai*, February 1979, 260–261.

10. Ibid., 249–250.

11. The Japanologist Winston Davis has written: "While Japan theory [*Nihonjinron*] is largely intuitive, generally anecdotal, and often ideologically motivated, I would contend that the theorists are trying to tell us, and their fellow Japanese, something important about their country, its tradition and basic values." Davis, *Japanese Religion*, at 267–268. I believe he is correct, and prefer to examine rather than to dismiss claims to uniqueness.

12. It should be noted that the current fascination with globalization is the most recent manifestation of interest in the cross-border transfer of legal rules and institutions.

13. Ugo Mattei, "Efficiency in Legal Transplants: An Essay in Comparative Law and Economics," *International Review of Law and Economics* 14 (1), March 1994, 3–4.

14. Bendix, *Nation-Building*, 413.

15. Ibid., 415.

16. Alan Watson, *Legal Transplants: An Approach to Comparative Law*, Charlottesville, VA: University Press of Virginia, 1974, 27; for a defense and elaboration of the idea of legal transplants, see, Alan Watson, "Legal Change, Sources of Law and Legal Culture," *University of Pennsylvania Law Review* 131(5), April 1983, 1121–1157.

17. Ibid., 20.

18. Chalmers Johnson, "The Foundations of Japan's Wealth and Power and Why They Baffle the United States," presented to the Workshop on "Japan as Techno-Economic Superpower: Implications for the United

States," Los Alamos National Laboratory, Santa Fe, New Mexico, November 1993, 22.

19. Lawrence M. Friedman, "Legal Culture and Social Development," *Law and Society Review* 4, 1969, 29–44, 34; Lawrence M. Friedman, *Total Justice*, New York: Russell Sage Foundation, 1985, 31. Either implicitly or explicitly, most studies of legal culture have taken a narrow view of law, treating it as constituting the formal decisions of state agencies bounded by explicit rules. Robert Ellickson of Yale Law School, for example, defines law as rules that emanate from government. (Robert Ellickson, *Order Without Law: How Neighbors Settle Disputes*, Cambridge, MA: Harvard University Press, 1991, 127.) John O. Haley treats law as consisting of two aspects, "a corpus of legitimate rules," and "a coercive command at least in enforcement." (John O. Haley, *Authority Without Power: Law and the Japanese Paradox*, New York: Oxford University Press, 1991, 13; see his discussion of the definition of law at 5–13.) By creating a sharp distinction between law and non-law, both Ellickson and Haley implicitly reject the insights of legal anthropologists and legal sociologists who stress that the rules and norms of non-state bodies are also law, as are other concepts and doctrines that may be evolving but are not enshrined in the state's corpus of formal rules. The "legal" in legal culture should be thought of in its broadest sense – rules and norms of state and non-state bodies that are created, exist, and are enforced in formal and informal ways. The boundaries between law and non-law are more practical than theoretical. Where the boundaries are drawn, if they are drawn, and the process through which they are drawn is product of each legal culture and will differ between them.

20. Austin Sarat, "Studying American Legal Culture: An Assessment of Survey Evidence," *Law and Society Review* 11, 1977, 427.

21. Henry W. Ehrmann, *Comparative Legal Cultures*, Englewood Cliffs, NJ: Prentice-Hall, Inc., 1976, 9.

22. John Henry Merryman, *The Civil Law Tradition*, Stanford, CA: Stanford University Press, 1969, 2.

23. Ehrmann, *Comparative Legal Cultures*, 13. Ehrmann's four "families" of legal culture are Romano-Germanic, common law, socialist law, and non-Western law.

24. Friedman, in *Total Justice*, at several junctures discusses the inaccuracy of writing about *the* American legal culture, but having done so he continues with his analysis of American legal character and culture.

25. James L. Gibson and Gregory A. Caldeira, "The Legal Cultures of Europe," *Law and Society Review* 30, 1996, 55.

26. Joseph Sanders and V. Lee Hamilton, "Legal Cultures and Punishment Repertoires in Japan, Russia, and the United States," *Law and Society Review*, 1992, 117; Gunter Bierbrauer, "Toward an Understanding of Legal Culture: Variations in Individualism and Collectivism between Kurds, Lebanese, and Germans," *Law and Society Review* 28, 1994, 243.

27. Thomas W. Church, Jr., "Examining Local Legal Culture," *American Bar Foundation Research Journal* 3, 1986, 449; Patricia Ewick and Susan

S. Silbey, "Conformity, Contestation, and Resistance: An Account of Legal Consciousness," *New England Law Review* 26, 1992, 731.

28. Eckstein, *Regarding Politics*, 267.
29. Friedman, *Total Justice*, 34.
30. Sarat, "American Legal Cultures," 430.
31. *Ibid.*, 431.
32. One of the most stimulating debates about legal culture can be found in David Nelken, ed., *Comparing Legal Cultures*, Aldershot: Dartmouth, 1997, which captures an exchange between David Nelken and Erhard Blankenburg about how to conceptualize, analyze, and measure legal culture comparatively.
33. Roger Cotterrell, "The Concept of Legal Culture," in Nelken, ed., *Comparing Legal Cultures*, 15.
34. David Nelken, "Disclosing/Invoking Legal Culture: An Introduction," *Social and Legal Studies* 4, 1995, 435.
35. Ruth Benedict, *The Chrysanthemum and the Sword: Patterns of Japanese Culture*, Boston: Houghton Mifflin Co., 1946.
36. Robert E. Ward, "Japan: The Continuity of Modernization," in Lucian W. Pye and Sidney Verba, eds., *Political Culture and Political Development*, Princeton, NJ: Princeton University Press, 1965, 27–82. Other studies of Japanese political culture include Ishida Takeshi, *Japanese Political Culture*, New Brunswick, NJ: Transaction Books, 1983; and Bradley Richardson, *The Political Culture of Japan*, Berkeley, CA: University of California Press, 1974.
37. Susan Pharr, *Losing Face: Status Politics in Japan*, Berkeley, CA: University of California Press, 1990 28–29.
38. Koga Masayoshi, "Kenri Ishiki ni Tsuite," *Hanrei Taimuzu (Bessatsu)* 3, 1977, 17.
39. Dave Barry, *Dave Barry Does Japan*, New York: Fawcett Columbine, 1992, 63.
40. For an historical discussion of individualism in Japan, with emphasis on the way in which it has changed in recent decades, see Yamazaki Masakazu, "Atarashii Kojinshugi no Yochō," *Chūō Kōron* 98, August 1983, 62–88.
41. Hironaka Toshio, "Hō Ishiki Kenkyū no Mondai," *Hō Shakaigaku* 35, 1983, 5–13, explicitly makes this point.
42. Pharr, *Losing Face*, 182–183.
43. Kawashima and others write about *hō ishiki* [legal consciousness] and *hō bunka* [legal culture] interchangeably. A good overview of the themes of the literature can be found in Murakami Junichi, *Kenri no Tame no Tōsō o Yomu*, Tokyo: Iwanami, 1983, 267–288; Frank Upham surveys and analyzes the field of Japanese legal sociology in "What's Happening in Japan, Sociolegalwise," *Law and Society Review* 23(5), 1989.
44. Kawashima Takeyoshi, *Nihonjin no Hō Ishiki*, Tokyo: Iwanami, 1967, 5.
45. Miyazawa Setsuo, "Taking Kawashima Seriously: A Review of Japanese Research on Japanese Legal Consciousness and Disputing Behavior," *Law and Society Review* 21(2), 1987, 220.

46. Kawashima Takeyoshi, "The Status of the Individual in the Notion of Law, Right, and Social Order in Japan," in Charles A. Moore, ed., *The Japanese Mind: Essentials of Japanese Philosophy*, Honolulu: East-West Center Press, University of Hawaii Press, 1967, 274.

47. George Sansom, *The Western World and Japan*, New York: Alfred A. Knopf, 1950, 446.

48. Kawashima, "The Status of the Individual," 280.

49. Kawashima, *Nihonjin no Hō Ishiki*, 17.

50. Rokumoto Kahei, *Hō Shakaigaku*, Tokyo: Yūhikaku, 1986, ch. 5, 189–232.

51. Miyazawa, "Taking Kawashima Seriously," 222.

52. Ibid., 237.

53. Rokumoto Kahei, "Nihonjin no Hō Ishiki no Chōsa," *Hōgaku Kyōshitsu* 109, October 1989, 97.

54. Toshitani Nobuyoshi, "Kokumin Seikatsu to Hōritsu no Hedatari: Nihonjin no Hō Ishiki," *Tōki no Hōrei*, Tokushō, 1236, 1985, 8–24, 10–11.

55. This study was described by Miyazawa in his review of the literature on Japanese legal culture, supra note 45.

56. Miyazawa, "Taking Kawashima Seriously," 234.

57. Ibid., 223.

58. Wada Yasuhiro, "Nichijyo no Naka no Funsō Shōri," *Tokyo Toritsu Daigaku Hō Gakkai Zasshi* 24(2), 25(1), 1983–1984, 1–73, 41–119.

59. Miyazawa, "Taking Kawashima Seriously," 236.

60. Ibid., 226–227.

61. Ibid., 228, 232.

62. One long study of legal consciousness that relies almost entirely on such methods is Nihon Bunka Kaigi, *Gendai Nihonjin no Hō Ishiki*, Tokyo: Daiichi Hōki, 1982.

63. Miyazawa, "Taking Kawashima Seriously," 227.

64. Rokumoto Kahei, "Hō Ishiki no Sokutei," in Yamauchi Toshio, ed., *Noda Yoshiyuki sensei Koki Kinen: Tozai Hō Bunka no Hikaku to Kōryu*, Tokyo: Yūhikaku, 1983, 21–44.

65. Ōki Masao, *Nihonjin no Hō Gainen*, Tokyo: Tokyo University Press, 1983.

66. Ibid., 218–219.

67. Ibid., 26.

68. Mizubayashi Takeshi, "'Nihonteki Hō Ishiki' no Rekishiteki Kiso," *Hō Shakaigaku* 35, 1983, 34–47.

69. Kumagai Kaisaku, "'Nihonteki Hō Ishiki' Keisei no Rekishi Katei no Ichirei," *Hō Shakaigaku* 36, 1984, 24–36.

70. John O. Haley, "The Myth of the Reluctant Litigant," *Journal of Japanese Studies* 4(2), 1978, 359.

71. Ibid., 366–367.

72. John O. Haley, "Sheathing the Sword of Justice in Japan: An Essay on Law Without Sanctions," *Journal of Japanese Studies* 8(2) 1982, 281.

73. Miyazawa, "Taking Kawashima Seriously," 222.

74. Haley, *Authority Without Power*, 7, 13.
75. Michael Thompson, Richard Ellis, and Aaron Wildavsky, *Cultural Theory*, San Francisco, CA: Westview Press, 1990, 21.
76. Robert Putnam, *Making Democracy Work: Civic Traditions in Modern Italy*, Princeton, NJ: Princeton University Press, 1993, 181–182.
77. Aaron Wildavsky, "Choosing Preferences by Constructing Institutions: A Cultural Theory of Preference Formation," *American Political Science Review* 81(1), March 1987, 3–21, 8.
78. Frank Upham, *Law and Social Change in Postwar Japan*, Cambridge, MA: Harvard University Press, 1987, 25.
79. J. Mark Ramseyer, *Odd Markets in Japanese History: Law and Economic Growth*, New York: Cambridge University Press, 1996, 8.
80. J. Mark Ramseyer, "Reluctant Litigant Revisited: Rationality and Disputes in Japan," *Journal of Japanese Studies* 14, 111, 1988.
81. Ibid.
82. Upham, in *Law and Social Change*, and Pharr, in *Losing Face*, both discuss women and Burakumin, and Upham also discusses environmental conflict. While neither of them treats rights assertion as an analytical focus – indeed, while Upham clearly assumes that rights are powerful, he devotes little attention to them, and Pharr is openly skeptical of the relevance of rights in the Japanese context – their books can both be seen as laying the groundwork for an examination of rights in the cases they present.
83. See Upham, "Japanese Legal Studies."
84. John Haley argues that prior to the influence of Western law in China, Korea, and Japan, "there were no rights only duties." *Authority Without Power*, 11. Although I do not agree with his assessment that there was no concept of rights in Japan until the adaptation of Western law, I do agree that the link between rights and duties may be illuminated by examining Japanese law.
85. Eric A. Feldman, "Mirroring Minds: Recruitment and Promotion in Japan's Law Faculties," *American Journal of Comparative Law* 41, 1993, 468.

BIBLIOGRAPHY

Abe, Yasutaka, "Kenri no Keisei to Hatten" [The Constitution of Rights and its Development], *Hō Shakaigaku* 39, 1987, 17–27.

Akatsu, Haruko, "The Heart, the Gut, and Brain Death in Japan," *Hastings Center Report*, March/April 1990.

Anesaki, Masaharu, *History of Japanese Religion with Special Reference to the Social and Moral Life of the Nation*, London: K. Paul, Trench, Trubner & Co., 1930.

Aoki, Kōji, *Hyakushō Ikki no Sōgō Nempyō* [An Integrated Chronoogical Table of Peasant Rebellions], Tokyo: Sanichi Shobo, 1971.

Awaji, Takehisa, "Minji Hō no Ryōiki" [The Domain of Civil Law], *Hō Shakaigaku* 38, 1986, 8–18.

Bai, Kōichi, *Iji Hōgaku e no Ayumi* [The Road to Medical Jurisprudence], Tokyo: Iwanami, 1970 (originally published 1965).

　Iryō to Jinken [Health Care and Human Rights], Tokyo: Chūō Hōki Shuppan, 1985.

　"Nōshi Riron no Ronri: 'Saigo Hōkokusho' Hihan" [The Logic of Brain Death: Criticism of the Final Report], *Sekai*, October 1988, 32–46.

Bai, Kōichi and Hirabayashi Katsumasa, "The Legal Situation in Japan" and "Whose Consent Shall Make Organ Removal Lawful," in "Symposium: A Comparative Legal Study of Organ Transplantation: Requirements for Organ Removal from Cadavers," *Comparative Law Journal* 46, 1984.

Barry, Dave, *Dave Barry Does Japan*, New York: Fawcett Columbine, 1992.

Barshay, Andrew, *State and Intellectual in Imperial Japan: The Public Man in Crisis*, Berkeley, CA: University of California Press, 1988.

Bayer, Ronald, *Private Acts, Social Consequences: AIDS and the Politics of Public Health*, New York: The Free Press, 1989.

Beasley, W. G., *The Rise of Modern Japan*, London: Weidenfeld and Nicolson, 1990.

Bendix, Reinhard, *Nation-Building and Citizenship: Studies in Our Changing Social Order*, Berkeley, CA: University of California Press, 1964.

Benedict, Ruth, *The Chrysanthemum and the Sword: Patterns of Japanese Culture*, Boston: Houghton Mifflin Co., 1946.

Bierbrauer, Gunter, "Toward an Understanding of Legal Culture: Variations in Individualism and Collectivism between Kurds, Lebanese, and Germans," *Law and Society Review* 28, 1994.

Bix, Herbert, *Peasant Protest in Japan, 1590–1884*, New Haven, CT: Yale University Press, 1986.

Blacker, Carmine, *The Japanese Enlightenment: A Study of the Writings of Fukuzawa Yūkichi*, Cambridge: Cambridge University Press, 1964.

Blood Services Department, Japanese Red Cross Society, *Blood Services*, Tokyo: Japanese Red Cross Society, 1993.

Bohannan, Paul, *Justice and Judgment Among the Tiv*, London: Oxford University Press for the African Institute, 1957.

Boling, Patricia, "Private Interest and the Public Good in Japan," *The Pacific Review* 3(2), 1990.

Bowen, Roger W., *Rebellion and Democracy in Meiji Japan: A Study of Commoners in the Popular Rights Movement*, Berkeley, CA: University of California Press, 1980.

Broadbent, Jeffery, *Environmental Politics in Japan: Networks of Power and Protest*, New York: Cambridge University Press, 1998.

Calman, Donald, *The Nature and Origins of Japanese Imperialism*, New York: Routledge, 1992.

Church, Jr., Thomas W., "Examining Local Legal Culture," *American Bar Foundation Research Journal* 3, 1986, 449.

Cotterrell, Roger, "The Concept of Legal Culture," in David Nelken, ed., *Comparing Legal Cultures*, Aldershot: Dartmouth Publishing Company, 1997.

Dale, Peter, *The Myth of Japanese Uniqueness*, New York: St. Martin's Press, 1986.

Dando, Shigemitsu, *Japanese Criminal Procedure*, trans. B. J. George, South Hackensack, NJ: Fred B. Rothman & Co., 1965.

"System of Discretionary Prosecution in Japan," *American Journal of Comparative Law* 18, 1970, 518–531.

Davis, Winston, *Japanese Religion and Society: Paradigms of Structure and Change*, Albany, NY: State University of New York Press, 1992.

Dower, John, *War Without Mercy: Race and Power in the Pacific War*, New York: Pantheon, 1986.

Dunn, John, "Rights and Political Conflict," in Larry Gostin, ed., *Civil Liberties in Conflict*, New York: Routledge, 1988.

Duus, Peter, *The Rise of Modern Japan*, Boston: Houghton Mifflin Co., 1976.

Ebashi, Takashi, "Kansenbyō Taisaku to Jinken" [Infectious Disease Policy and Human Rights], in Yamada Takao, Ōi Gen, Negishi Masayoshi, et al., *AIDS ni Manabu* [Studying AIDS], Tokyo: Nihon Hyōronsha, 1991, 151–170.

Eckstein, Harry, *Regarding Politics: Essays on Political Theory, Stability, and Change*, Berkeley, CA: University of California Press, 1992.

Ehrmann, Henry W., *Comparative Legal Cultures*, Englewood Cliffs, NJ: Prentice-Hall, 1976.

Ellickson, Robert C., *Order Without Law: How Neighbors Settle Disputes*, Cambridge, MA: Harvard University Press, 1991.

Epstein, Steven, *Impure Science: AIDS, Activism, and the Politics of Knowledge*, Berkeley, CA: University of California Press, 1996.

Ewick, Patricia and Susan S. Silbey, "Conformity, Contestation, and Resistance: An Account of Legal Consciousness," *New England Law Review* 26, 1992.

Feeley, Malcolm M., "Hollow Hopes, Flypaper, and Metaphors," *Law and Social Inquiry* 17(4), Fall 1992, 745–760.

Feldman, Eric A., "Mirroring Minds: Recruitment and Promotion in Japan's Law Faculties," *American Journal of Comparative Law* 41, 1993, 465–479.

"Culture, Conflict, and Cost: Perspectives on Brain Death in Japan," *International Journal of Technology Assessment in Health Care* 10, 1994, 447–463.

"Legal Transplants, Organ Transplants: The Japanese Experience," *Social and Legal Studies* 3, 1994, 71–91.

"Over My Dead Body: The Enigma and Economics of Brain Death in Japan," in Ikegami Naoki and John C. Campbell, eds., *Containing Health Care Costs in Japan*, Ann Arbor, MI: University of Michigan Press, 1996.

"Patients' Rights, Citizens' Movements, and Japanese Legal Culture," in David Nelken, ed., *Comparing Legal Cultures*, Aldershot: Dartmouth Publishing Company, 1997.

"HIV and Blood in Japan: Transforming Private Conflict into Public Scandal," in Eric A. Feldman and Ronald Bayer, eds., *Blood Feuds: AIDS, Blood, and the Politics of Medical Disaster*, New York: Oxford University Press, 1999.

Feldman, Eric A. and Yonemoto Shohei, "Japan: AIDS as a Non-issue," in David L. Kirp and Ronald Bayer, eds., *AIDS in the Industrial Democracies: Passion, Politics, and Policies*, New Brunswick, NJ: Rutgers University Press, 1992.

Field, Norma, *In the Realm of a Dying Emperor: A Portrait of Japan at Century's End*, New York: Pantheon, 1991.

Fisher, Jerry K., "The Meirokusha and the Building of a Strong and Prosperous Nation," in Harry Wray and Hilary Conroy, eds., *Japan Examined: Perspectives on Modern Japanese History*, Honolulu: University of Hawaii Press, 1983, 83–97.

Foote, Daniel H., "The Benevolent Paternalism of Japanese Criminal Justice," *California Law Review* 80, 1992, 317–390.

Friedman, Lawrence M., "Legal Culture and Social Development," *Law and Society Review* 4, 1969, 29–44.

Total Justice, New York: Russell Sage Foundation, 1985.

Fujimoto, Teruo, "Hōken Shoken Kara Mita Shin Ishoku" [Heart Transplants from the Perspective of Autopsy], *Saishin Igaku* [Modern Medicine], March 1969.

Fukuzawa, Yūkichi, *An Encouragement of Learning*, trans. David A. Dilworth and Hirano Umeyo, Tokyo: Sophia University Press, 1969.

An Outline of a Theory of Civilization, trans. David A. Dilworth and G. Cameron Hurst, Tokyo: Sophia University, 1973.

Gekkan Asahi, "Zōki Ishoku ni Gō Sign wa Detaka?" [Has the Go Sign been Given for Organ Transplantation?], interview with Ōta Kazuo and Nishioka Yoshiki, March 1992.

George, Jr., B. J., "Discretionary Authority of Public Prosecutors in Japan," *Law in Japan* 17, 1984, 42–76.

Gibson, James L. and Gregory A. Caldeira, "The Legal Cultures of Europe," *Law and Society Review* 30, 1996, 55.

Glendon, Mary Ann, *Abortion and Divorce in Western Law*, Cambridge, MA: Harvard University Press, 1987.

Rights Talk: The Impoverishment of Political Discourse, New York: The Free Press, 1991.

Gluck, Carol, *Japan's Modern Myths: Ideology in the Late Meiji Period*, Princeton, NJ: Princeton University Press, 1985.

Gluckman, Max, "Natural Justice in Africa," in Csaba Varga, ed., *Comparative Legal Cultures*, New York: New York University Press, 1992.

Goodman, Marcia E., "The Exercise and Control of Prosecutorial Discretion in Japan," *UCLA Pacific Basin Law Journal* 5, 1986.

Greenhouse, Carol J., "Interpreting American Litigiousness," in June Starr and Jane F. Collier, eds., *History and Power in the Study of Law*, Ithaca, NY: Cornell University Press, 1989, 252–273.

Gresser, Julian, Fujikura Kōichiro, and Morishima Akio, *Environmental Law in Japan*, Cambridge, MA: MIT Press, 1981.

Grossberg, Kenneth, ed. and trans., *The Laws of the Muromachi Bakufu*, Tokyo: Monumenta Nipponica, 1981.

Haley, John O., "The Myth of the Reluctant Litigant," *Journal of Japanese Studies* 4(2), 1978, 359–390.

"Sheathing the Sword of Justice in Japan: An Essay on Law Without Sanctions," *Journal of Japanese Studies* 8(2), 1982, 265–281.

Authority Without Power: Law and the Japanese Paradox, New York: Oxford University Press, 1991.

Hall, John Carey, *Japanese Feudal Law*, Washington, DC: University Publications of America, 1979.

Hall, John W., *Japan from Prehistory to Modern Times*, New York: Dell Publishing Co., 1970, 71.

Hane, Mikiso, "The Movement for Liberty and Popular Rights," in Harry Wray and Hilary Conroy, eds., *Japan Examined: Perspectives on Modern Japanese History*, Honolulu: University of Hawaii Press, 1983.

Harootunian, Harry, "Ideology as Conflict," in Najita Tetsuo and J. Victor Koschmann, eds., *Conflict in Modern Japanese History*, Princeton, NJ: Princeton University Press, 1982, 31–36.

Hasegawa, Kōichi, "Gendaigata Soshō no Shakai Undōronteki Kōsatsu" [A Social Movement Inquiry into Contemporary Litigation], *Hōritsu Jihō* 61(12), October 1989, 65–71.

Hashimoto, Mitsuru, "The Social Background of Peasant Uprisings in Tokugawa Japan," in Najita and Koschmann, *Conflict in Modern Japanese History*, Princeton, NJ: Princeton University Press, 1982.

Hatakeyama, Takemichi, "AIDS Hōan o Meguru Sho Mondai" [Various Problems of the AIDS Bill], *Jurisuto* 888, June 15, 1987, 83–87.

Hearn, Lafcadio, *Japan: An Attempt at Interpretation*, Rutland, VT: Charles C. Tuttle Co., 1955 (originally published 1904).

Henderson, Dan Fenno, *Conciliation and Japanese Law: Tokugawa and Modern*, Washington: University of Washington Press, 1965, 2 volumes.

Herbert, Jean, *Shintō*, New York: Stein and Day, 1967.

Higuchi, Norio, "The Patient's Right to Know of a Cancer Diagnosis: A Comparison of Japanese Paternalism and American Self-Determination," *Washburn Law Journal* 31(3), 1992, 455–473.

Hirasawa, Masao, "Iryō Henkaku to Shimin Undō" [Health Care Reform and People's Movements], in *Jurisuto*, Tokushū, *Iryō to Jinken* [Health Care and Human Rights], 548, November 25, 1973, 273–277.

Hironaka, Toshio, "Hō Ishiki Kenkyū no Mondai" [The Problem of Studying Legal Consciousness], *Hō Shakaigaku* 35, 1983, 5–13.

HIV Soshō Benkyo Kai, "44 Ki Shihō Shūshūsei Natsu no Shūkai Hōkokushū" [A Collection of Reports of the 44th Judicial Apprentices' Summer Meeting], Kyoto, April 27–28, 1991, 96–117.

Honda, Katsunori and Andō Hiroyuki, "Brain Death and Patients' Rights," paper presented at the International Conference on Health Law and Medicine, Sydney, Australia, August 20, 1986.

Hozumi, Nobushige, *Ancestor Worship and Japanese Law*, New York: Books for Libraries Press, 1912 (reprinted 1973).

Huffman, James L., "The Popular Rights Debate: Political or Ideological?," in Harry Wray and Hilary Conroy, eds., *Japan Examined: Perspectives on*

Modern Japanese History, Honolulu: University of Hawaii Press, 1983, 98–103.

Ihara, Saikaku, *The Great Mirror of Male Love*, trans. Paul Gordon Shalow, Stanford, CA: Stanford University Press, 1990.

Iizuka, Tomoyuki and Itō Toshikatsu, "Wakai Kankoku o Dō Miru Ka?" [How Should We Understand the Settlement Proposal?], *Hōgaku Seminā* 492, December 1995, 17–20.

Ike, Nobutaka, *The Beginnings of Political Democracy in Japan*, New York: Greenwood Press, 1969.

Ikeda, Daisaku, "Nōshi Mondai ni Kansuru Ichi Kōsatsu" [Thoughts on the Problems of Brain Death], *Tōyōgaku Kenkyū* [Journal of Oriental Studies], 26(2) 1987.

Ikegami, Naoki and John Creighton Campbell, eds., *Containing Health Care Costs in Japan*, Ann Arbor, MI: University of Michigan Press, 1996.

Ikenaga, Mitsuru, "'Kanja no Kenri Hō' Seitei Undō no Igi to Gen Dankai" [The Purpose and Current Situation of the Movement to Establish a "Patients' Rights Law"], *Iji Hōgaku* 7, June 1992, 72–78.

Ikoma, Iwao, "Tokyo HIV Soshō no Mezasumono" [Objectives of the Tokyo HIV Lawsuit], *Nihon no Kagakusha* 28, July 1993, 388–393.

Imai, Shōzō, "Nihon ni Okeru Jinken no Kenkyū Dōkō" [The Trend in Human Rights Research in Japan], in Hasegawa Masayasu, ed., *Gendai Jinken Ron (Kōho Jinken Ron I)*, Tokyo: Hōritsu Bunkasha, 1982, 277–291.

Inamoto, Yonosuke, " 'Atarashii Kenri' no Kategorii to Sōgō Sakuyō" [Categories of "New Rights" and their Misuse], *Hō Shakaigaku* 40, 1988, 2–8.

Inoue, Kyoko, *MacArthur's Japanese Constitution: A Linguistic and Cultural Study of Its Making*, Chicago: University of Chicago Press, 1991.

Inoue, Tatsuo, "The Poverty of Rights-Blind Communality: Looking Through the Window of Japan," *Brigham Young University Law Review* 1993, 517–551.

Institute of Medicine, National Academy of Sciences, *Mobilizing Against AIDS*, Cambridge, MA: Harvard University Press, 1986.

HIV and the Blood Supply, Washington, DC: National Academy Press, 1995.

Ishida, Takeshi, *Japanese Political Culture*, New Brunswick, NJ: Transaction Books, 1983.

Ishida, Yoshiaki, "Objection to the Legalization of AIDS Countermeasures," unpublished document, Kyoto Branch, Japanese Society of Friends of Hemophiliacs, 1987.

"AIDS Taisaku no Hō Seika ni Hantai," *Asahi Shimbun*, February 9, 1987.

Ishii, Ryōsuke, *Nihon Hōseishi Gaisetsu* [Survey of Japanese Legal History], Tokyo: Kōfundō, 2d ed., 1949.

Review, trans. K. Huff, of Dan Fenno Henderson's *Conciliation and*

Japanese Law – Tokogawa and Modern, in *Law in Japan: An Annual*, vol II, 1968, 198–224.

Jinken Yobō Sentā, "AIDS kara HIV e" [from AIDS to HIV], Tokyo, 1990.

Jiyū Jinken Kyōkai, "'AIDS Taisaku' wa Dō Aru Bekika" [What an AIDS Policy Should Be], Tokyo, March 10, 1988.

Johnson, Chalmers, "Trade, Revisionism, and the Future of Japanese–American Relations," in Yamamura Kōzō, ed., *Japan's Economic Structure: Should it Change?*, Seattle, WA: Society for Japanese Studies, 1990, 105–136.

"The Foundation of Japan's Wealth and Power and Why They Baffle the United States," presented to the workshop on "Japan as Techno-Economic Superpower: Implications for the United States," Los Alamos National Laboratory, Santa Fe, NM, November 18–19, 1993.

Japan: Who Governs, New York: W.W. Norton & Company, 1995.

Jowett, Benjamin, trans., *The Dialogues of Plato*, in *Great Books of the Western World*, ed. Robert Maynard Hutchins, Chicago: Encyclopaedia Britannica, 1952.

Kamei, Masateru, "HIV Soshō no Gaiyō" [Summary of the HIV Litigation], *Hōgaku Seminā* 481, January 1995, 22–26.

Kanja no Kenri Hō o Tsukuru Kai, *Kanja no Kenri Hō o Tsukuru* [Making a Patients' Rights Law], Tokyo: Meiseki Shoten, 1992.

Kass, Leon, "Is There a Right to Die?," *Hastings Center Report*, January/February 1993.

Katahira, Kiyohiko and Satō Tsugumichi, "AIDS as Drug-Induced Suffering in Japan," in S. Araki, ed., *Behavioral Medicine: An Integrated Biobehavioral Approach to Health and Illness*, Dordrecht: Elsevier Science Publishers, 1992.

"AIDS Hassei no Shoki ni Okeru Nihon no Ketsuyūbyō-Ketsueki Seizai Kankeisha no Ninshiki to Taiō" [The Awareness and Responses of People Associated with Hemophiliacs and Blood Products in the Early Stages of the AIDS Epidemic in Japan], *Nihon no Kagakusha* 28 (306), July 1993, 17–22.

Katahira, Kiyohiko et al., "Improvement of the Law and Procedures to Relieve Drug-Induced Suffering and to Prevent its Occurrence: Lessons from the Clioquinol Lawsuit and Other Cases in Japan," Proceedings of the Kyoto International Conference Against Drug-Induced Suffering, April 14–18, 1979, International Congress Series 513.

Katō, Ichirō, *Nōshi Zōki Ishoku to Jinken* [Brain Death, Organ Transplantation, and Human Rights], Tokyo: Yūhikaku, 1986.

"Nōshi Mondai: Shakai teki Gōi wa Shinkirō" [Brain Death: Social Consensus is a Mirage], *Bungei Shunjyū* 4, 1988, 106–115.

Katō, Ichirō et al., "Nōshi Rinchō Saishū Tōshin o Megutte" [On the Final Report of the Ad Hoc Committee], *Jurisuto* 1001, June 1, 1992, 9–34.

Kawaguchi, Takao, "The Conversation: Minami Teishiro," *Tokyo Journal*, August 1992, 23–25.

Kawashima, Takeyoshi, *Nihonjin no Hō Ishiki* [The Legal Consciousness of the Japanese], Tokyo: Iwanami, 1967.

"The Status of the Individual in the Notion of Law, Right, and Social Order in Japan," in Charles A. Moore, ed., *The Japanese Mind: Essentials of Japanese Philosophy*, Honolulu: East-West Center Press, University of Hawaii Press, 1967.

"Nihonjin no Gengo Ishiki to Hōritsu" [Law and the Linguistic Consciousness of the Japanese], *Sekai*, February 1979.

Kierstead, Thomas, *The Geography of Power in Medieval Japan*, Princeton, NJ: Princeton University Press, 1992.

Kihara, Masahiro, "Saikin Nihon Gaikokujin HIV Kansenshasū no Zōka o Dō Miruka" [Interpreting the Recent Increase of HIV Infection Rates among Foreigners in Japan], *Nihon Kōshū Eisei Zasshi* 40 (11), November 15, 1993, 1001–1005.

Kihara, Masahiro and Kihara Masako, "Wagakuni no HIV Kansen Hayari no Ekigaku" [Epidemiology of HIV Infection Rates in Japan], *Kikan Rōdōhō* 168, 1993, 34–42.

Kimura, Rihito, "Bioethics as Prescription for Civic Action: The Japanese Interpretation," *The Journal of Medicine and Philosophy* 12, 1987, 267–277.

Kirp, David L. and Ronald Bayer, eds., *AIDS in the Industrialized Democracies: Passions, Politics, and Policies*, New Brunswick, NJ: Rutgers University Press, 1992.

Kobayashi, Naoki, "Atarashii Kihonken no Tenkai" [Development of New Fundamental Law], *Jurisuto* 606, February 15, 1976, 15–27.

Koga, Masayoshi, "Kenri Ishiki ni Tsuite" [About Rights Consciousness], in *Hanrei Taimuzu (Bessatsu)* 3, 1977.

Konishi, Minoru, "Kenri Gainen o Meguru Ichi Kōsatsu" [One Inquiry Into the Concept of Rights], in Inoue Shigeru, *Gendai no Hō Tetsugaku*, Tokyo: Yūhikaku, 1981, 266–284.

Kōsei Kei Kyōkai, "Kōsei no Shihyō" [The Welfare Index], Tokyo: 1989.

Krauss, Ellis S., Thomas P. Rohlen, and Patricia G. Steinhoff, *Conflict in Japan*, Honolulu: University of Hawaii Press, 1984.

Kumagai, Kaisaku, "Nihonteki Hō Ishiki Keisei no Rekishi Katei no Ichirei" [One Example of the Historical Process of Formulating Japanese-style Legal Consciousness], *Hō Shakaigaku* 36, 1984.

LaFleur, William R., "Japan," in Frederick H. Holck, ed., *Death and Eastern Thought: Understanding Death in Eastern Religions and Philosophies*, Nashville, TN: Abingdon Press, 1974.

Lebra, Takie S., *Japanese Patterns of Behavior*, Honolulu: University of Hawaii Press, 1976.

Leflar, Robert B., "Informed Consent and Patients' Rights in Japan," *Houston Law Review* 3(1), 1996, 1–112.

Lewis, Michael, *Rioters and Citizens: Mass Protest in Imperial Japan*, Berkeley, CA: University of California Press, 1990.

Lock, Margaret and Christina Honde, "Reaching Consensus about Death: Heart Transplants and Cultural Identity in Japan," in G. Weisz, ed., *Social Science Perspectives on Medical Ethics*, Dordrecht, 1990.

McCann, Michael W., "Reform Litigation on Trial," *Law and Social Inquiry* 17(4), Fall 1992, 715–743.

    Rights at Work: Pay Equity Reform and the Politics of Legal Mobilization, Chicago: University of Chicago Press, 1994.

McKean, Margaret A., *Environmental Protest and Citizen Politics in Japan*, Berkeley, CA: University of California Press, 1981.

Maeda, Masaharu, "Kenri to Kenri Kakusho" [A Note on the Legal Terms "Kenri" and "Kenri"], *Hō to Seiji* 25, 1975, 347–386.

von Mehren, Arthur Taylor, ed., *Law in Japan: The Legal Order in a Changing Society*, Cambridge, MA: Harvard University Press, 1963.

Meiji Japan through Contemporary Sources, vol. II, *1844–1882*, compiled and published by The Centre for East Asian Cultural Studies, Tokyo, 1970.

Maruyama, Eiji, "Informed Consent: Ishi no Setsumei to Kanja no Shōdaku," *Hōgaku Kyōiku* 120, September 1990.

    "Japanese Law of Informed Consent," *Kobe University Law Review* 25, 1991, 39–43.

    "History and Theories of Brain Death in Japan Since 1985," *Journal of Behavioral and Social Sciences* (*Kōdō Kagaku Kenkyū*) 41, 1992, 45–57.

Maruyama, Masao, *Thought and Behavior in Modern Japanese Politics*, ed. Ivan Morris, New York: Oxford University Press, 1969.

Mass, Jeffery P., *The Development of Kamakura Rule*, Stanford, CA: Stanford University Press, 1979.

Matano, Hansuke, *Etō Nampaku*, Hara Shobō, 1914 (2nd ed. 1968).

Mattei, Ugo, "Efficiency in Legal Transplants: An Essay in Comparative Law and Economics," *International Review of Law and Economics* 14(1), March 1994, 3–19.

Melnick, R. Shep, "Separation of Powers and the Strategy of Rights: The Expansion of Special Education," in Marc K. Landy and Martin A. Levin, eds., *The New Politics of Public Policy*, Baltimore, MD: Johns Hopkins University Press, 1995, 23–46.

Merryman, John Henry, *The Civil Law Tradition*, Stanford, CA: Stanford University Press, 1969.

Minear, Richard, *Japanese Tradition and Western Law: Emperor, State, and Law in the Thought of Hozumi Yatsuka*, Cambridge, MA: Harvard University Press, 1970.

Ministry of Health and Welfare, "AIDS Control in Japan," May 1993.

AIDS Report, August 1997.

Ministry of Justice, *White Paper on Crime*, 1989.

Miyahara, Mitsuo, "Shinzō Ishoku Tōki ni Okeru Seishi Hantei" [Determination of Life and Death at the Time of Heart Transplants], in *Naika* [Internal Medicine], special issue, "Rinshōka no Tame no Seishi Hantei" [For Clinicians who make Determinations of Life and Death], May 1969.

Miyazawa, Setsuo, "Taking Kawashima Seriously: A Review of Japanese Research on Japanese Legal Consciousness and Disputing Behavior," *Law and Society Review* 21 (2), 1987, 219–241.

"Kenri Keisei/Tenkai no Shakai Undō Moderu o Mezashite" [Aiming for a Social Movement Model of Rights Formation/Process], *Hō Shakaigaku* 40, 1988, 33–46.

"Social Movements and Contemporary Rights in Japan: Relative Success Factors in the Field of Environmental Law," *Kobe University Law Review* 22, 1988.

Miyoshi, Masao, *Off Center: Power and Culture Relations between Japan and the United States*, Cambridge, MA: Harvard University Press, 1991.

Mizubayashi, Takeshi, "'Nihonteki Hō Ishiki' no Rekishiteki Kiso" [Historical Basis of Japanese-style Legal Consciousness], *Hō Shakaigaku* 35, 1983, 34–47.

Mizuno, Hajime, *Nōshi to Zōki Ishoku* [Brain Death and Organ Transplantation], Tokyo: Kinokuniya, 1991.

Murakami, Junichi, *Kenri no tame no Tōsō o Yomu* [Interpreting the Battle for Rights], Tokyo: Iwanami, 1983.

Namba, Nobuo, "Hyakushō Ikki no Hōishiki" [The Legal Consciousness of Peasant Rebellions], in Aoki Michio, ed., *Ikki*, vol. IV, of *Seikatsu, Bunka, Shisō*, Tokyo: University of Tokyo Press, 1981, 43–88.

Nelken, David, "Disclosing/Invoking Legal Culture: An Introduction," *Social and Legal Studies* 4, 1995.

Nelken, David, ed., *Comparing Legal Cultures*, Aldershot: Dartmouth Publishing Company, 1997.

Nihon Bunka Kaigi, *Gendai Nihonjin no Hō Ishiki* [The Legal Consciousness of Contemporary Japanese], Tokyo: Daiichi Hōki, 1982.

Nihon Hō Shakaigaku Kaihen, "Shimpojyūmu: Hō Ishiki o Meguru Shomondai" [Symposium: Various Problems Regarding Legal Consciousness], *Hō Shakaigaku*, 1984–1986.

Nihon Ishikai Seimei Rinri Kondankai, "Nōshi Oyobi Zōki Ishoku ni Tsuite" [Japan Medical Association Life Ethics Deliberative Council, "Concerning Brain Death and Organ Transplantation"], Chukan Hōkoku [Interim Report], Tokyo, March 25, 1987.

"Setsumei to Dōi' ni tsuite no Hōkoku" [Report on Informed Consent], *Jurisuto* 950, February 15, 1990, 149–157.

Niwayama Shōichiro, "Kokkai Tsūka o Isoida AIDS Yobō Hōan no Kiken-sei" [The Dangers of the AIDS Prevention Law which was Rushed through the Diet], *Shin Iryō*, December 1988, 34–36.

Noda, Yoshiyuki, *Introduction to Japanese Law*, ed. and trans. Anthony H. Angelo, Tokyo: University of Tokyo Press, 1976.

"Kenri to yū Kotoba no Imi ni Tsuite" [About the Word "Right"], *Gaku-shūin Daigaku Hōgakubu Kenkyūbu Kenkyū Nempō* 14, 1979.

Norman, E. H., *Origins of the Modern Japanese State*, ed. John W. Dower, New York: Pantheon, 1975.

Nudeshima, Jirō, *Nōshi/Zōki Ishoku to Nihon Shakai* [Brain Death, Organ Transplantation, and Japanese Society], Tokyo: Kōbundo, 1991.

Ohnuki-Tierney, Emiko, *Illness and Culture in Contemporary Japan*, New York: Cambridge University Press, 1984.

"Socio-cultural Dimensions of Renal Transplants in Japan," *Health Policy* 6, 1986.

Ōiwa, Yūri, "Nihon no Gei" [Gays in Japan], *Aera*, August 27, 1991, 18–22.

Ōki, Masao, *Nihonjin no Hō Gainen* [The Legal Outlook of the Japanese], Tokyo: Tokyo University Press, 1983.

Osaka Byōin "Nōshi" to Zōki Ishoku no Mondai o Sasaeru Kai, *Zōki Teki-shutsu wa Tadashikatta ka?*, [Was the Removal of the Organs Right?], Tokyo: Azusa Shoten, 1991.

Osaka Tomo no Kai, "Osaka Tomo no Kai Nyūsu" [Newsletter of the Osaka Friends Association], 65, May 1987.

Ōta Tomoyuki, "Kenri to yū Kotoba no Imi ni Tsuite" [On the Meaning of the Word "Right"], *Shisō* 5 (479), 1964, 25–35.

Pharr, Susan, *Losing Face: Status Politics in Japan*, Berkeley, CA: University of California Press, 1990.

Picken, Stuart D. B., "The Understanding of Death in Japanese Religion," *Japanese Religions* 9(4), July 1977.

Plath, David W., "Where the Family of God is the Family: The Role of the Dead in Japanese Households," *American Anthropologist* 66(2), April 1964.

Powell, Margaret and Anesaki Masahira, eds., *Health Care in Japan*, New York: Routledge, 1990.

Putnam, Robert, *Making Democracy Work: Civic Traditions in Modern Italy*, Princeton, NJ: Princeton University Press, 1993.

Pye, Lucian W. and Sidney Verba, *Political Culture and Political Development*, Princeton, NJ: Princeton University Press, 1965.

Ragin, Charles, *The Comparative Method: Moving Beyond Qualitative and Quantitative Strategies*, Berkeley, CA: University of California Press, 1987.

Ramseyer, J. Mark, *Odd Markets in Japanese History: Law and Economic Growth*, New York: Cambridge University Press, 1996.

"Water Law in Imperial Japan: Public Goods, Private Claims, and Legal Convergence," *The Journal of Legal Studies*, January 1989.

"Reluctant Litigant Revisited: Rationality and Disputes in Japan," *Journal of Japanese Studies* 14 (111), 1988.

Ramseyer, J. Mark and Nakazato Minoru, "The Rational Litigant: Settlement Amounts and Verdict Rates in Japan," *Journal of Legal Studies* 18, 1989, 263.

Reed, Stephen R., *Making Common Sense of Japan*, Pittsburgh, PA: University of Pittsburgh Press, 1993.

Richardson, Bradley, *The Political Culture of Japan*, Berkeley, CA: University of California Press, 1974.

Rimer, J. Thomas, ed., *Culture and Identity: Japanese Intellectuals During the Interwar Years*, Princeton, NJ: Princeton University Press, 1990.

Rinji Nōshi Oyobi Zōki Ishoku Chōsa Kai, "Nōshi Oyobi Zōki Ishoku ni Kansuru Jyūyō Jikō ni Tsuite (Chūkan Iken)" [Important Facts about Brain Death and Organ Transplantation], Kōseishō, June 14, 1991.

Robinson, Mark, "Making a Killing," *Tokyo Journal*, December 1994, 32–37.

Rokumoto, Kahei, "'Nihonjin no Hō Ishiki' Kenkyū Gaikan – Hō Kannen o Chūshin Toshite" [A General View of Research on Japanese Legal Consciousness – Focusing on the Concept of Law], *Hō Shakaigaku* 35, 1983, 14–33.

Hō Shakaigaku [Legal Sociology], Tokyo: Yūhikaku, 1986.

"Nihonjin no Hō Ishiki no Chōsa" [A Survey of the Legal Consciousness of the Japanese], *Hōgaku Kyōshitsu* 109, October 1989, 94–100.

"Hō Ishiki no Sokutei" [Measuring Legal Consciousness], in Yamauchi Toshio, ed., *Noda Yoshiyuki Sensei Koki Kinen: Tozai Hō Bunka no Hikaku to Kōryu*, Tokyo: Yūhikaku, 1983, 23–33.

Rosenberg, Gerald N., *The Hollow Hope: Can Courts Bring About Social Change?*, Chicago: University of Chicago Press, 1991.

"Hollow Hopes and Other Aspirations: A Reply to Feeley and McCann," *Law and Social Inquiry* 17(4), Fall 1992, 761–778.

Rothman, David J., "Three Views of History: View the First," *Hastings Center Report*, Special Supplement, November/December 1993, S11–S12.

Saitō, Tsuyoshi, *Meiji no Kotoba* [Words of the Meiji Era], Tokyo: Kōdansha, 1977.

Sanders, Joseph and V. Lee Hamilton, "Legal Cultures and Punishment Repertoires in Japan, Russia, and the United States," *Law and Society Review*, 1992, 117.

Sansom, George, *The Western World and Japan*, New York: Alfred A. Knopf, 1950.

Sarat, Austin, "Studying American Legal Culture: An Assessment of Survey Evidence," *Law and Society Review* 11, 1977, 427–488.

Satō, Shin'ichi and Ikeuchi Yoshisuke, comps., *Chūsei Hōsei Shiryōshū* [A

Collection of Data Regarding Medieval Legislation], vol. I, *Kamakura Bakufu Hō* [Laws of the Kamakura Shogunate], vol.II, *Muromachi Bakufu Hō* [Laws of the Muromachi Shogunate], Tokyo: Iwanami Shoten, 1955–1957.

Sawazaki, Yasushi, "Gay Men and HIV in Japan," in Mitchell Feldman, Eric Feldman, and Thomas Coates, eds., "Partners in AIDS Prevention: A U.S./Japan Collaboration," special supplement to *Journal of Acquired Immune Deficiency Syndromes and Human Retrovirology* 14 (Supplement 2), 1997, 47–50.

Scalapino, Robert, *Democracy and the Party Movement in Prewar Japan*, Berkeley, CA: University of California Press, 1967.

Scheiner, Irwin, "Benevolent Lords and Honorable Peasants: Rebellion and Peasant Consciousness in Tokugawa Japan," in Najita Tetsuo and Irwin Scheiner, eds., *Japanese Thought in the Tokugawa Period*, Chicago: University of Chicago Press, 1978.

Scheingold, Stewart, *The Politics of Rights: Lawyers, Public Policy, and Political Change*, New Haven, CT: Yale University Press, 1974.

Schuck, Peter H., "Rethinking Informed Consent," *Yale Law Journal* 103, 1993, 899.

Schultz, Marjorie Maguire, "From Informed Consent to Patient Choice: A New Protected Interest," *Yale Law Journal* 95, 1985.

Schwartz, Frank J., *Advice and Consent: The Politics of Consultation in Japan*, New York: Cambridge University Press, 1998.

Seimei Rinri Kenkyūkai, "Zōki no Tekishutsu ni Kansuru Hōritsu" (Shian) [Law Related to the Removal of Organs], *Jurisuto* 1001, June 1, 1992, 52–64.

"Setsumei to Dōi ni tsuite no Hōkoku," *Iji Hōgaku* [Report on Informed Consent] June 6, 1991, 164–168.

Shapiro, Martin, *Courts: A Comparative and Political Analysis*, Chicago: University of Chicago Press, 1981.

Shaw, William, *Human Rights in Korea: Historical and Policy Perspectives*, Cambridge, MA: Harvard University Press, 1991.

Silberman, Bernard S. and H. D. Harootunian, eds., *Japan in Crisis: Essays on Taisho Democracy*, Princeton, NJ: Princeton University Press, 1974.

Smith, J. C., "The Unique Nature of the Concepts of Western Law," *The Canadian Bar Review* 46(2), May 1968.

Smith, Thomas C., *The Agrarian Origins of Modern Japan*, Stanford, CA: Stanford University Press, 1959.

Soda, Kenji, "Present Situation of AIDS and HIV Infection in Japan," *HIV Ekigaku Kenkyūhan Kenkyū Hōkokusho* [Report of HIV Epidemic Study Group], March 1989.

Steenstrup, Carl, *A History of Law in Japan Until 1868*, New York: E. J. Brill, 1991.

"The Legal System of Japan at the End of the Kamakura Period from the Litigants' Point of View," in Brian E. McKnight, ed., *Law and the State in Traditional East Asia*, Honolulu: University of Hawaii Press, 1987, 73–109.

Stepanek, Marcia, "Japan's New Gay Activists Battle Bias, Indifference," *San Francisco Examiner*, May 26, 1991.

Suzuki, Shōji, *Nihon Kango to Chūgoku* [Japanese "Chinese Words" and China], Tokyo: Chūkōshinsho, 1981.

Suzuki, Toshihiro, "Kanja no Kenri Sengen" [Declaration of Patients' Rights], *Jurisuto* 826, December 1, 1984, 48–51.

"Atarashii Shimin Undō o Minna no Chikara de" [Joining Everyone's Strengths in the New Citizens' Movements], in Kanja no Kenri Hō o Tsukuru Kai, *Kanja no Kenri o Tsukuru* [Creation of Patients' Rights], Tokyo: Meiseki Shoten, 1992, 19–22.

Tachibana, Takashi, *Nōshi* [Brain Death], Chūō Kōron Shuppansha 1986.

"Nōshi to Hito no Shi" [Brain Death and Human Death], *Gekkan Asahi*, March 1992, 21–25.

Takasugi, Shingo, "Abe Takeshi: 'Watakushi wa AIDS Kansen no Dōgiteki Geshunin Da'" [Based on Moral Justice, I am the Perpetrator of AIDS Infection], *Gendai*, October 1987, 250–265.

Takayanagi, Kenzo, "A Century of Innovation: The Development of Japanese Law, 1868–1961," in Arthur Taylor von Mehren, ed., *Law in Japan: The Legal Order in a Changing Society*, Cambridge, MA: Harvard University Press, 1963, 5–40.

Takeda, Bin, "AIDS Kyōiku ni Motomerareru Mono" [What we Expect from AIDS Education], *Sekai*, October 1992, 68–71.

Tamashiro, Hidehiko, "21 Seiki ni wa, Ajia no Hasseisha Kazu wa Afurika yori Ōkunatte iru darō" [In the 21st Century the Number of Infected People in Asia Will Be Greater than in Africa], *Rengō*, November 1992, 4–7.

Tanaka, Shigeaki, "Hō, Kenri, Saiban ni tsuite no Ichi Kōsatsu" [An Inquiry into Law, Rights, and Courts], in Katō Shinpei, ed., *Hō Rigaku no Sho Mondai*, Tokyo: Yūhikaku, 1976, 101–129.

"Shimin Undō ni Okeru Kenri to Saiban: Sono Hōteki Senryaku no Haikei to Igi o Megutte" [Rights and Litigation in Citizens Movements: Focusing on their Background and Significance as a Legal Tactic], *Minshō Hō Zasshi* 76, 1977, 633 (part 1); 76, 1977, 779 (part 2); 77, 1977, 161 (part 3); 77, 1977, 321 (part 4).

Saiban o Meguru Hō to Seiji [Law and Politics in the Courts], Tokyo: Yūhikaku, 1979.

"Kenri, Gimu no Gainen" [The Concept of Rights and Duties], in Inoue Shigeru, ed., *Gendai no Hō Tetsugaku*, Tokyo: Yūhikaku, 1981, 285–310.

"Nihonjin no Hō Ishiki to sono Kenkyū no Genjyō ni tsuite" [The Legal Consciousness of the Japanese and the Present Situation of its Study], *Hō Shakaigaku* 37, 1985, 25–38.

Gendai Nihon Hō no Kōzu [The Composition of Contemporary Japanese Law], Tokyo: Kōtokusha Chikuma Shobō, 1987.

Tanase, Takao, "Kenri Seisei no Shisutemu Teki Kōsatsu," *Hō Shakaigaku* 39, 1987, 11–16.

Thompson, Michael, Richard Ellis, and Aaron Wildavsky, *Cultural Theory*, San Francisco, CA: Westview Press, 1990.

Tokyo Chihō Saibansho, *Wakaichōsho Kisai Jikō* [Contents of the Settlement Proposal], Hatasawa Preliminary Translation, Mr. Hatasawa Tamotsu, Hatasawa and Wakai Law Offices, Tokyo, Japan, April 5, 1996.

Toshitani, Nobuyoshi, "Kokumin Seikatsu to Hōritsu no Hedatari: Nihonjin no Hō Ishiki" [The Distance between Law and the Life of Citizens: Japanese Legal Consciousness], *Tōki no Hōrei*, Tokushū, 1236, 1985, 8–24.

Tsukamoto, Yasushi, "Arguments about the Criteria of Brain Death in Japan," *Journal of Behavioral and Social Sciences (Kōdō Kagaku Kenkyū)* 41, 1992, 24–38.

Umehara, Takeshi, "Gendaijin no Sei to Shi" [The Life and Death of Contemporary People], *This Is* 6(10), 1989, 20–26.

"Watakushi wa Naze, 'Nōshi = Ningen no Shi' ni Shitsuyō ni Hantaishi Tsuzukeru no ka" [Why Is it that I Continue to Obstinately Oppose the Idea of Brain Death as Equal to Human Death?], *Sapio*, January 9, 1992, 76–80.

Upham, Frank, *Law and Social Change in Postwar Japan*, Cambridge, MA: Harvard University Press, 1987.

"What's Happening in Japan, Sociolegalwise," *Law and Society Review* 23(5), 1989.

"The Development of Japanese Legal Studies in American Law Schools," prepared for the Reischauer Institute 25th Anniversary Symposium on the Postwar Development of Japanese Studies, Fall, 1996.

Verwayen, Frans B., "Early Transplantations of Dutch Law Texts," Paper Presented at the Japan–Netherlands Institute, November 16, 1992.

Vlastos, Gregory, "Justice and Equality," in Jeremy Waldron, *Theories of Rights*, New York: Oxford University Press, 1984, 41–76.

Vlastos, Stephen, "*Yonaoshi* in Aizu," in Najita Tetsuo and J. Victor Koschmann, ed., *Conflict in Modern Japanese History: The Neglected Tradition*, Princeton, NJ: Princeton University Press, 1982.

Wada, Yasuhiro, "Nichijyō no naka no Funsō Shori" [Conflict Management in Daily Life], *Tokyo Toritsu Daigaku Hō Gakkai Zasshi* 24(2), 25(1), 1983–1984, 1–73, 41–119.

Walthall, Anne, *Social Protest and Popular Culture in Eighteenth-Century Japan*, Tucson, AZ: University of Arizona Press, 1986.

Waswo, Ann, *Modern Japanese Society, 1968–1984*, New York: Oxford University Press, 1996.

Watson, Alan, *Legal Transplants: An Approach to Comparative Law*, Charlottesville, VA: University Press of Virginia, 1974.

"Legal Change, Sources of Law and Legal Culture," *University of Pennsylvania Law Review* 131(5), April 1983, 1121–1157.

Weatherall, William, "Japan Curses Gaijin and AIDS Still Spreads," *Far Eastern Economic Review*, April 9, 1987, 111.

Wildavsky, Aaron, "Choosing Preferences by Constructing Institutions: A Cultural Theory of Preference Formation," *American Political Science Review* 81(1), March 1987, 3–21.

van Wolferen, Karel, *The Enigma of Japanese Power*, New York: Alfred A. Knopf, 1989.

Yamada, Takao, "Kenri no Katarogu Zukuri ni Mukete" [Making a Catalogue of Rights], *Hō Shakaigaku* 39, 1987, 2–10.

Yamauchi, Masaya, "Transplantation in Japan," *British Medical Journal* 301, 507, 1988.

Yamazaki, Masakazu, "Atarashii Kojinshugi no Yochō" [The Events Surrounding the Rise of New Individualism], *Chūō Kōron*, 98, August 1983, 62–88.

Yanabu, Akira, *Honyaku no Shisō: Shizen to Nature* [The Intellectual Thought of Translation: "Shizen" and "Nature"], Tokyo: Heibunsha, 1977.

Honyakugo Seiritsu Jijyō [Circumstances of the Formulation of Translated Words], Tokyo: Iwanami Shoten, 1982.

Yasuda, Yukuo, "AIDS Higai to Kuni no Sekinin" [AIDS Victims and the Nation's Responsibility], *Hōgaku Seminā* 406, October 1988, 14–17.

Yokoyama, Toshio, *Hyakushō Ikki to Gimin Denshō* [The Legend of a Public-spirited Man of the People and Peasant Rebellions], Tokyo, 1977.

Yonemoto, Shōhei, *Sentan Kakumei Iryō* (Advanced Medical Revolution), Tokyo: Chūō Kōron Shupansha, 1988.

INDEX

214

Japan Medical Association, 95–97
  journalistic opposition to, 97–98
  Life Ethics Problem Study
    Parliamentarians League, 93
  legislation, enactment of, 108
  rights, assertion of, 83–85, 90–93, 96–97,
    100, 102–10
  values, traditional and religious
    brain death, organ transplantation, and,
      85,
      89–92, 94–95, 105
    death, 85–89, 94–75, 105
  Wada case, 83, 98, 132–36

Centers for Disease Control, 114–15, 119
Chūkaku-ha, 103–04
Code of Criminal Procedure, 131–32
Code of Patients' Rights, 49
concentrates and cryoprecipitate, 112–113,
  115
confidentiality, see privacy and
  confidentiality
courts, see litigation and the courts
Criminal Law Academy, 105, 108
cryoprecipitate and concentrates, 112–113,
  115
Cutter Japan, 114

Declaration for Patients' Rights, 48
Declaration of a Right to Health, 49
Declaration of the Rights of Hospital
  Patients, 136
Declaration on Private Practice Physicians,
  49
Diet (Japanese legislature)
  AIDS legislation, 67, 70–72
  AIDS public health policy, 73
  brain death and organ transplantation, 82,
    93, 108, 136, 139
  hemophiliacs' demands for compensation,
    122
  self-sufficiency in blood products, 118
Doctors Law, 61

estate (shōen) system (medieval), 21–22
Etō Shimpei, 28–29

factors 8 and 9, 112–13, 115
feudalism, 20–27
Food and Drug Administration (of US),
  119–20
Fujimoto Teruo, 135

Fukuzawa Yūkichi, 29, 31–32

Green Cross Corporation, 114, 119, 126–29
Gunji Atsuaki, 125–26

Hara Hideo, 101
Hashimoto Ryūtaro, 123–24
Heart Transplant Study Society,
  95
Hirano Ryūichi, 138
Hironaka Junichirō, 139
HIV–Human Rights Information Center, 55,
  74, 80
HIV Infection Investigation Team, 124
HIV Litigation Support Group, 121
Honda Katsunori, 137
Hori Toshikatsu, 90
Hurley, Robert, 127

Immigration Act, 61, 65, 75
Infectious Disease Department (of MHW),
  60
Infectious Disease Prevention Law, 63
informed consent
  brain death, organ transplantation, and,
    84–85, 90, 96, 101–08, 135
  codes proposed by professional groups,
    48–49
  definition of, 44–45
  institutional barriers to implementing,
    45–47
  Organization to Establish a Patients'
    Rights Law and,
    49–50
  progress in implementation, assessment of,
    49–50
International Friends, 58
Investigative Panel on Brain Death and Life
  Ethics (of LDP), 99
Ishida Yoshiaki, 66, 70
Itagaki Taisuke, 27
Itami Jūzō, 89

Japan Civil Liberties Union, 67
Japan Electroencephalography Association,
  92–94
Japan Federation of Bar Associations (JFBA)
  consulted on the Wada case, 136
  opposition to brain death, 92,
    96–98, 101, 103
  support of patients' rights, 49–50
Japan Hospital Association, 50, 79, 118

215